ECONOMIC JUSTICE IN PERSPECTIVE

A BOOK OF READINGS

JERRY COMBEE

Grove City College

EDGAR NORTON

Fairleigh Dickinson University

 Prentice Hall, Englewood Cliffs, New Jersey 07632

Library of Congress Cataloging-in-Publication Data

Economic justice in perspective : a book of readings / [edited by] Jerry Combee, Edgar Norton.
   p.   cm.
ISBN 0-13-223686-9
   1. Economics—Moral and ethical aspects.   2. Communism—Moral and ethical aspects.
3. Capitalism—Moral and ethical aspects.
I. Combee, Jerry. II. Norton, Edgar.
HB72.E264 1991
174—dc20   90-38311
                                       CIP

Editorial/production supervision and interior design: Joanne Palmer
Cover design: Mike Fender Design
Prepress buyer: Trudy Pisciotti
Manufacturing buyer: Robert Anderson

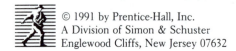 © 1991 by Prentice-Hall, Inc.
A Division of Simon & Schuster
Englewood Cliffs, New Jersey 07632

Printed in the United States of America

10 9 8 7 6 5 4 3 2 1

ISBN 0-13-223686-9

PRENTICE-HALL INTERNATIONAL (UK) LIMITED, London
PRENTICE-HALL OF AUSTRALIA PTY. LIMITED, Sydney
PRENTICE-HALL CANADA INC., Toronto
PRENTICE-HALL HISPANOAMERICANA, S.A., Mexico
PRENTICE-HALL OF INDIA PRIVATE LIMITED, New Delhi
PRENTICE-HALL OF JAPAN, INC., Tokyo
SIMON & SCHUSTER ASIA PTE. LTD., Singapore
EDITORA PRENTICE-HALL DO BRASIL, LTDA., Rio de Janeiro

To Daneille, Trevor, and Cara

Jerry

To my wife, Becky, and our wonderful children, Matthew and Amy

Edgar

Contents

v

THE NINETEENTH CENTURY

THE TWENTIETH CENTURY

Preface

Economic justice is a concept that is not easily defined. Philosophers, economists, and theologians have grappled with the notion of justice for several millennia. Current debate on the topic of justice deals with complex issues of equality, equity, fairness, opportunity, and oppression. With the increasing number of articles, books, authors, and politicians addressing the issues of economic justice, it is easy to lose sight of the forest because of the trees. Increasingly complex models of economic equilibrium or mathematical statements of "fairness" provide little insight into how the world really works and how justice in the realm of economics can best be attained.

Debate on the topic of economic justice cannot be fully appreciated or understood by reading only the thoughts of present day thinkers. When classical sources are not read and injected into the debate, the same arguments occur over and over again on issues that were addressed perhaps hundreds of years ago. Modern men and women have no monopoly on influential ideas and arguments. In fact, modern thought loses some of its luster and impact when compared to the society-shaping philosophies and the influence on humankind that some of the classical thinkers have had. The issues and arguments presented by Plato, the Old and New Testament scriptures, Clement of Alexandria, Aquinas, Molinaeus, Locke, and Smith on the topics of property, wealth, usury, and justice are timeless. The thoughts expressed by these and other classical writers are still relevant and their insights need to be appreciated anew.

Major differences exist between this readings book and other readings books in economics. First, rather than dealing with current, "trendy" issues, this book deals with such eternal questions in economics as what is the most just mode of production? What is the ideal economic man presupposed or encouraged by each model of an economic system? This latter question is one which has been largely ignored in discussions of economic systems and economic justice. In order to try to resolve the "trendy" issues, one must first have an understanding and appreciation of the issues discussed and the philosophies expounded in the debate of these eternal questions.

Second, this book focuses on the classics. Most readings books concentrate on current writings over, say, a five- to twenty-five-year period, with perhaps some classical writings placed here and there. About two-thirds of the excerpts in this book were written before the twentieth century; their significance and importance in the debate on economic justice has stood the test of time. Modern writers have been included to the extent that they give a clear statement of modern thought on the topic of economic justice and that they appear to have a major influence on modern society and its beliefs.

Third, primary readings are used in this book. Rather than being a textbook description of what somebody thinks about what someone else wrote, here the writers "speak" for themselves. Individuals reading this book can acquire a flavor and a sense of appreciation for these classics that reading a textbook just cannot provide. Headnotes were written to assist the reader in appreciating the importance of the discussion and arguments made by each writer.

Fourth, no one doctrine or perspective in economic justice is thrust upon the reader. The excerpts contain a wide variety of points of view. By giving fair coverage to a variety of perspectives, the reader can study the arguments presented and formulate his/her own thoughts and ideas on the topic of economic justice.

What is contained in this reader is a comprehensive assembly of excerpts from classical sources and influential modern thought on the topic of economic justice superior to that presently found in other readings books. Unfortunately, in any readings book, some deserving excerpts must be excluded due to space and cost considerations. The editors apologize to those who feel we erred by omitting an excerpt or a piece written by such and such an author.

Any book project involves many people in addition to those who have their names on the cover. We wish to extend our thanks and acknowledge the assistance of the following: Bill Webber and Whitney Blake, our Prentice Hall editors; Joanne Palmer, who oversaw the production process; Dan Pellow, our Prentice Hall book representative, who encouraged us to assemble and submit a book proposal to Prentice Hall; Debbie Anthony, for typing assistance during the early stages of the book; William Snavely and Kevin Clauson, for helpful, illuminating discussions on economic justice; and Nida Wed-Ang, for assistance in assembling some of the excerpts. Finally, we must thank our wives and children for supporting and encouraging us through this project.

Jerry Combee

Edgar Norton

Introduction

In his 1987 best-selling *The Closing of the American Mind,*[1] Allan Bloom decries the failure of American colleges and universities to have students confront the "great books" and therefore the "great issues." In a similar vein, former United States Secretary of Education William Bennett, a proponent of the classics, criticizes "textbook-driven" education.[2] Bloom, Bennett, and other like-minded critics of American higher education charge the contemporary college curriculum with favoring ephemeral over eternal questions. They harken to a past when students read primary rather than secondary sources . . . Plato, Aristotle, and other great minds behind the great books.

Among the social sciences, at least, economics has perhaps recently neglected the primary sources more than any other discipline. Just as graduate students in physics can earn Ph.D.s without reading Newton and Einstein, economists can complete doctoral work and perhaps not be exposed to the primary fountainhead

---

[1]Allan Bloom, *The Closing of the American Mind: How Higher Education Has Failed Democracy and Impoverished the Souls of Today's Students* (New York: Simon and Schuster, 1987).

[2]For Bennett's views on American education, see his speeches in William Bennett, *Our Children and Our Country: Improving America's Schools and Affirming the Common Culture* (New York: Simon and Schuster, 1988).

texts of Adam Smith, Karl Marx, or even Keynes in the original. Often at best they read *about* Smith, Marx, and Keynes; most of their studies center on mathematical manipulations of quantifiable phenomena. And in the name of scientific method, economists, both as researchers and teachers, typically avoid "value judgments" and such ethical issues as the nature of economic justice, a prime topic in the classics of economic literature.

Economics has entered the stage of an academic discipline similar to what physics entered with the triumph of the theories of Isaac Newton in the seventeenth century, after which physicists read *about* Newton but largely stopped reading Newton himself. As Thomas Kuhn describes in *The Structure of Scientific Revolutions,*[3] in physics, chemistry, and the other hard sciences, after "paradigms" or such basic philosophical frameworks as Newton's theories are adopted, they become unquestioned assumptions or presuppositions. When a given paradigm triumphs, the concepts, categories, criteria, and canons defined in the reigning framework tightly govern research. With the philosophical issues alive in the classics seemingly dead, standardized scientific textbooks dominate. In such social sciences as psychology, sociology, and political science, nothing resembling the paradigm status of Newton's ideas has emerged. In economics, however, the ideas of an Alfred Marshall or a John Maynard Keynes have indeed achieved something close to the level of acceptance the Newtonian paradigm once enjoyed in physics.

In Kuhn's analysis, paradigms are overthrown only when anomalies that do not fit the governing model are found as the outcome of investigation, inquiry, and research. After enough anomalies appear, the time ripens for new paradigms to challenge the existing one by better explaining the anomalies. Something like that happened in economics during the 1970s when, not long after Pres. Richard Nixon's famous declaration that "we are all Keynesians now," it became clear that with simultaneous inflation and unemployment, something had gone awry in the Keynesian paradigm.

As a byproduct of the breakdown of the Keynesian paradigm, interest has revived in the ethical issues that Keynesians essentially took for granted. Though seemingly purely "scientific," Keynesianism also *implicitly* answered fundamental questions about economic justice. For example, Keynesianism assumed that government should guarantee full employment; and most Keynesians tended to be redistributionists ("liberals" as opposed to "conservatives") to one degree or another. With the breakdown of the Keynesian paradigm, however, such issues entered center stage as other paradigms such as monetarism and supply-side theory competed for dominance in the discipline of economics.

In a bibliographic essay in the *Human Studies Review,*[4] Tyler Cowen cites the "rediscovery" of "normative inquiry" once part of economics during its classical days when economics was tightly tied to political philosophy:

[3]Thomas Kuhn, *The Structure of Scientific Revolutions,* 2nd ed. (Chicago: University of Chicago Press, 1970).

[4]Tyler Cowen, "Political Philosophy and Welfare Economics," *Humane Studies Review,* 4, no. 3 (Summer 1987), 1–2, 13–15.

Ever since the pioneering work of Robert Nozick and John Rawls, the field of overlap between political economy and political philosophy has been one of the fastest growing and most exciting areas in the social sciences. Many of the world's leading economists and philosophers have exchanged ideas on the nature of the good society and its justification.

Before the initiation of these debates in the early 1970's, both political philosophy and welfare economics were in a relatively stagnant state. The period between Sidgwick [late nineteenth-century English ethical philosopher] and Rawls yielded little significance in political philosophy, perhaps due to the influence of positivism. Likewise, the "new welfare economics" dating from the 1930's had developed into a super-refined mathematical structure that was largely irrelevant to many interesting normative questions.

Developments in the 1970's and 1980's can be interpreted as a rediscovery of the aims of political philosophy as it was developed in the post Renaissance period by such figures as Hobbes, Locke, Rousseau, and Kant. Normative inquiry should be directed at obtaining useful knowledge about the structure and nature of available alternatives, rather than the analysis of linguistic propositions or refining the art of model-building for its own sake. . . .

The resurgence of normative moral and political philosophy in recent decades owes much to the crossfertilization of two hitherto independent fields of thought. The new political economy emerging from this development offers many exciting opportunities for classical liberal scholarship.[5]

At the same time as these developments in economic and political philosophy, challenges to welfare state assumptions from the Right during the Reagan era, matched by more consistently statist, if not socialist, arguments from the Left, have thrust the theme of economic justice to the center of American public policy debate. The struggle of competing values and policy paradigms in the public sector increasingly challenges the discipline of economics to return to the neglected themes of economic justice.

But why try to reinvent the wheel? Why try to rethink everything without, at first, looking at what has been thought before? The classical literature of political economy, whether authored by those who would be called economists, philosophers, or theologians, is rich with thoughts about the issues that are again coming to the forefront of the discipline of economics. Reviewing the thoughts of the past on the fundamental questions of economic justice will enrich present discussion, increasing the probability that current debate will reach depths of which it might otherwise fall short.

It is, of course, in the classics of economic thought that one finds the "classic" treatments of moral issues that contemporary economics until quite recently seemed largely content to ignore. The history of economic thought reveals eternal themes of economic justice—issues as old as Aristotle and as recent as the pastoral letter of the Catholic bishops on the United States economy.

[5]Ibid.

What is the most just mode for the production and distribution of wealth? That question points to alternative economic systems and their evaluation by the criteria of justice. It also involves the justice of interest (or "usury") and profit, plus the issue of equality versus inequality of property so central to the contemporary socialism/capitalism debate.

What is the ideal economic man? While keeping the question of the most just mode for the production and distribution of wealth above the level of consciousness, economists have seldom if ever explicitly dealt with "ideal economic man"— more often the theme of political philosophers and theologians. Contemporary economics, taking for granted the "homo economicus" model of man as rational decision maker seeking to maximize business profits and personal utility, has failed to consider the moral desirability of such a human type. Concern for the human consequences of economics, however, requires one to address the kind of human being an economic system presupposes or encourages.

It was Socrates in Plato's *Republic* who said that "it is necessary that there also be as many forms of human characters as there are forms of regimes."[6] Such questions figure prominently in debate across the centuries about economic justice. Indeed, the kinds of human beings accompanying economic systems can more greatly influence preferences for economic systems than do results measured by efficiency and utility, as the ideal of "socialist man," a driving force in contemporary radical socialism, illustrates. While defenders of capitalism most commonly mount their arguments in terms of their favored system's greater economic efficiency or the need for concessions to human nature, radical socialism's vision of "socialist man," originated by Karl Marx, has permitted its advocates to mount more morally based arguments.

As far back as Aristotle's defense of private property against Socrates in terms of the "wickedness" of human nature[7] and as recently as Michael Novak's case for capitalism as a necessary concession to "sin" (1982),[8] socialism has commonly succeeded in occupying the moral high ground. Socrates' case for communism as the appropriate economic arrangement for a society that aspires to perfect justice is of a piece with Marx's predictions of perfection through the actualization of "socialist man" in a future communist millennium.

For a period of several centuries, however, beginning with the Protestant Reformation of the sixteenth century, a different model of man—an ideal human type, admired and praised as the manifestation of true humanity—morally (and religiously) undergirded capitalism. Max Weber's "Protestant ethic" thesis captured an aspect of this extraordinary phenomena. But it was nineteenth-century German philosopher G. W. F. Hegel who painted a much fuller picture of "bourgeois man," the ideal human type presupposed and encouraged by capitalism. Hegel

[6]Plato, *Republic*, trans. Allan Bloom (New York: Basic Books, 1968), p. 222.
[7]Aristotle, *Politics*, p. 1263b.
[8]Michael Novak, *The Spirit of Democratic Capitalism* (New York: Touchstone Books, 1982).

traced "bourgeois man" back to his roots in the Reformation. "It is more consonant with justice that he who has money should spend it even in luxuries, than that he should give it away to idlers and beggars," as Hegel described Martin Luther's view of economic justice, "for he bestows it upon an equal number of persons by so doing, and these must at any rate have worked diligently for it." Beginning with the Reformation, Hegel argued, "Industry, crafts and trades now have their moral validity recognized, and the obstacles to their prosperity which originated with the [medieval] Church, have vanished."[9]

In contrast to "socialist man"—a moral vision so powerful that it causes many advocates of socialism to overlook that system's widely admitted failures of efficiency—there is much less awareness that capitalism, too, has its ideal human type. Hence the failure of capitalism's contemporary defenders to contest the moral high ground.[10]

The contemporary quarrel between socialism and capitalism—and the debate over economic justice across the centuries—has to some extent turned on disagreement about the more morally desirable kind of human being—or "state of soul," as Plato would have said. By confronting the classics of economics, perhaps the next generation of citizens, rather than being blown by whatever winds of ideology, whether from the Left or the Right, prevail at the moment, will possess convictions about economic justice informed by the great thoughts of the great minds on all sides of all the issues.

[9]G. W. F. Hegel, *The Philosophy of History*, trans. J. Sibree (New York: Dover, no date), pp. 81–95.

[10]Norman Podhoretz, "The New Defenders of Capitalism," *Harvard Business Review*, 59 (March-April 1981).

CHAPTER 1

Aristotle on Communism and Private Property

The debate over economic justice began in antiquity with the Greek philosophers, the first persons to engage in systematic inquiry into economic justice. Their writings, particularly those of Plato and Aristotle, constitute *the* classical references in the literature of economic justice. They set the tone for dialogue that continued during the Christian era and throughout the Middle Ages, when Christian philosophers tried to tie together Hellenistic thinking and the teachings of Christ.

The *Republic*, magnum opus of Greek philosopher Plato (428?–347 B.C.) and a fountainhead of Western philosophy, contains one of the first philosophical treatments of economic justice. Plato depicts his mentor, the philosopher Socrates, in conversation with others, discussing justice. In a society aspiring to perfect justice, Socrates is made to argue, the nature of things requires total communism.

In his work, the *Politics*, excerpted here, Aristotle (384–322 B.C.), Plato's greatest pupil and second only to Plato in philosophical influence on Western civilization, summarizes Socrates' advocacy of communism and offers a rebuttal. In this early and classic critique of communism, Aristotle, advocating the need for incentives, frames the issue of the justice of private property. Arguing that "wicked" human nature requires the incentives that a system of private property provides,

Aristotle contends that persons will be tempted to shirk work under communism, since they still can have access to material goods.

By basing his argument on the *practical,* not moral, necessity for private property, however, Aristotle leaves the moral high ground to Socrates. His silence implies that perfect justice, even though impractical, would require the abolition of private property. Aristotle thus begins a pattern of reasoning frequently repeated in the history of economic thought—practical necessity (the reality of human nature) requires something less than perfection in economics, while in terms of ethical absolutes, communism suggests true justice.

Another often repeated theme appears in Aristotle's treatment of economic justice—disdain for economic activity. *Economics,* originally a Greek word, literally meant "household management," with the "household" consisting of husband, wife, offspring, and slaves. In the cultural perspective of classical Greece, what we today call "economic production" should be confined to the household, where it is most properly the work of slaves, not free persons. Paralleling his culture, Aristotle exalts the ideal of the aristocratic gentleman—the man of "nobility" for whom the proper activities are war, politics, and philosophy, *not* economic activity. Aristotle depicts economic activity as in tension with the concept of completed human nature and perfected man because of the intrinsic nature of work (especially manual labor, which he labels "illiberal") and the logic of economic motives that leads to greed and obsession with the low, the material, the base. Economics thus represents the antithesis of the "virtue" characteristic of the ideal human type Aristotle wishes to encourage.

It is in the context of exaltation of the aristocratic gentleman for whom economic activity is "unnatural" (at odds with the "virtue" that is the perfection of human nature) that Aristotle's condemnation of profits and usury (the earning of interest on money) must be seen. Usury is "unnatural," according to Aristotle, because the true purpose of money is to serve as a medium of exchange. Aristotle explicitly argues from the premise that any use of a thing for something other than its "proper" purpose is "unnatural." But Aristotle's deeper meaning—and one that sounds less strange to modern ears—appears to be that profit and usury are "unnatural" because the motives that drive them clash with the notion of perfected *human nature* that he favored.

As the teacher and sometime companion of Alexander the Great, Aristotle influenced the world of his time with his ideas on many subjects (economic justice included). But Aristotle's views on the justice of private property, profit, and usury, and on the moral effect of economic activities upon human beings also had a substantial impact upon the succeeding Christian era.

Politics

Aristotle

Our purpose is to consider what form of political community is best of all for those who are most able to realize their ideal of life. . . .

We will begin with the natural beginning of the subject. Three alternatives are conceivable: The members of a state must either have (1) all things or (2) nothing in common, or (3) some things in common and some not. That they should have nothing in common is clearly impossible, for the state is a community, and must at any rate have a common place—one city will be in one place, and the citizens are those who share in that one city. But should a well-ordered state have all things, as far as may be, in common, or some only and not others? For the citizens might conceivably have wives and children and property in common, as Socrates proposes in the Republic of Plato. Which is better, our present condition, or the proposed new order of society?

Next let us consider what should be our arrangements about property: should the citizens of the perfect state have their possessions in common or not? This question may be discussed separately from the enactments about women and children. Even supposing that the women and children belong to individuals, according to the custom which is at present universal, may there not be an advantage in having and using possessions in common? Three cases are possible: (1) the soil may be appropriated, but the produce may be thrown for consumption into the common stock; and this is the practice of some nations. Or (2), the soil may be common, and may be cultivated in common, but the produce divided among individuals for their private use; this is a form of common property which is said to exist among certain barbarians. Or (3), the soil and the produce may be alike common.

When the husbandmen are not the owners, the case will be different and easier to deal with; but when they till the ground themselves the question of ownership will give a world of trouble. If they do not share equally in enjoyments and toils, those who labour much and get little will necessarily complain of those who labour little and receive or consume much. There is always a difficulty in men living together and having things in common, but especially in their having common property. The partnerships of fellow-travellers are an example to the point; for they generally fall out by the way and quarrel about any trifle which turns up. So with servants: we are most liable to take offence at those with whom we most frequently come into contact in daily life.

These are only some of the disadvantages which attend the community of

---

Aristotle, Politics *translated by Benjamin Jowett. Oxford: Clarendon Press, 1885.*

property; the present arrangement, if improved as it might be by good customs and laws, would be far better, and would have the advantages of both systems. Property should be in a certain sense common, but, as a general rule, private; for, when every one has a distinct interest, men will not complain of one another, and they will make more progress, because every one will be attending to his own business. And yet among the good, and in respect of use, 'Friends,' as the proverb says, 'will have all things common.' Even now there are traces of such a principle, showing that it is not impracticable, but, in well-ordered states, exists already to a certain extent and may be carried further. For, although every man has his own property, some things he will place at the disposal of his friends, while of others he shares the use with them. The Lacedaemonians, for example, use one another's slaves, and horses, and dogs, as if they were their own; and when they happen to be in the country, they appropriate in the fields whatever provisions they want. It is clearly better that property should be private, but the use of it common; and the special business of the legislator is to create in men this benevolent disposition. Again, how immeasurably greater is the pleasure, when a man feels a thing to be his own; for the love of self is a feeling implanted by nature and not given in vain, although selfishness is rightly censured; this, however, is not the mere love of self, but the love of self in excess, like the miser's love of money; for all, or almost all, men love money, and other such objects in a measure. And further, there is the greatest pleasure in doing a kindness or service to friends or guests or companions, which can only be rendered when a man has private property. The advantage is lost by the excessive unification of the state. Two virtues are annihilated in such a state: first, temperance towards women (for it is an honourable action to abstain from another's wife for temperance sake); secondly, liberality in the matter of property. No one, when men have all things in common, will any longer set an example of liberality or do any liberal action; for liberality consists in the use which is made of property.

Such legislation may have a specious appearance of benevolence; men readily listen to it, and are easily induced to believe that in some wonderful manner everybody will become everybody's friend, especially when some one is heard denouncing the evils now existing in states, suits about contracts, convictions for perjury, flatteries of rich men and the like, which are said to arise out of the possession of private property. These evils, however, are due to a very different cause—the wickedness of human nature. Indeed, we see that there is much more quarrelling among those who have all things in common, though there are not many of them when compared with the vast numbers who have private property.

CONDEMNATION OF TRADE AND USURY

Seeing then that the state is made up of households, before speaking of the state, we must speak of the management of the household. The parts of the household are the persons who compose it, and a complete household consists of slaves and freemen. Now we should begin by examining everything in its least elements; and the first and least parts of a family are master and slave, husband and wife, father and children. We have therefore to consider what each of these three relations is and ought to be:—I mean the relation of master and servant, of husband and wife, and thirdly of parent and child. And there is another element of a household, the so-called art of money-making, which, according to some, is identical with household management, according to others, a principal part of it; the nature of this art will also have to be considered by us. . . .

Of the art of acquisition then there is one kind which is natural and is a part of the management of a household. Either we must suppose the necessaries of life to exist previously, or the art of household management must provide a store of them for the common use of the family or state. They are the elements of true wealth; for the amount of property which is needed for a good life is not unlimited, although Solon in one of his poems says that

No bound to riches has been fixed for man.

But there is a boundary fixed, just as there is in the arts; for the instruments of any art are never unlimited, either in number or size, and wealth may be defined as a number of instruments to be used in a household or in a state. And so we see that there is a natural art of acquisition which is practised by managers of households and by statesmen, and what is the reason of this.

There is another variety of the art of acquisition which is commonly and rightly called the art of making money, and has in fact suggested the notion that wealth and property have no limit. Being nearly connected with the preceding, it is often identified with it. But though they are not very different, neither are they the same. The kind already described is given by nature, the other is gained by experience and art.

Let us begin our discussion of the question with the following considerations:

Of everything which we possess there are two uses: both belong to the thing as such, but not in the same manner, for one is the proper, and the other the improper or secondary use of it. For example, a shoe is used for wear, and is used for exchange; both are uses of the shoe. He who gives a shoe in exchange for money or food to him who wants one, does indeed use the shoe as a shoe, but this is not its proper or primary purpose, for a shoe is not made to be an object of barter. The same may be said of all possessions, for the art of exchange extends to all of them, and it arises at first in a natural manner from the circumstance that some have too little, others too much. Hence we may infer that retail trade is not a natural part of the art of money-making; had it been so, men would have ceased to exchange when they had enough. And in the first community, which is the family, this art is obviously of no use, but only begins to be useful when the society increases. For the members of the family originally had all things in common; in a more divided state of society they still shared in many things, but they were different things which they had to give in exchange for what they wanted, a kind of barter which is still practised among barbarous nations who exchange with one another the necessaries of life and nothing more; giving and receiving wine, for example, in exchange for corn and the like. This sort of barter is not part of the money-making art and is not contrary to nature, but is needed for the satisfaction of men's natural wants. The other or more complex form of exchange grew out of the simpler. When the inhabitants of one country became more dependent on those of another, and they imported what they needed, and exported the surplus, money necessarily came into use. For the various necessaries of life are not easily carried about, and hence men agreed to employ in their dealings with each other something which was intrinsically useful and easily applicable to the purposes of life, for example, iron, silver, and the like. Of this the value was at first measured by size and weight, but in process of time they put a stamp upon it, to save the trouble of weighing and to mark the value.

When the use of coin had once been discovered, out of the barter of necessary articles arose the other art of money-making, namely, retail trade; which was at first probably a simple matter, but became more complicated as soon as men learned by experience whence and by what exchanges the greatest profit might be made. Originating in the use of coin, the art of money-making is generally thought to be chiefly concerned with it, and to be the art which produces wealth and money; having to consider how they may be accumulated. Indeed, wealth is assumed by many to be only a quantity of coin, because the art of money-making and retail trade are concerned with coin. Others maintain that coined money is a mere sham, a thing not natural, but conventional only, which would have no value or use for any of the purposes of daily life if another commodity were substituted by the users. And, indeed, he who is rich in coin may often be in want of necessary food. But how can that be wealth of which a man may have a great abundance and yet perish with hunger, like Midas in the fable, whose insatiable prayer turned everything that was set before him into gold?

Men seek after a better notion of wealth and of the art of making money than the mere acquisition of coin, and they are right. For natural wealth and the natural art of money-making are a different thing; in their true form they are part of the management of a household; whereas retail trade is the art of producing wealth, not in every way, but by exchange. And it seems to be concerned with coin; for coin is the beginning of exchange and the measure or limit of it. And there is no bound to the wealth which springs from this art of money-making. As in the art of medicine there is no limit to the pursuit of health, and as in the other arts there is no limit to the pursuit of their several ends, for they aim at accomplishing their ends to the uttermost; (but of the means there is a limit, for the end is always the limit), so, too, in this art of money-making there is no limit of the end, which is wealth of the spurious kind, and the acquisition of money. But the art of household management has a limit; the unlimited acquisition of money is not its business. And, therefore, in one point of view, all wealth must have a limit; nevertheless, as a matter of fact, we find the opposite to be the case; for all money-makers increase their hoard of coin without limit. The source of the confusion is the near connexion between the two kinds of money-making; in either, the instrument [i.e., wealth] is the same, although the use is different, and so they pass into one another; for each is a use of the same property, but with a difference: accumulation is the end in the one case, but there is a further end in the other. Hence some persons are led to believe that making money is the object of household management, and the whole idea of their lives is that they ought either to increase their money without limit, or at any rate not to lose it. The origin of this disposition in men is that they are intent upon living only, and not upon living well; and, as their desires are unlimited, they also desire that the means of gratifying them should be without limit. Even those who aim at a good life seek the means of obtaining bodily pleasures; and, since the enjoyment of these appears to depend on property, they are absorbed in making money: and so there arises the second species of money-making. For, as their enjoyment is in excess, they seek an art which produces the excess of enjoyment; and, if they are not able to supply their pleasures by the art of money-making, they try other arts, using in turn every faculty in a manner contrary to nature. The quality of courage, for example, is not intended to make money, but to inspire confidence; neither is this the aim of the general's or of the physician's art; but the one aims at victory and the other at health. Nevertheless, some men turn every quality or art into a means of making money; this they conceive to be the end, and to the promotion of the end all things must contribute.

Thus, then, we have considered the art of money-making, which is unnecessary, and why men want it; and also the necessary art of money-making, which we have seen to be different from the other, and to be a natural part of the art of managing a household, concerned with the provision of food, not, however, like the former kind, unlimited, but having a limit.

And we have found the answer to our original question, whether the art of money-making is the business of the manager of a household and of the statesman or not their business?—viz. that it is an art which is presupposed by them. For political science does not make men, but takes them from nature and uses them; and nature provides them with food from the element of earth, air, or sea. At this stage begins the duty of the manager of a household, who has to order the things which nature supplies;—he may be compared to the weaver who has not to make but to use wool, and to know what sort of wool is good and serviceable or bad and unserviceable. Were this otherwise, it would be difficult to see why the art of money-making is a part of the management of a household and the art of medicine not; for surely the members of a household must have health just as they must have life or any other necessary. And as from one point of view the master of the house and the ruler of the state have to consider about health, from another point of view not they but the physician; so in one way the art of household management, in another way the subordinate art, has to consider about money. But strictly speaking, as I have already said, the means of life must be provided beforehand by nature; for the business of nature is to furnish food to that which is born, and the food of the offspring always remains over in the parent. Wherefore the art of making money out of fruits and animals is always natural.

Of the two sorts of money-making one, as I have just said, is a part of household management, the other is retail trade: the former necessary and honourable, the latter a kind of exchange which is justly censured; for it is unnatural, and a mode by which men gain from one another. The most hated sort, and with the greatest reason, is usury, which makes a gain out of money itself, and not from the natural use of it. For money was intended to be used in exchange, but not to increase at interest. And this term usury (*τόκος*) which means the birth of money from money, is applied to the breeding of money because the offspring resembles the parent. Wherefore of all modes of making money this is the most unnatural.

Enough has been said about the theory of money-making; we will now proceed to the practical part. The discussion of such matters is not unworthy of philosophy, but to be engaged in them practically is illiberal and irksome.

CHAPTER *2*

The Judeo-Christian Scriptures

After the passing of its founder in the first century A.D., the new religion of Christianity, as it rapidly expanded throughout the ancient Roman Empire, brought new perspectives on economic justice. Greek philosophy continued to challenge the best minds to grapple with the issues of the most just economic system and ideal human characteristics. But now ethical disputation was compelled to confront Christianity's ethical imperatives and new notions of nobility.

The Judeo-Christian scriptures have much to say on property, poverty, and proper human responses to each. Two-thirds of the parables of Jesus Christ in the gospels of the New Testament deal with money or wealth in one way or another, even if only as metaphor. The teachings of the law and prophets in the Old Testament also address economic issues. Not surprisingly, participants in the debate over economic justice since the Christian era began have cited verses from the Bible, claiming the force of special revelation (the Word of God) as well as reason (natural revelation) for their arguments.

Advocates of extreme views, whether in favor of private property or communism, have found seemingly supportive verses and lines of thought. For example, St. John Chrysostom (347–407 A.D.) argues:

Tell me, whence are you rich? From whom have you received? From your grandfather, you say; from your father. Are you able to show, ascending in the order of generation, that that possession is just throughout the whole series of preceding generations? Its beginning and root grew necessarily out of injustice. Why? Because God did not make this man rich and that man poor from the beginning. Nor, when He created the world, did He allot much treasure to one man, and forbid another to seek any. He gave the same earth to be cultivated by all. Since, therefore, His bounty is common, how comes it that you have so many fields, and your neighbor not even a clod of earth? . . . But, as I have already said, how can he who has riches be just? He certainly is not. He is good only if he distributes them to others: if he is without riches he is good; but as long as he retains them, he is not good. Can a thing be good, the possession of which makes men unjust, the distribution of which makes them just? It is not good, therefore, to have money; not to have it manifests the just man.[1]

Likewise, St. Ambrose (340–397 A.D.) also strongly argues against the claim of private property and wealth accumulation, commenting on Christ's Sermon on the Mount:

They are a great example truly, and one worthy of our faithful imitation, for if God's Providence never fails to supply the fowls of Heaven albeit they use no husbandry, and trouble nothing about the prospects of the harvest, the true cause of our want would seem to be avarice. It is for this reason that they have an abundance of suitable food, because they have not learnt to claim as their private and peculiar property the fruits of the earth which have been given to them in common for their food. We have lost common property by the claims of private property.

How far will your mad lusts take you, ye rich people, till you dwell alone upon the earth? Why do you at once turn nature out of doors, and claim the possession of her for your own selves? The land was made for all: why do you rich men claim it as your private property? Nature knows nothing of rich men; she bore us all poor.

Nature lavished all things for all in common, so likewise God made all things to be produced, that all should have common pasture, and the land should be a kind of property common to all men.

Nature then produced common property.

Robbery made private property.[2]

However, not all of the early church fathers favored communism and the abolition of private property. Most notably, Clement of Alexandria (?—215 A.D.) explicitly favored private property, as seen in the excerpt below. In *The Rich Man's Salvation*, Clement is discussing the exchange between Christ and the rich young ruler found in Matthew 19:16–26. Clement argues that a prerequisite for helping one's fellow man is the possession of wealth and private property.

[1]John Ryan, *Alleged Socialism of the Church Fathers* (St. Louis: B. Herder, 1913).

[2]Conrad Noel, *Socialism in Church History* (London: F. Palmer, 1910).

And how much more useful is the opposite condition, when by possessing a sufficiency a man is himself in no distress about money-making and also helps those he ought? For what sharing would be left among men, if nobody had anything? And how could this doctrine be found other than plainly contradictory to and at war with many other noble doctrines of the Lord? . . . How could we feed the hungry and give drink to the thirsty, cover the naked and entertain the homeless, with regard to which deeds He threatens fire and the outer darkness to those who have not done them, if each of us were himself already in want of all these things?[3]

Readers who bring to the Judeo-Christian scriptures no particular ideological bias discover balance. The Bible does indeed defend private property, but couples it with protection of the poor. While some New Testament verses may suggest the virtues of communism, certainly no *state* system of socialism is ever implied; rather, at most, a private and voluntary one in the church. And perhaps what at first glance appears to be flirtation with communism is actually celebration of charity. Certainly with Christianity a new ideal human type, very different from the Greek gentleman, begins to appear in Western civilization—a person who finds not degradation but dignity in work, and for whom the fruit of labor, encouraged by a system of incentives, provides the opportunity, through free giving, for tangible expression of an otherwise abstract love for humanity.

[3]Clement of Alexandria, *The Rich Man's Salvation*, trans. G. Butterworth (Cambridge, Mass.: Harvard University Press, 1919).

The Ten Commandments and the Right to Private Property

Exodus 20:1–17

Writers from a Judeo-Christian perspective frequently refer to verse 15 and verse 17 as evidence supporting the right to private property and possessions. Verse 15 warns against taking private property that belongs to others. Verse 17 gives an even stronger warning: We should not desire to have the personal property, belongings, or possessions that belong to others.

And God spake all these words, saying,

2 I am the Lord thy God, which have brought thee out of the land of Egypt, out of the house of bondage.

3 Thou shalt have no other gods before me.

4 Thou shalt not make unto thee any graven image, or any likeness of any thing that is in heaven above, or that is in the earth beneath, or that is in the water under the earth:

5 Thou shalt not bow down thyself to them, nor serve them: for I the Lord thy God am a jealous God, visiting the iniquity of the fathers upon the children unto the third and fourth generation of them that hate me;

6 And showing mercy unto thousands of them that love me, and keep my commandments.

7 Thou shalt not take the name of the Lord thy God in vain; for the Lord will not hold him guiltless that taketh his name in vain.

8 Remember the sabbath day, to keep it holy.

9 Six days shalt thou labour, and do all thy work:

10 But the seventh day is the sabbath of the Lord thy God: in it thou shalt not do any work, thou, nor thy son, nor thy daughter, thy manservant, nor thy maidservant, nor thy cattle, nor thy stranger that is within thy gates:

11 For in six days the Lord made heaven and earth, the sea, and all that in them is, and rested the seventh day: wherefore the Lord blessed the sabbath day, and hallowed it.

12 Honour thy father and thy mother: that thy days may be long upon the land which the Lord thy God giveth thee.

13 Thou shalt not kill.

14 Thou shalt not commit adultery.

15 Thou shalt not steal.

16 Thou shalt not bear false witness against thy neighbour.

17 Thou shalt not covet thy neighbour's house, thou shalt not covet thy neighbour's wife, nor his manservant, nor his maidservant, nor his ox, nor his ass, nor any thing that is thy neighbour's.

Sanctions for Property, But Warnings against Usury and Harming the Poor
Exodus 22:1-15, 25-27

Verses 1 through 15 illustrate the protection of private property in the Mosaic law. Those harmed, whether by accident or purposeful theft, were to receive compensation for their loss of property.

Verse 25 contains an admonition against usury (charging interest) on money lent to the poor. If a person's coat is held as collateral or security for a loan (verses 26–27), the lender is required to ensure the borrower's warmth and comfort by returning it to him for use during the night.

If a man shall steal an ox, or a sheep, and kill it, or sell it; he shall restore five oxen for an ox, and four sheep for a sheep.

2 If a thief be found breaking up, and be smitten that he die, there shall no blood be shed for him.

3 If the sun be risen upon him, there shall be blood shed for him; for he should make full restitution; if he have nothing, then he shall be sold for his theft.

4 If the theft be certainly found in his hand alive, whether it be ox, or ass, or sheep; he shall restore double.

5 If a man shall cause a field or vineyard to be eaten, and shall put in his beast, and shall feed in another man's field; of the best of his own field, and of the best of his own vineyard, shall he make restitution.

6 If fire break out, and catch in thorns, so that the stacks of corn, or the standing corn, or the field, be consumed therewith; he that kindled the fire shall surely make restitution.

7 If a man shall deliver unto his neighbour money or stuff to keep, and it be stolen out of the man's house; if the thief be found, let him pay double.

8 If the thief be not found, then the master of the house shall be brought unto the judges, to see whether he have put his hand unto his neighbour's goods.

9 For all manner of trespass, whether it be for ox, for ass, for sheep, for raiment, or for any manner of lost thing, which another challengeth to be his, the cause of both parties shall come before the judges; and whom the judges shall condemn, he shall pay double unto his neighbour.

10 If a man deliver unto his neighbour an ass, or an ox, or a sheep, or any beast, to keep; and it die, or be hurt, or driven away, no man seeing it:

11 Then shall an oath of the Lord be between them both, that he hath not put his hand unto his neighbour's goods; and the owner of it shall accept thereof, and he shall not make it good.

12 And if it be stolen from him, he shall make restitution unto the owner thereof.

13 If it be torn in pieces, then let him bring it for witness, and he shall not make good that which was torn.

14 And if a man borrow aught of his neighbour, and it be hurt, or die, the owner thereof being not with it, he shall surely make it good.

15 But if the owner thereof be with it, he shall not make it good: if it be an hired thing, it came for his hire. . . .

25 If thou lend money to any of my people that is poor by thee, thou shalt not be to him as an usurer, neither shalt thou lay upon him usury.

26 If thou at all take thy neighbour's raiment to pledge, thou shalt deliver it unto him by that the sun goeth down:

27 For that is his covering only, it is his raiment for his skin: wherein shall he sleep? and it shall come to pass, when he crieth unto me, that I will hear; for I am gracious.

The Gleaning Law

Leviticus 19:9–10

Property owners (specifically farmers) were to provide for the needs of the poor. When harvesting their crop, they were to leave part of the crop in their fields so the poor could gather food for sustenance.

9 And when ye reap the harvest of your land, thou shalt not wholly reap the corners of thy field, neither shalt thou gather the gleanings of thy harvest.

10 And thou shalt not glean thy vineyard, neither shalt thou gather every grape of thy vineyard; thou shalt leave them for the poor and stranger: I am the Lord your God.

The Sabbatic Year and the Jubilee Year
Leviticus 25:1–43

The symbolism of God's six days of labor and seventh day of rest during the creation of the heavens and earth (Genesis chapters 1 and 2) was to be an integral part of the economic system under Mosaic law. Every seven years, during the Sabbatic year, the land was to lie fallow and not be farmed (verses 1–7). A "Sabbath of Sabbatic years" occurred after seven sabbatic years (49 years). This was the Jubilee year, during which land was to lie fallow and possessions that were traded during the previous fifty years were to be returned to their original owner (verses 8–13). Due to the reversion of property in the Jubilee year, property bought and sold was to be priced according to the length of time to the next Jubilee (verses 14–16). The basic impetus for the Jubilee reversion is found in verse 23.

One exception to the reversion rule was the sale of a house in a walled city. The seller could "redeem" the house (retake possession of it, with recompense to the buyer) up to a year after the sale. After a year, however, it belonged to the person who bought it and was not to be returned to the original owner in the Jubilee year (verses 29–30).

The passage closes with admonitions concerning the poor (verses 35–43).

And the Lord spake unto Moses in mount Sinai, saying,

2 Speak unto the children of Israel, and say unto them, When ye come into the land which I give you, then shall the land keep a sabbath unto the Lord.

3 Six years thou shalt sow thy field, and six years thou shalt prune thy vineyard, and gather in the fruit thereof;

4 But in the seventh year shall be a sabbath of rest unto the land, a sabbath for the Lord: thou shalt neither sow thy field, nor prune thy vineyard.

5 That which groweth of its own accord of thy harvest thou shalt not reap, neither gather the grapes of thy vine undressed: for it is a year of rest unto the land.

6 And the sabbath of the land shall be meat for you; for thee, and for thy servant, and for thy maid, and for thy hired servant, and for thy stranger that sojourneth with thee,

7 And for thy cattle, and for the beast that are in thy land, shall all the increase thereof be meat.

8 And thou shalt number seven sabbaths of years unto thee, seven times seven years; and the space of the seven sabbaths of years shall be unto thee forty and nine years.

9 Then shalt thou cause the trumpet of the jubilee to sound on the tenth day of the seventh month, in the day of atonement shall ye make the trumpet sound throughout all your land.

10 And ye shall hallow the fiftieth year, and proclaim liberty throughout all the land unto all the inhabitants thereof: it shall be a jubilee unto you; and ye shall return every man unto his possession, and ye shall return every man unto his family.

11 A jubilee shall that fiftieth year be unto you: ye shall not sow, neither reap that which groweth of itself in it, nor gather the grapes in it of thy vine undressed.

12 For it is the jubilee; it shall be holy unto you: ye shall eat the increase thereof out of the field.

13 In the year of this jubilee ye shall return every man unto his possession.

14 And if thou sell aught unto thy neighbour, or buyest aught of thy neighbour's hand, ye shall not oppress one another:

15 According to the number of years after the jubilee thou shalt buy of thy neighbour, and according unto the number of years of the fruits he shall sell unto thee:

16 According to the multitude of years thou shalt increase the price thereof, and according to the fewness of years thou shalt diminish the price of it: for according to the number of the years of the fruits doth he sell unto thee.

17 Ye shall not therefore oppress one another; but thou shalt fear thy God: for I am the Lord your God.

18 Wherefore ye shall do my statutes, and keep my judgments, and do them; and ye shall dwell in the land in safety.

19 And the land shall yield her fruit, and ye shall eat your fill, and dwell therein in safety.

20 And if ye shall say, What shall we eat the seventh year? behold, we shall not sow, nor gather in our increase:

21 Then I will command my blessing upon you in the sixth year, and it shall bring forth fruit for three years.

22 And ye shall sow the eighth year, and eat yet of old fruit until the ninth year; until her fruits come in ye shall eat of the old store.

23 The land shall not be sold for ever: for the land is mine; for ye are strangers and sojourners with me.

24 And in all the land of your possession ye shall grant a redemption for the land.

25 If thy brother be waxen poor, and hath sold away some of his possession, and if any of his kin come to redeem it, then shall he redeem that which his brother sold.

26 And if the man have none to redeem it, and himself be able to redeem it;

27 Then let him count the years of the sale thereof, and restore the overplus unto the man to whom he sold it; that he may return unto his possession.

28 But if he be not able to restore it to him, then that which is sold shall remain in the hand of him that hath bought it until the year of jubilee: and in the jubilee it shall go out, and he shall return unto his possession.

29 And if a man sell a dwelling house in a walled city, then he may redeem it within a whole year after it is sold; within a full year may he redeem it.

30 And if it be not redeemed within the space of a full year, then the house that is in the walled city shall be established for ever to him that bought it throughout his generations: it shall not go out in the jubilee.

31 But the houses of the villages which have no wall round about them shall be counted as the fields of the country: they may be redeemed, and they shall go out in the jubilee.

32 Notwithstanding the cities of the Levites, and the houses of the cities of their possession, may the Levites redeem at any time.

33 And if a man purchase of the Levites, then the house that was sold and the city of his possession, shall go out in the year of jubilee: for the houses of the cities of the Levites are their possession among the children of Israel.

34 But the field of the suburbs of their cities may not be sold; for it is their perpetual possession.

35 And if thy brother be waxen poor, and fallen in decay with thee; then thou shalt relieve him: yea, though he be a stranger, or a sojourner; that he may live with thee.

36 Take thou no usury of him, or increase: but fear thy God; that thy brother may live with thee.

37 Thou shalt not give him thy money upon usury, nor lend him thy victuals for increase.

38 I am the Lord your God, which brought you forth out of the land of Egypt, to give you the land of Canaan, and to be your God.

39 And if thy brother that dwelleth by thee be waxen poor, and be sold unto thee; thou shalt not compel him to serve as a bondservant:

40 But as an hired servant, and as a sojourner, he shall be with thee, and shall serve thee unto the year of jubilee:

41 And then shall he depart from thee, both he and his children with him, and shall return unto his own family, and unto the possession of his fathers shall he return.

42 For they are my servants, which I brought forth out of the land of Egypt: they shall not be sold as bondmen.

43 Thou shalt not rule over him with rigour; but shalt fear thy God.

Further Instruction on the Sabbatic Year, Treatment of the Poor, and Taking of Another's Property

Deuteronomy 15:1–18

In addition to letting the land lie fallow, all debts were to be forgiven during the Sabbatic year. An exception was that debt to "foreigners" (non-Israelites), at the option of the Israelite lender, did not have to be forgiven (verses 1–4). Those who had wealth to lend were not to withhold lending as the Sabbatic year approached. Though such debt was to be forgiven in the soon-coming Sabbatic year, God promises his blessings to repay such unselfish lenders (verses 7–11).

Verses 12–18 explain what was to be done with Hebrew slaves during the Sabbatic year. Those slaves desiring freedom were to be set free with adequate provisions to ensure their near-term survival. Slaves desiring to stay with their masters were to receive a sign and remain with their master "for ever."

At the end of every seven years thou shalt make a release.

2 And this is the manner of the release: Every creditor that lendeth aught unto his neighbour shall release it; he shall not exact it of his neighbour, or of his brother; because it is called the Lord's release.

3 Of a foreigner thou mayest exact it again: but that which is thine with thy brother thine hand shall release;

4 Save when there shall be no poor among you; for the Lord shall greatly bless thee in the land which the Lord thy God giveth thee for an inheritance to possess it:

5 Only if thou carefully hearken unto the voice of the Lord thy God, to observe to do all these commandments which I command thee this day.

6 For the Lord thy God blesseth thee, as he promised thee: and thou shalt lend unto many nations, but thou shalt not borrow; and thou shalt reign over many nations, but they shall not reign over thee.

7 If there be among you a poor man of one of thy brethren within any of thy gates in thy land which the Lord thy God giveth thee, thou shalt not harden thine heart, nor shut thine hand from thy poor brother:

8 But thou shalt open thine hand wide unto him, and shalt surely lend him sufficient for his need, in that which he wanteth.

9 Beware that there be not a thought in thy wicked heart, saying, The seventh year, the year of release, is at hand; and thine eye be evil against thy poor brother, and thou givest him nought; and he cry unto the Lord against thee, and it be sin unto thee.

10 Thou shalt surely give him, and thine heart shall not be grieved when thou givest unto him: because that for this thing the Lord thy God shall bless thee in all thy works, and in all that thou puttest thine hand unto.

11 For the poor shall never cease out of the land: therefore I command thee, saying, Thou shalt open thine hand wide unto thy brother, to thy poor, and to thy needy, in thy land.

12 And if thy brother, an Hebrew man, or an Hebrew woman, be sold unto thee, and serve thee six years; then in the seventh year thou shalt let him go free from thee.

13 And when thou sendest him out free from thee, thou shalt not let him go away empty:

14 Thou shalt furnish him liberally out of thy flock, and out of thy floor, and out of thy winepress: of that wherewith the Lord thy God hath blessed thee thou shalt give unto him.

15 And thou shalt remember that thou wast a bondman in the land of Egypt, and the Lord thy God redeemed thee: therefore I command thee this thing today.

16 And it shall be, if he say unto thee, I will not go away from thee; because he loveth thee and thine house, because he is well with thee;

17 Then thou shalt take an awl, and thrust it through his ear unto the door, and he shall be thy servant for ever. And also unto thy maidservant thou shalt do likewise.

18 It shall not seem hard unto thee, when thou sendest him away free from thee; for he hath been worth a double hired servant to thee, in serving thee six years: and the Lord thy God shall bless thee in all that thou doest.

A Rebuke to the Rich

Nehemiah 5:1-13

After the Babylonian captivity of the Jewish people, some Hebrews returned to what was formerly Jerusalem to rebuild the city walls and the Temple. Evidently some Israelites were taking advantage of their brethren by charging usury and forcing some to become slaves. Nehemiah, as a leader of the former exiles, reminds the wealthy of the Mosaic law and their duty to the poor.

And there was a great cry of the people and of their wives against their brethren the Jews.

2 For there were that said, We, our sons, and our daughters, are many: therefore we take up corn for them, that we may eat, and live.

3 Some also there were that said, We have mortgaged our lands, vineyards, and houses, that we might buy corn, because of the dearth.

4 There were also that said, We have borrowed money for the king's tribute, and that upon our lands and vineyards.

5 Yet now our flesh is as the flesh of our brethren, our children as their children: and, lo, we bring into bondage our sons and our daughters to be servants, and some of our daughters are brought unto bondage already: neither is it in our power to redeem them; for other men have our lands and vineyards.

6 And I was very angry when I heard their cry and these words.

7 Then I consulted with myself, and I rebuked the nobles, and the rulers, and said unto them, Ye exact usury, every one of his brother. And I set a great assembly against them.

8 And I said unto them, We after our ability have redeemed our brethren the Jews, which were sold unto the heathen; and will ye even sell your brethren? or shall they be sold unto us? Then held they their peace, and found nothing to answer.

9 Also I said, It is not good that ye do: ought ye not to walk in the fear of our God because of the reproach of the heathen our enemies?

10 I likewise, and my brethren, and my servants, might exact of them money and corn: I pray you, let us leave off this usury.

11 Restore, I pray you, to them, even this day, their lands, their vineyards, their olive-yards, and their houses, also the hundredth part of the money, and of the corn, the wine, and the oil, that ye exact of them.

12 Then said they, We will restore them, and will require nothing of them; so will we do as thou sayest. Then I called the priests, and took an oath of them, that they should do according to this promise.

13 Also I shook my lap, and said, So God shake out every man from his house, and from his labour, that performeth not this promise, even thus be he shaken out, and emptied. And all the congregation said, Amen, and praised the Lord. And the people did according to this promise.

Laziness and Poverty, Work and Wealth

Proverbs 20:13, Proverbs 23:21, Proverbs 24:30–34,
Proverbs 28:19–20

These verses contain teaching that poverty is not necessarily due to personal misfortune, but rather laziness. Hard work will lead to success.

13 Love not sleep, lest thou come to poverty; open thine eyes, and thou shalt be satisfied with bread.

21 For the drunkard and the glutton shall come to poverty: and drowsiness shall clothe a man with rags.

30 I went by the field of the slothful, and by the vineyard of the man void of understanding;
31 And, lo, it was all grown over with thorns, and nettles had covered the face thereof, and the stone wall thereof was broken down.
32 Then I saw, and considered it well: I looked upon it, and received instruction.
33 Yet a little sleep, a little slumber, a little folding of the hands to sleep:
34 So shall thy poverty come as one that travelleth; and thy want as an armed man.

19 He that tilleth his land shall have plenty of bread: but he that followeth after vain persons shall have poverty enough.
20 A faithful man shall abound with blessings: but he that maketh haste to be rich shall not be innocent.

A Warning against Desire for Things of This World

Matthew 6:19-34

This excerpt is from Jesus' Sermon on the Mount. Jesus warns against setting one's desires on earthly treasures and needs. He admonishes to "lay up treasures in heaven" and to not worry about adequate food and clothing, as the heavenly Father will provide for one's needs. The concept of the ideal Christian economic man can perhaps be summarized by verse 33; it is one who seeks God, rather than wealth. This thought also seems to be implicit in much of the Mosaic law previously excerpted. The New Testament excerpts to follow also seem to agree with Jesus' concept of ideal economic man.

19 Lay not up for yourselves treasures upon earth, where moth and rust doth corrupt, and where thieves break through and steal:

20 But lay up for yourselves treasures in heaven, where neither moth nor rust doth corrupt, and where thieves do not break through nor steal:

21 For where your treasure is, there will your heart be also.

22 The light of the body is the eye: if therefore thine eye be single, thy whole body shall be full of light.

23 But if thine eye be evil, thy whole body shall be full of darkness. If therefore the light that is in thee be darkness, how great is that darkness!

24 No man can serve two masters: for either he will hate the one, and love the other; or else he will hold to the one, and despise the other. Ye cannot serve God and mammon.

25 Therefore I say unto you, Take no thought for your life, what ye shall eat, or what ye shall drink; nor yet for your body, what ye shall put on. Is not the life more than meat, and the body than raiment?

26 Behold the fowls of the air: for they sow not, neither do they reap, nor gather into barns; yet your heavenly Father feedeth them. Are ye not much better than they?

27 Which of you by taking thought can add one cubit unto his stature?

28 And why take ye thought for raiment? Consider the lilies of the field, how they grow; they toil not, neither do they spin:

29 And yet I say unto you, That even Solomon in all his glory was not arrayed like one of these.

30 Wherefore, if God so clothe the grass of the field, which today is, and tomorrow is cast into the oven, shall he not much more clothe you, O ye of little faith?

31 Therefore take no thought, saying, What shall we eat? or, What shall we drink? or, Wherewithal shall we be clothed?

32 (For after all these things do the Gentiles seek:) for your heavenly Father knoweth that ye have need of all these things.

33 But seek ye first the kingdom of God, and his righteousness; and all these things shall be added unto you.

34 Take therefore no thought for the morrow: for the morrow shall take thought for the things of itself. Sufficient unto the day is the evil thereof.

Christ and the Rich Young Ruler

Matthew 19:16–26

This exchange between Jesus and the rich young ruler seems to imply that wealth and salvation are contradictory. Many writers of socialism and communism use this dialogue as evidence of the evilness of wealth and concomitant selfishness.

Clement of Alexandria, however, interprets this passage differently, concluding that wealth is not inherently sinful. What is sinful, in Clement's view, is the selfish possession and pursuit of wealth and the refusal to use one's private possessions to ease the suffering and needs of others.

16 And, behold, one came and said unto him, Good Master, what good thing shall I do, that I may have eternal life?

17 And he said unto him, Why callest thou me good? there is none good but one, that is, God: but if thou wilt enter into life, keep the commandments.

18 He saith unto him, Which? Jesus said, Thou shalt do no murder, Thou shalt not commit adultery, Thou shalt not steal, Thou shalt not bear false witness,

19 Honour thy father and thy mother: and, Thou shalt love thy neighbour as thyself.

20 The young man saith unto him, All these things have I kept from my youth up: what lack I yet?

21 Jesus said unto him, If thou wilt be perfect, go and sell that thou hast, and give to the poor, and thou shalt have treasure in heaven: and come and follow me.

22 But when the young man heard that saying, he went away sorrowful: for he had great possessions.

23 Then said Jesus unto his disciples, Verily I say unto you, That a rich man shall hardly enter into the kingdom of heaven.

24 And again I say unto you, It is easier for a camel to go through the eye of a needle, than for a rich man to enter into the kingdom of God.

25 When his disciples heard it, they were exceedingly amazed, saying, Who then can be saved?

26 But Jesus beheld them, and said unto them, With men this is impossible; but with God all things are possible.

Parable of the Kingdom of Heaven

Matthew 25:14-27

Though interpreters of scripture typically discuss this parable for the Christian doctrine it contains, it is interesting to note the setting of the parable. The parable contains references to private property, and business transactions, as well as the receipt of usury. We leave it to the reader to ponder whether this implies Jesus' approval of these arrangements.

14 For the kingdom of heaven is as a man travelling into a far country, who called his own servants, and delivered unto them his goods.

15 And unto one he gave five talents, to another two, and to another one; to every man according to his several ability; and straightway took his journey.

16 Then he that had received the five talents went and traded with the same, and made them other five talents.

17 And likewise he that had received two, he also gained other two.

18 But he that had received one went and digged in the earth, and hid his lord's money.

19 After a long time the lord of those servants cometh, and reckoneth with them.

20 And so he that had received five talents came and brought other five talents, saying, Lord, thou deliveredst unto me five talents: behold, I have gained beside them five talents more.

21 His lord said unto him, Well done, thou good and faithful servant: thou hast been faithful over a few things, I will make thee ruler over many things: enter thou into the joy of thy lord.

22 He also that had received two talents came and said, Lord, thou deliveredst unto me two talents: behold, I have gained two other talents beside them.

23 His lord said unto him, Well done, good and faithful servant; thou has been faithful over a few things, I will make thee ruler over many things: enter thou into the joy of thy lord.

24 Then he which had received the one talent came and said, Lord, I knew thee that thou art an hard man, reaping where thou hast not sown, and gathering where thou hast not strawed:

25 And I was afraid, and went and hid thy talent in the earth: lo, there thou hast that is thine.

26 His lord answered and said unto him, Thou wicked and slothful servant, thou knewest that I reap where I sowed not, and gather where I have not strawed:

27 Thou oughtest therefore to have put my money to the exchangers, and then at my coming I should have received mine own with usury.

Communism in the Jerusalem Church

Acts 2:41–47, Acts 4:32–37, Acts 5:1–11

These excerpts are widely quoted by socialist and communist philosophers who seek a foundation for their views in the Christian scriptures. These excerpts describe the economic condition of the Christian church shortly after Christ's resurrection and ascension. Believers "sold their possessions" and "had all things common." The excerpt from chapter 5 is sometimes used as an example of the punishment coming to those who are selfish. But a careful reading of the passage shows that Ananias and Sapphira were not struck dead because they retained some of their wealth, but because they lied about it (verses 4 and 9).

41 Then they that gladly received his word were baptized: and the same day there were added unto them about three thousand souls.

42 And they continued steadfastly in the apostles' doctrine and fellowship, and in breaking of bread, and in prayers.

43 And fear came upon every soul: and many wonders and signs were done by the apostles.

44 And all that believed were together, and had all things common;

45 And sold their possessions and goods, and parted them to all men, as every man had need.

46 And they, continuing daily with one accord in the temple, and breaking bread from house to house, did eat their meat with gladness and singleness of heart,

47 Praising God, and having favour with all the people. And the Lord added to the church daily such as should be saved.

32 And the multitude of them that believed were of one heart and of one soul: neither said any of them that aught of the things which he possessed was his own; but they had all things common.

33 And with great power gave the apostles witness of the resurrection of the Lord Jesus: and great grace was upon them all.

34 Neither was there any among them that lacked: for as many as were possessors of lands or houses sold them, and brought the prices of the things that were sold,

35 And laid them down at the apostles' feet: and distribution was made unto every man according as he had need.

36 And Joses, who by the apostles was surnamed Barnabas, (which is, being interpreted, The son of consolation,) a Levite, and of the country of Cyprus,

37 Having land, sold it, and brought the money, and laid it at the apostles' feet.

But a certain man named Ananias, with Sapphira his wife, sold a possession,

2 And kept back part of the price, his wife also being privy to it, and brought a certain part, and laid it at the apostles' feet.

3 But Peter said, Ananias, why hath Satan filled thine heart to lie to the Holy Ghost, and to keep back part of the price of the land?

4 Whiles it remained, was it not thine own? and after it was sold, was it not in thine own power? why hast thou conceived this thing in thine heart? thou hast not lied unto men, but unto God.

5 And Ananias hearing these words fell down, and gave up the ghost: and great fear came on all them that heard these things.

6 And the young men arose, wound him up, and carried him out, and buried him.

7 And it was about the space of three hours after, when his wife, not knowing what was done, came in.

8 And Peter answered unto her, Tell me whether ye sold the land for so much? And she said, Yea, for so much.

9 Then Peter said unto her, How is it that ye have agreed together to tempt the Spirit of the Lord? behold, the feet of them which have buried thy husband are at the door, and shall carry thee out.

10 Then fell she down straightway at his feet, and yielded up the ghost: and the young men came in, and found her dead, and, carrying her forth, buried her by her husband.

11 And great fear came upon all the church, and upon as many as heard these things.

Charity in the Early Church
Acts 6:1-7, 1 Corinthians 16:1-2

Despite the voluntary communal sharing described in Acts chapters 2 and 4, the excerpt from Acts 6 shows the early church had some problems. Some Christians were not receiving their fair share of the offerings; therefore seven men, the first deacons, were appointed to ensure that the needy received sustenance.

The passage from 1 Corinthians states the teaching of the apostle Paul on offerings.

And in those days, when the number of the disciples was multiplied, there arose a murmuring of the Grecians against the Hebrews, because their widows were neglected in the daily ministration.

2 Then the twelve called the multitude of the disciples unto them, and said, It is not reason that we should leave the word of God, and serve tables.

3 Wherefore, brethren, look ye out among you seven men of honest report, full of the Holy Ghost and wisdom, whom we may appoint over this business.

4 But we will give ourselves continually to prayer, and to the ministry of the word.

5 And the saying pleased the whole multitude: and they chose Stephen, a man full of faith and of the Holy Ghost, and Philip, and Prochorus, and Nicanor, and Timon, and Parmenas, and Nicolas a proselyte of Antioch:

6 Whom they set before the apostles: and when they had prayed, they laid their hands on them.

7 And the word of God increased; and the number of the disciples multiplied in Jerusalem greatly; and a great company of the priests were obedient to the faith.

Now concerning the collection for the saints, as I have given order to the churches of Galatia, even so do ye.

2 Upon the first day of the week let every one of you lay by him in store, as God hath prospered him, that there be no gatherings when I come.

Warnings about Work

2 Thessalonians 3:7-12

This teaching from Paul to the church at Thessalonica shows that sharing private goods and possessions does have its limits. Such goods were not to be provided to those who, though presumably physically able to work, did not work.

7 For yourselves know how ye ought to follow us: for we behaved not ourselves disorderly among you;

8 Neither did we eat any man's bread for nought; but wrought with labour and travail night and day, that we might not be chargeable to any of you:

9 Not because we have not power, but to make ourselves an example unto you to follow us.

10 For even when we were with you, this we commanded you, that if any would not work, neither should he eat.

11 For we hear that there are some which walk among you disorderly, working not at all, but are busybodies.

12 Now them that are such we command and exhort by our Lord Jesus Christ, that with quietness they work, and eat their own bread.

Warnings to the Rich

1 Timothy 6:17–19, James 5:1–5

As Clement's interpretation of the exchange between Jesus and the rich young ruler shows, wealth is not inherently evil. Wealth can be used to meet the needs of others. The excerpt from James shows the dangers of the pursuit of wealth for selfish and personal ends.

17 Charge them that are rich in this world, that they be not highminded, nor trust in uncertain riches, but in the living God, who giveth us richly all things to enjoy;

18 That they do good, that they be rich in good works, ready to distribute, willing to communicate;

19 Laying up in store for themselves a good foundation against the time to come, that they may lay hold on eternal life.

Go to now, ye rich men, weep and howl for your miseries that shall come upon you.

2 Your riches are corrupted, and your garments are motheaten.

3 Your gold and silver is cankered; and the rust of them shall be a witness against you, and shall eat your flesh as it were fire. Ye have heaped treasure together for the last days.

4 Behold, the hire of the labourers who have reaped down your fields, which is of you kept back by fraud, crieth: and the cries of them which have reaped are entered into the ears of the Lord of sabaoth.

5 Ye have lived in pleasure on the earth, and been wanton; ye have nourished your hearts, as in a day of slaughter.

CHAPTER *3*

Medieval Christian Views of Economic Justice

During the Middle Ages, with the renewed availability of classical texts, particularly Aristotle's, Christian thinkers felt increasingly compelled to consider Greek philosophy as well as scripture. St. Thomas Aquinas (1225–1274) undertook the most ambitious effort of the age to develop a comprehensive and systematic Christian theology by synthesizing special revelation with Aristotle, whom he treated authoritatively as "the Philosopher." One would be hard pressed to name a topic— the great questions of economic justice included—untouched by Aquinas' *Summa Theologica*.

It has been argued that "we find in the writings of St. Thomas Aquinas the economic doctrines of Aristotle reproduced with a partial infusion of Christian elements."[1] Certainly Aristotle's influence amply evinces itself in Aquinas' defense of private property and condemnation of trade, profit, and usury. To be sure, Aquinas includes a distinctively Christian insistence on the necessity for charity if economic justice is to be done. Otherwise, the views of Aquinas on economic justice seem scarcely distinguishable from Aristotle's.

During the Middle Ages, the intellectual force of Greek philosophy and the

---

[1]Quoted in George O'Brien, *An Essay on Mediaeval Economic Teaching* (London: Longmans, Green & Co., 1920, reprinted 1967), p. 17.

moral power of Christianity combined to determine the governing views of economic justice in Western civilization. The reigning view justified private property, but only as a necessary concession to human nature, and granted the moral legitimacy of economic activity only if confined to bare necessities.

In economics, at least, the human ideal types of classical Greek and medieval Christendom, otherwise so divergent, converged remarkably. The Greek gentleman viewed economic production as beneath dignity; the medieval monk, exalting poverty, considered work—with the aim of necessity, of course, and not profit—to be grim punishment. Though they lived worlds and ages apart, the Greek gentleman and the Christian monk both disdained the frankly economic motives that would typify the modern era and would even receive theological sanction from a radically redirected, de-Hellenized Christian tradition.

Summa Theologica

Thomas Aquinas

THE RIGHT TO PROPERTY

Man's Control over Nature.   Material things may be considered under two aspects. First, as to their nature: and this in no way lies within human power, but only within the divine power whose wish all things obey. Secondly, as to the use of such things. And in this respect, man has a natural control over material things; for he can, in virtue of his reason and will, make use of material things for his own benefit, as though they were created for this purpose: for imperfect things exist to serve the advantage of the more perfect as we have already seen. On this principle the Philosopher proves (I, *Politics*), that the possession of material things is natural to man. And this natural dominion which man has over other creatures, in virtue of reason which makes him the image of God, is clearly shown in the creation of man (*Genesis* I) where it is said: 'Let us make man to our own image and likeness, and he shall rule over the fish of the sea,' etc.

The Limits of Private Property.   With respect to material things there are two points which man must consider. First, concerning the power of acquisition and disposal; and in this respect private possession is permissible. It is also necessary to human life for three reasons. First, because every one is more concerned with the obtaining of what concerns himself alone than with the common affairs of all or of many others: for each one, avoiding extra labour, leaves the common task to the next man; as we see when there are too many officials. Secondly, because human affairs are dealt with in a more orderly manner when each has his own business to go about: there would be complete confusion if every one tried to do everything. Thirdly, because this leads to a more peaceful condition of man; provided each is content with his own. So we see that it is among those who possess something jointly and in common that disputes most frequently arise.

The other point which concerns man with regard to material things is their use. As to this, men should not hold material things as their own but to the common benefit: each readily sharing them with others in their necessity. So the Apostle says (I *Tim.*, ult.): 'Charge the rich of this world to give easily, to communicate to others.'

Aquinas: Selected Political Writings, *ed. A. P. D'Entreves, trans. J. G. Dawson (Oxford: Basil Blackwell, 1978), pp. 167–175. Permission granted by Basil Blackwell, Inc., and by Barnes & Noble Books, Totowa, New Jersey.*

The Right to Private Property Derives from Human Law. The common possession of things is to be attributed to natural law, not in the sense that natural law decrees that all things are to be held in common and that there is to be no private possession: but in the sense that there is no distinction of property on grounds of natural law, but only by human agreement; and this pertains to positive law, as we have already shown. Thus private property is not opposed to natural law, but is an addition to it, devised by the human reason.

The Duty of Charity. What pertains to human law can in no way detract from what pertains to natural law or to divine law. Now according to the natural order, instituted by divine providence, material goods are provided for the satisfaction of human needs. Therefore the division and appropriation of property, which proceeds from human law, must not hinder the satisfaction of man's necessity from such goods. Equally, whatever a man has in superabundance is owed, of natural right, to the poor for their sustenance. So Ambrosius says, and it is also to be found in the *Decretum Gratiani* (Dist. XLVII): 'The bread which you withhold belongs to the hungry; the clothing you shut away, to the naked; and the money you bury in the earth is the redemption and freedom of the penniless.' But because there are many in necessity, and they cannot all be helped from the same source, it is left to the initiative of individuals to make provision from their own wealth, for the assistance of those who are in need. If, however, there is such urgent and evident necessity that there is clearly an immediate need of necessary sustenance,—if, for example, a person is in immediate danger of physical privation, and there is no other way of satisfying his need,—then he may take what is necessary from another person's goods, either openly or by stealth. Nor is this, strictly speaking, fraud or robbery.

USURY

The Profit Motive. Traders are those who apply themselves to the exchange of goods. But as the Philosopher says (I *Politics*, ch. 3) there are two reasons for the exchange of things. The first may be called natural and necessary; and obtains when exchange is made either of goods against goods, or of goods against money, to meet the necessities of life. Such exchange is not, strictly speaking, the business of traders; but is rather the province of the steward or politician whose duty it is to see that the household or the state obtain the necessities of life. The other form of exchange, either of money against money or of any sort of goods against money, is carried on not for the necessary business of life, but for the sake of profit. And it is this form of exchange which would seem, strictly speaking, to be the business of traders. Now, according to the Philosopher, the first form of exchange, because it serves natural necessity, is praiseworthy. But the second form is rightly condemned; for of itself it serves only the desire for gain, which knows no bounds but spreads always further. Therefore trading, considered in itself, always implies a certain baseness, in that it has not of itself any honest or necessary object.

Though profit, which is the object of trading does not of itself imply any honest or necessary aim, neither does it imply anything vicious or contrary to virtue. So there is nothing to prevent its being turned to some honest or necessary object. In this way trading is made lawful. As, for example, when a person uses a moderate profit, which he seeks from trading, for the upkeep of his household, or for assisting the poor, or again, when a person carries on trade for the public welfare, and to provide the country with the necessities of life; and when he seeks profit, not for its own sake, but as a reward for his labour.

Usury Never Permissible on Moral Grounds. To accept usury for the loan of money is in itself unjust; because this is selling what does not exist, and must obviously give rise to inequality, which is contrary to justice. For the better understanding of this point it should be noted that there are some things whose use lies in their consumption: as, for example, wine is consumed when it is used as drink, and wheat is consumed when it is used for food. In such cases the use of the thing and the thing itself cannot be separately taken into account, so that whenever the use of the thing is granted to some one the thing itself is given at the same time. For this reason ownership is transferred by a loan in such cases. If a man were to sell separately both the wine and the use of the wine he would be selling the same thing twice over; that is he would be selling what does not exist: and he would clearly be sinning against justice. For the same reason he commits an injustice who requires two things in return for the loan of wine or wheat, namely the return of an equal quantity of the thing itself and the price of its use. This is what is called usury.

There are other things whose use does not lie in the consumption of the thing itself; as for instance the use of a house, which lies in the living in it and not in its destruction. In such cases both the use and the thing itself can be separately granted; as when, for instance, some one passes the ownership of a house to another, but reserves to himself the right to live there for a certain time; or on the other hand when some one grants the use of a house to another, reserving to himself its ownership. For this reason it is permissible for a man to accept a price for the use of a house, and in addition to sell the freehold of the house itself, as is clear in the sale and leasing of houses.

Now money, according to the Philosopher in the *Ethics* (V, 5) and *Politics* (1, 3), is devised mainly to facilitate exchange; and therefore the proper and principal use of the money lies in its consumption or expenditure in the business of exchange. For this reason, therefore, it is wrong to accept a price, or money, for the use of a sum of money which is lent. And just as a man is bound to make restitution of other things which he has unjustly acquired, so also must he restore the money he has obtained from usury.

Human laws allow certain sins to go unpunished because of the imperfection of man's condition which brings it about that much which is useful would be prevented if all sins were separately punished by explicit penalties. Therefore human law permits usury, not as though considering it to be just, but to avoid interference with the useful activities of many persons. So in Roman law itself we read that, 'things consumed in use do not bear usufruct either upon natural or upon civil grounds': and that the Senate did not grant usufruct upon such things, nor indeed had it power to do so: but that it did institute a quasi-usufruct, by permitting usury. And the Philosopher, arguing from natural reason, says in the first book of the *Politics* (ch. 3) that the acquisition of money by usury is wholly contrary to nature.

CHAPTER *4*

Reformation Beginnings

The earliest challenge to the world-view of the Middle Ages appeared during the Renaissance, a cultural movement which began in Italy in the 1300s. Renaissance painters, poets, and philosophers, questioning the other worldliness of medieval religion, celebrated the values of *this* life. Yet because the Renaissance, a name that means "rebirth," represented a return to the classical tradition of Greece and Rome, no new moral or religious vision of economic life appeared.

On the other hand, the Protestant Reformation, a revolt against the Catholic church that began during the 1500s in Germany and spread through many parts of Europe, did offer new *moral* and *theological* perspectives on life, economics included. An ethical vision with significant long-run implications for economics—particularly a spirit that would favor the developing capitalist system—surfaced in Protestant thought.

Nineteenth-century German philosopher G. W. F. Hegel, who viewed the Reformation as the true beginning point of modernity, saw new human ideals in the thoughts of the Protestant leaders. For example, Hegel found in Martin Luther's view of wealth and poverty a perspective very different from that current in medieval Christendom; as Hegel described Luther's opinions, "It is more consonant with justice that he who has money should spend it even in luxuries, than that he should give it away to idlers and beggars, for he bestows it upon an equal number of persons by so doing, and these must at any rate have worked diligently for it." Hegel argued that beginning with the Reformation, "Industry, crafts and trades now have their moral validity recognized, and their obstacles to their prosperity which originated with the [medieval] Church, have vanished."[1]

Hegel glimpsed in the Reformation the birth of a new ideal human type that would morally undergird capitalism. The classical analysis of Reformation economic ideals, however, appeared much later in the essays of German sociologist Max Weber (1864–1920). Weber traced to the Reformation a new moral perspective subsequently known as the "Protestant ethic." As Weber described the capitalist economic system, "Man is dominated by the making of money, by acquisition as the ultimate purpose of his life" rather than as an activity "subordinated to man as the means for the satisfaction of his material needs." And this acquisition, Weber argued, "is closely connected with certain religious ideals": that "The earning of money . . . is, so long as it is done legally, the result and expression of virtue and proficiency in a calling." Acquiring wealth came to be viewed as "one's duty in a calling"—a duty owed to God. As Weber pointed out, "The conception of money-making as an end in itself to which people were bound, as a calling, was contrary to the ethical feelings of whole epochs."

> The peculiarity of this philosophy of avarice appears to be the ideal of the honest man of recognized credit, and above all the idea of a duty of the individual towards the increase of his capital, which is assumed as an end in itself. Truly what is . . . preached is not simply a means of making one's way in the world, but a peculiar ethic. The infraction of its rules is . . . forgetfulness of duty. That is the essence of the matter. It is not mere business astuteness—that sort of thing is common enough; it is an ethos.

Such a "state of mind," Weber continued, "would both in ancient times and in the Middle Ages have been proscribed as the lowest sort of avarice and as an attitude entirely lacking in self-respect." How different is the new view of work and wealth that came in with the Reformation—ennoblement of work "for the provision of humanity with material goods," accompanied by "the joy and pride of having given employment to numerous people."[2]

Weber's critics contend that the first Protestant leaders—notably Martin Luther and John Calvin—in many respects maintained an essentially medieval approach to economics; for example, both condemned usury. Yet perhaps the issue is not so much what Luther and Calvin themselves thought as what others would deduce in the atmosphere created by the Reformation challenge to medieval Christian interpretations. Thus in 1546, less than thirty years after Luther's nailing of the Ninety-Five Theses to the church door at Wittenburg, French jurist Carolus

[1]G. W. F. Hegel, *The Philosophy of History*, trans. J. Sibree (New York: Dover, no date), p. 423.
[2]Stranislav Andreski, ed. and trans., *Max Weber on Capitalism, Bureaucracy and Religion* (Unwin Hyman, Ltd., London 1972), pp. 113–115, 124–125.

Molinaeus (1500–1566) wrote a controversial tract, excerpted here, challenging the theological and biblical accuracy of the condemnation of usury by earlier Christian thinkers. New views on the justice of usury—the borrowing of money for interest—were essential for the removal of no small moral obstacle to the unleashing of business activity in early capitalism. Molinaeus justifies usury by demonstrating from the utility of the use of money the justice of charging for the loan of it, but more importantly, by boldly opposing the overarching Christian principle of "charity"—benevolence—against particular scriptural texts hitherto used to condemn the earning of interest.

A Treatise on Contracts and Usury

Carolus Molinaeus

Here it is to be noted* that Scholastic theologians, as well as canonists & jurists, considering the letter rather than the spirit or intent & purpose of the divine law, have believed there was something peculiarly & inherently vicious about usury or usurious gains, more than in unjust, deceitful sales, or other similar kinds of fraud. And this, not because one's neighbor is more harmed thereby; but because in a loan something more than the principal is received; as if usury *per se* were more detestable & more wicked, or *per se* more unlawful. Thus some hold (Bernardi., *de Contract.*) that, although usury may sometimes not be contrary to charity, as if it were harmful, still there is always something rather dishonorable about it; or again (Petr. Anchar.), that the prohibition of usury is so strict according to divine law that it cannot be modified by legislation, even in cases where it is a question of public utility & the common good, & the civil amity which nature has established among men. Hence they have fallen into the infinite evasions & numerous errors & fallacies with which their very confused books are filled; all because they have not considered the purpose of the divine law, which is charity, as Christ himself testifies (Matth. 7): *All things, therefore, whatsoever you would that men should do to you, do you also to them. For this is the law & the prophets.* That is to say, this is its purpose. And St. Paul (I Timothy): *The end of the law is charity.* Also Romans 13 & Galatians 5: *He who loveth his neighbor hath fulfilled the law.* Therefore, usury is not forbidden & unlawful according to divine law, except insofar as it is contrary to charity. Since, however, usury is taken in many ways, that form alone is prohibited & condemned which offends against charity & love of one's neighbor. This is the interpretation of the passages cited & all similar passages of Scripture.

Suppose a merchant of means borrows money in order to make a profit from legitimate business, & promises to pay usury monthly or annually, instead of a portion of the expected profit: Should you say that the creditor, if unable to prove

---

*This passage is preceded by a summary of the chief scriptural texts cited by opponents of usury.— Ed.

Carolus Molinaeus, "A Treatise on Contracts and Usury," in Early Economic Thought, *ed. A. E. Monroe (Cambridge, Mass.: Harvard University Press, 1924). Reprinted by permission of the publisher.*

his claim to that much *interest,* [a] or perhaps any *interest* at all, cannot lawfully contract for or receive such usury without injury to the debtor? Whatever all this crowd may have written, I see no harm in this, nothing contrary to divine or natural law; since nothing is done in it contrary to charity, but rather from mutual charity. It is plain that one grants the favor of a loan from his property; the other remunerates his benefactor with a part of the gain derived therefrom, without suffering any loss. Therefore the creditor lawfully receives more than his principal; & by the same reasoning, he may from the beginning covenant to this effect, within legitimate limits, however, & provided that the one who covenants does not plan any fraud against his neighbor, or demand usury unfairly. Indeed he should not receive it at all, if the debtor would suffer a loss by giving it; but he should take & exact only as much as he, in good faith & fair judgment, would wish to have taken or exacted from him, if he were in the same circumstances, or caught in a similar emergency. I know what these sophists prattle in reply (such as Conrad, *de Contract.,* quaest. 22): that the debtor, forsooth, cannot give a part of his gain without suffering loss to that extent, even if he keeps the greater part of it; since all the gain belongs to him, inasmuch as it is not derived from the property of the creditor, but from property or money which is now wholly the property of the debtor alone. But the answer is easy: that this subtlety is not based upon any divine or natural precepts, but upon human & positive interpretations; nay, not upon any human light or law, but upon the confused dreamings of certain ill-informed men. Therefore it cannot prevail against us. Moreover, I prove that it is pure sophistry, by the argument that the creditor, by making the loan, furnishes the immediate & efficacious cause, or, as the popular saying is, the *sine qua non* of this gain; hence he seems to give the gain itself. Therefore, he can covenant for a part of the gain, at least if there is any, according to divine & natural law, even according to civil regulations. And since the debtor makes a greater profit out of the loan, even with this burden, than if he had not had the loan, it is plain that the loan with this burden is an advantage to the debtor & not a disadvantage. Finally, since by hypothesis the debtor has the wherewithal to return the principal with usury, conveniently & retaining the better part of the gain, it follows that usury of this kind does not injure or defraud one's neighbor, but rather works to his not inconsiderable advantage. So far is it, then, from being in any way contrary to charity or love of one's neighbor: therefore it is not contrary to divine or natural laws; & hence it is lawful in conscience, which strictly follows correct reasoning—a kind of divine thing—& clings to pure truth, limiting the scope of artificial law, as Baldus says, most philosophic of professors of law. Again, he says, *Conscience does not bind those whom nature does not oblige.* What they

---

[a] *Tanti sua intersit.* The word *interesse* has no exact English equivalent. It is used by Molinaeus to refer to loss sustained or gain prevented through delay in repaying the principal. *Interusurii* has a similar meaning. See below, pp. 114–118.

have written & taught hitherto, therefore, is not true but erroneous & superstitious: that usury or any other return whatever received by a creditor for the lending of money is condemned by divine law; for usury is not condemned unless it defrauds or oppresses one's neighbor.

The general negative (Luke 6): *hoping for nothing thereby*, is not opposed to this conclusion: for in this passage Christ is speaking, not of usury, but of the repayment of the principal or the return of the favor. This is evident, because He is speaking there against men who lend only to those who are expected to return equal amounts, as Heathens & sinners do. But He teaches & requires fuller justice from His people; namely, to lend to those in need, with the feeling that, even if they are not likely to return anything, you rejoice in assisting a neighbor. So far is the benefit from perishing, He teaches, that God will repay it the more abundantly as it was less repaid & expected by men. As Christ, therefore, does not wish us to lend only when there is certain hope of repayment, but to consider how we can aid the needy, rather than how we can be sure of our money, so if your brother is not so much in need as to prevent his returning the principal with interest to his benefactor with profit to himself, He does not prohibit it, as He does not prohibit demanding back the principal, even in the public courts. But He desires that charity toward one's poor neighbor be always & everywhere considered. And He teaches often with what kindness we should deal with the poor who cannot pay at all or conveniently. Therefore, it is not the receiving of any usury whatever that conflicts with brotherly love, but receiving it to the injury of one's brother. If, therefore, your brother acquires gain by means of your money, & gives you a part of the gain, you are not sharing in a divine blessing that belongs to another; nor is the offense of usury to be estimated from the amount which you receive, but from the harm done to your neighbor, the debtor; so long as the limits fixed by laws or public ordinances are not exceeded. This opinion appears to be accepted by Innocent & Aretino. And this is what I have written elsewhere, myself, concerning the true & simple law of contracts, rejecting the nice distinctions made by others, briefly indeed (as suited that discussion), but in equally effective language. . . .

It is agreed by all learned & good authors, & the derivation of the word indicates, that usury is not taken for the thing but for the use of the thing. Now this (to demand payment for the use of a thing or principal) the scholastic theologians declare to be inherently evil & unjust, in the case of a loan, and contrary to natural law, basing this conclusion upon several reasons, but chiefly these three. The first is Thomas Aquinas's argument that the usurer sells that which does not exist or sells the same thing twice, or receives double compensation for the same thing. This he proves as follows. In loans the use of the thing is the consumption of it, & therefore it cannot be separated or computed apart from the thing itself: consequently he who receives anything over & above the sum lent, either receives it for the use of the thing & for nothing, or for what does not exist; or he receives it for the principal, & thus sells twice or receives double compensation for the same thing. The second reason is Scotus's point that I ought not to sell you what is not mine but yours: but in a loan there is a transfer of ownership, as shown by the derivation of the word (*mutuum*) from *meum* & *tuum*. Hence for the use of money which is already yours, I cannot demand any payment from you. The third reason is also from Scotus: that money lent is not of itself reproductive, even if we grant that it remains the property of the lender. Therefore, since the principal remains intact, it is not lawful to demand anything more than the principal: because that would be to receive gain, not from money (which is barren), but from the industry of another. These are the three principal reasons of the Theologians. For all their other reasons are derived from these, however much the verbal forms may seem to be multiplied & diversified. For example, the three arguments advanced by Petrus de Palude. First, that in commutative justice one man should not receive more from another than he gave him in value: but this is the same as the first argument above from Thomas. Second, that in a loan I transfer ownership, & therefore I ought not to sell you what is yours, namely, the use of your money: but this is the same as the second argument above from Scotus. Third, following Durand, that it is not lawful to sell one thing as two, & to receive two for one: but this is no different from the first argument above from Thomas, except for the shell & the sound of the words. Similarly, the twenty-five arguments recently collected by Conrad in his treatise on contracts may for the most part be reduced to the three given above. The others, indeed, are irrelevant to a natural process of reasoning. He even, with ridiculous pedantry, gives the same argument with slight verbal changes seven times: namely, his first, fifth, sixth, ninth, tenth, & eleventh. Let him who has leisure look them up; I do not care to pursue them in further detail, lest I fall myself into the pedantry I have criticized, & delay our argument. So much for the arguments of the sophists. I pass over their opinion that usury is wholly prohibited by divine law, according to the passages cited above, which they apply to loans in the strict sense only, & according to the custom of the people, who do not realize there is usury in anything but formal or suspected loans, not observing that the Holy Scriptures mean by the word usury any superabundance & excess in dealing with one's neighbor, as Jerome declares in commenting on Ezechiel, & likewise the ancient canons (14, q.3; 14, q.4). I also pass over many absurd suggestions, which men unmindful of the limits of speech & unacquainted with civil laws & business have foolishly made in this connection.

Another & fourth argument, which is more plausible than the foregoing, is advanced by John Teutonicus, an old canonist, who says that when the money is at the risk of the borrower from the beginning, it is improper to put any further burden on him & to look for additional gain. Other more reasonable arguments are advanced by philosophers & men of experience, which may be reduced to two, namely (continuing the previous series, for the sake of more convenient numbering) fifth, with reference to the interest of the state: lest men abandon agriculture, commerce, & other useful & necessary arts, or attend to them less carefully, enticed by the richer & easier gains from usury; or lest a few usurers absorb the property of all other men. Innocent treats this explicitly, & is of the opinion of Aristotle. For the business of usury is not like trade in commodities, by means of which a state is preserved: since in the latter trade an equivalent is always given & received; while in usury, though the use of the money gives the user a greater advantage for a time than does the use of merchandise for the same period, still it is not perpetual, & yet the interest continues until the principal is returned intact. Thus, in the course of time, if usury multiplied & continued, the result would be that the property of all would be transferred to the usurers. Sixth, with reference to the origin and development of the practice & the order & end of nature: that money was not devised as an end but as a means of acquisition, & so it should not be a merchandise, but a price; therefore usury is especially contrary to nature, which is the original & explicit opinion of Aristotle. I add a seventh: that the more usury takes advantage of the poverty or need of men, so much the more should it be excluded. And the more frequent & common is the necessity of borrowing money, so much the less should it be permitted to seek gain therefrom, & to render such necessary transactions difficult.

Analyzing the arguments outlined above, the first three can be refuted in almost the same way, inasmuch as they all err on one point especially. For they do not distinguish between the use, or the benefit accruing from the use, of the principal for a time, and the principal itself. But not only civil laws but also experience & common sense demonstrate that the use or fruition of money has a utility suitable & valuable for the uses of men, over & above the amount or restitution of the principal itself. And so there is no force in the first argument that the lender sells what does not exist or the same thing twice; for it is plainly false, provided that what he takes in addition to the principal for the use thereof does not exceed the just *interest*: for this is not selling the principal, inasmuch as payment is not received for the principal; nor is it selling nothing, but a true & real benefit, due, moreover, to him to whom the principal is due, & which meanwhile, in addition to the principal itself, & pending its repayment, is out of the possession of the creditor & in the hands of the debtor. Thus it is childish to say that the use of money cannot be considered apart from the principal, on the ground that the use of money is the consumption of it; for the use & fruition of money consists not only in the first momentary spending or disposal of it, but also in the ensuing use of the merchandise or things purchased with it, or replaced by it, or preserved in one's patrimony, which otherwise would have had to be disposed of, had not assistance been received from the money of another, or would have to be sold, if the money had to be returned at once. . . . Indeed, the dictum of Thomas & all the Scholastics is refuted by himself, & he is not consistent; for he admits, & they all agree, that one may lawfully sell the use of money lent, say, for the purpose of display, the ownership being retained: therefore, if the ownership of the same money is transferred, so that the recipient can have the use of it more freely & more profitably, until he has to return an equal sum, them then there will be much stronger grounds for selling the use & benefit of money in this case than in the former, in proportion as a greater & richer benefit is transferred in this case than in the former. Nor is it a valid objection to say that in the former case the money is at the risk of its owner, the creditor, but in the latter case is at the risk of the debtor: first, because it is lawful in the first case to covenant that the money be at the risk of the borrower or hirer (& the contract will be valid), along with a contract to pay for the use; & second, because the lender or lessor can obtain security against the risk by pledges or otherwise. It is true that, insofar as the risk falls upon the user, the payment for the use, or usury, should be that much smaller, just as it may reasonably be greater, when the risk falls upon the creditor, as in the case of bottomry loans. And thus the transfer of ownership does not, of itself, prevent the use from being sold in addition to the principal. And thus the first argument is completely overthrown, along with all those depending upon it.

The second argument, about what is not mine but thine, is easy to answer: if, however, you owe me a debt unconditionally, I can sell it to you; in fact, even if it is only a conditional debt, I can sell it to you. But the use of money which you owe me unconditionally is likewise owed to me unconditionally; therefore I can sell it to you. Likewise the claim itself, or the benefit of it, can be sold to the debtor himself, or to anyone else.

The answer to the third argument is evident from the foregoing, & everyday commercial practice shows that the utility of the use of a considerable sum of money is not slight, & in law it is often called the product. Nor does it avail to say that money by itself does not fructify: for even fields do not fructify by themselves, without expense, labor, & the industry of men; money, likewise, even when it has to be returned after a time, yields meanwhile a considerable product through the industry of man. Indeed, without gain-seeking activity, the mere delay itself yields a not inconsiderable profit, since the debtor can meanwhile procure enough from the product of his estates or otherwise to pay back the principal without any grievous & irreparable breaking-up of his patrimony. And sometimes it deprives the creditor of as much as it brings to the debtor.

The three principal arguments being refuted, all the other subtleties of the sophists, which depend on them, fall too. To the fourth I reply, in the first place, that it merely leads to the conclusion that not all the product should go to the creditor who does not share the risk, nor as much as if he retained or shared in the risk, for which even the civil law provides. And so it is not inappropriate that some part of the profit be given to the creditor: since in giving an appreciable use of money, he does give something, though he does not bear the risk. In the second place, I answer that to escape risk is of the very nature of the material involved, which is loaned on condition, not that the identical bodies, but the same amount in kind, is owed. Moreover, it does not ordinarily happen that money perishes & becomes useless to the debtor, but on the contrary, it is utilized for the advantage of the debtors in the majority of cases. Hence usury should not be universally prohibited, on account of what happens only rarely & unexpectedly; for laws ought to be adapted to what happens frequently, not to what happens rarely. And yet it is sometimes true that, when it is established that the debtor has lost all the money as a result of an accident, it is not proper for the creditor to demand usury, or even the principal in some cases.

The fifth argument proves nothing except that usury should not be excessive: for the disadvantages of discouraging the desirable arts & of disturbing the condition of the state cannot result from small & moderate usury.

Similarly the sixth & seventh arguments prove nothing except that usury is hated & should be restricted, especially the more extreme & immoderate; but they do not make out a case for the complete exclusion of even moderate & reasonable usury. Therefore, all just hating, condemning & punishing of usury should be understood as applying to excessive & unreasonable, not to moderate & acceptable usury. . . .

CHAPTER 5

Private Property as a Moral Right

The modern moral approbation of economic activity—both the justice of private property and the ethical approval of acquisition—reached a climactic moment in the writings of English philosopher John Locke (1632–1704). Locke summarized and systematized the new views on the most just mode of production and distribution of wealth and the ideal human type that had been developing since the Reformation. His views on economic justice are as important an influence on the modern period as Aristotle's were on antiquity and the Middle Ages and therefore deserve extensive treatment.

In the *Second Treatise of Civil Government* (1688), reflecting and refining what had become the dominant opinions of his time, Locke builds the case for private property on moral high ground. He defends the right to accumulate property as intrinsically moral rather than a merely prudentially necessary concession to human nature. In the course of his argument, Locke also sketches the outline of a new ideal human type–the "rational and industrious." Locke's "rational and industrious" live the logic of the "Protestant ethic," the religiously rooted moral ideal that drove early capitalism.

Locke develops his case for the moral foundations of private property in the context of his treatment of the "state of nature." The "state of nature" refers not to an actual historical circumstance but rather to a hypothetical condition that aids in understanding the basis for private property, other human rights, and the principle of limited government based upon consent of the governed. With the "state of nature" concept, Locke answers the question: What would life be like without civil government? By finding a right to property that would exist in a state of nature, Locke demonstrates that the property right is God-given, not government-given, hence grounded in the moral order of the universe, which government does not create but rather exists to protect and respect.

In his moral argument for private property, Locke gives himself the most difficult starting point possible—and one that addresses Christian-based communistic arguments. Locke proposes that we presume that God has given the world to human beings to own in common. He demonstrates how, from an assumption of initial total communism of property in a state of nature, the logical move to private property can be made.

While arguing the justice of private property, Locke introduces one of his chief contributions to discourse on economic justice; the labor theory of ownership and value. In a state of nature, he reasons, when an individual mixes *his* labor, the energy of *his* body, with the raw material of nature, that part of material nature with which he has mixed his labor becomes *his* private property. It becomes the individual's private property because it becomes something uniquely his—his labor.

In the logic of Locke's argument, the input of labor brings a segment of external nature out of the common possession, making it something a person may call with justice *his* private property. Imagine an individual in a state of nature walking through a wild apple grove and reaching to pick an apple or two. In the act of picking, he mixes his labor, the energy of his body, with a part of external material nature. That apple becomes his because it contains not only nature (the apple itself), but something that is without question his—the labor (energy) of his body. Similarly, imagine an individual in a state of nature deciding to use the arts of agriculture to work a piece of land and grow a crop. The land and crops become his private property because he has mixed his labor with them. Locke's argument suggests that if someone else says "Give me that apple," or "Give me those crops," he lays claim not to something that is his but rather to something that belongs to another. If he takes the apple or the crop, he is guilty of theft in violation of the laws of nature and God.

As Locke explains, theft would be very tempting in a state of nature. In the absence of prospective punishment for wrongdoing, how tempting it would be to steal from someone who has just exerted the labor to pick apples or harvest crops! That temptation explains why a state of nature would tend to turn into a state of war and why, to protect their property rights, people would consent to the establishment of civil government.

Locke's labor theory of ownership is also a labor theory of economic value. Locke maintains that nature itself, the mere raw material, is of no real value to anyone until someone mixes his labor with it—the apple on the tree is of no value until picked, and the land is of no value until a person mixes his labor with it to grow crops. For nature to be increased in value therefore requires much labor. Thus for the betterment of mankind, the great economic challenge is to provide conditions in which people have incentives to engage in labor.

In his treatment of property, a new ideal human type emerges as Locke begins to distinguish between the "industrious and rational" versus the "quarrelsome and contentious." The "industrious and rational" would like to engage extensively in economic activity and accumulate much material wealth. The "quarrelsome and contentious," on the other hand, would prefer to steal from the "industrious and rational." As Locke's argument unfolds, the chief problem becomes one of protecting the industrious and rational from the quarrelsome and contentious. If the industrious and rational are protected, the total amount of wealth (defined as nature plus "mixed-in" labor) will increase.

According to Locke, two factors in a state of nature put moral limits on the right to accumulate property—spoilage and scarcity.

The fundamental foundation of the right to property is the right of a person to mix his labor with nature for his preservation and contentment. There is thus no right in a state of nature to pick more apples than can be eaten before they spoil—no right to accumulate more material wealth than can be consumed before spoilage. There is, to put it simply, no right to waste.

There also must be, as Locke says in the *Second Treatise,* "as much and as good left over for others." Assume that one individual has picked a number of apples that he can consume before they spoil, but has left very few on the tree. If apples are the only source of food, the individual has no right to pick more than would leave "as much and as good left over for others." In Locke's analysis, the private property right derives from the right to life and the means to preserve life. Everyone retains the right to life. Therefore, if someone happened to pick five apples and not leave enough for others, then those others retain rights to the five apples. One person has no right to all five apples in such conditions of scarcity.

A *practical* limit on the accumulation of private property in Locke's state of nature is crime. Why be "industrious and rational" if the fruit of one's labor is likely to be taken away? Crime constitutes a serious practical limit on the accumulation of property in Locke's state of nature, and the protection of private property provides the main motivation for leaving the state of nature and establishing civil government.

Locke explains how the invention of money effectively removes the spoilage limit on the industrious and the rational. Money is a commodity that we agree to accept in exchange for other commodities—a medium of exchange. The most common form of money through the ages has been precious metals, which can be accumulated infinitely without violating the spoilage rule. If one can exchange the fruit of one's labor for money, the spoilage rule ceases to limit production and productivity. If one can exchange apples for money, then there is no moral limit on the number of apples, as far as spoilage is concerned, that one can accumulate. If one works a segment of land and produces abundant crops—much more than can be used before spoilage—one can exchange the crops for precious metals that will not spoil.

According to Locke, by agreeing to a monetary system we implicitly consent to inequality of possessions—to a condition that makes it moral for one person to accumulate as much money as he can. The inevitable result is inequality of property. By consenting to money, mankind has therefore consented to economic inequality.

The invention of money, by increasing the incentives for productivity and hence tempting the "quarrelsome and contentious" to steal from the "industrious and rational" all the more, creates a very strong need for civil government. As soon as money is invented, according to Locke's analysis, civil government quickly follows. The government's main purpose is to protect the inequality of possessions that results from money.

According to Locke, then, the invention of money removes the spoilage limitation of accumulation of wealth. But what of the requirement that there be "as much and as good left over for others"?

Imagine a civil society in which a few people accumulate so much wealth that there is not enough left over for the rest of the members of society to obtain the means of subsistence. While Locke does not explicitly address this issue, it would seem compatible with his principles to say that a starving person retains the fundamental right to life, and if there is not "as much and as good left over for others," he can reach out and take a piece of bread from the rich man.

But Locke would probably argue that such conditions are less likely to occur when the industrious and the rational have incentives to engage in economic activities. Civil government, by protecting the property of the industrious and rational, guarantees infinite acquisitiveness (made moral because of the invention of money). The resultant economic expansion tends to raise the economic well-being of society as a whole.

What is the main justification for inequality of possessions in civil society? To put the same question another way: What is the moral foundation for the right to private property in the sense of a right to infinite accumulation? The Lockean logic reduces to this: Not only is there enough and as good left over, there is more and more left over for others due to the actions of the industrious and rational. Granted, there is inequality. But as long as there is enough and as good left over or, in fact, more and more left over for others, inequality—the fruit of morally praiseworthy human endeavor—can only be attacked on the basis of envy, not "justice."

Second Treatise

John Locke

OF PROPERTY

Whether we consider natural reason, which tells us that men, being once born, have a right to their preservation, and consequently to meat and drink, and such other things as nature affords for their subsistence; or revelation, which gives us an account of those grants God made of the world to Adam, and to Noah and his sons; it is very clear that God, as King David says (Psalm cxv. 16), "has given the earth to the children of men," given it to mankind in common. But this being supposed, it seems to some a very great difficulty how any one should ever come to have a property in anything. I will not content myself to answer that if it be difficult to make out property upon a supposition that God gave the world to Adam and his posterity in common, it is impossible that any man but one universal monarch should have any property upon a supposition that God gave the world to Adam and his heirs in succession, exclusive of all the rest of his posterity. But I shall endeavor to show how men might come to have a property in several parts of that which God gave to mankind in common, and that without any express compact of all the commoners.

God, who has given the world to men in common, has also given them reason to make use of it to the best advantage of life and convenience. The earth, and all that is therein, is given to men for the support and comfort of their being. And though all the fruits it naturally produces and beasts it feeds belong to mankind in common, as they are produced by the spontaneous hand of nature; and nobody has originally a private dominion exclusive of the rest of mankind in any of them, as they are thus in their natural state; yet being given for the use of men, there must of necessity be a means to appropriate them some way or other before they can be of any use or at all beneficial to any particular man. The fruit or venison which nourishes the wild Indian, who knows no enclosure and is still a tenant in common, must be his, and so his, i. e., a part of him, that another can no longer have any right to it before it can do him any good for the support of his life.

Though the earth and all inferior creatures be common to all men, yet every man has a property in his own person: this nobody has any right to but himself. The labor of his body and the work of his hands, we may say, are properly his. Whatsoever then he removes out of the state that nature has provided, and left

John Locke, Two Treatises on Civil Government, *The Works of John Locke,* Vol. II, London: Awnsham Churchill, 1722.

it in, he has mixed his labor with, and joined to it something that is his own, and thereby makes it his property. It being by him removed from the common state nature has placed it in, it has by this labor something annexed to it that excludes the common right of other men. For this labor being the unquestionable property of the laborer, no man but he can have a right to what that is once joined to, at least where there is enough and as good left in common for others.

He that is nourished by the acorns he picked up under an oak, or the apples he gathered from the trees in the wood, has certainly appropriated them to himself. Nobody can deny but the nourishment is his. I ask then, When did they begin to be his? When he digested or when he ate or when he boiled or when he brought them home? Or when he picked them up? And it is plain, if the first gathering made them not his, nothing else could. That labor put a distinction between them and common; that added something to them more than nature, the common mother of all, had done; and so they became his private right. And will anyone say he had no right to those acorns or apples he thus appropriated because he had not the consent of all mankind to make them his? Was it a robbery thus to assume to himself what belonged to all in common? If such a consent as that was necessary, man had starved, notwithstanding the plenty God had given him. We see in commons, which remain so by compact, that it is the taking any part of what is common and removing it out of the state nature leaves it in, which begins the property, without which the common is of no use. And the taking of this or that part does not depend on the express consent of all the commoners. Thus the grass my horse has bit, the turfs my servant has cut, and the ore I have digged in any place where I have a right to them in common with others, become my property, without the assignation or consent of anybody. The labor that was mine, removing them out of that common state they were in, has fixed my property in them.

By making an explicit consent of every commoner, necessary to any one's appropriating to himself any part of what is given in common, children or servants could not cut the meat, which their father or master had provided for them in common, without assigning to every one his peculiar part. Though the water running in the fountain be every one's, yet who can doubt but that in the pitcher is his only who drew it out? His labor has taken it out of the hands of nature where it was common, and belonged equally to all her children, and has thereby appropriated it to himself.

Thus this law of reason makes the deer that Indian's who has killed it; it is allowed to be his goods who has bestowed his labor upon it, though before it was the common right of every one. And amongst those who are counted the civilized part of mankind, who have made and multiplied positive laws to determine property, this original law of nature, for the beginning of property in what was before common, still takes place; and by virtue thereof, what fish any one catches in the ocean, that great and still remaining common of mankind, or what ambergris any one takes up here, is by the labor that removes it out of that common state nature left it in, made his property who takes that pains about it. And even amongst us, the hare that anyone is hunting is thought his who pursues her during the chase. For, being a beast that is still looked upon as common and no man's private possession, whoever has employed so much labor about any of that kind as to find and pursue her has thereby removed her from the state of nature, wherein she was common, and has begun a property.

It will perhaps be objected to this that "if gathering the acorns, or other fruits of the earth, etc., makes a right to them, then any one may engross as much as he will." To which I answer: not so. The same law of nature that does by this means give us property does also bound that property, too. "God has given us all things richly" (I Tim. vi. 17), is the voice of reason confirmed by inspiration. But how far has he given it us? To enjoy. As much as any one can make use of to any advantage of life before it spoils, so much he may by his labor fix a property in: whatever is beyond this is more than his share and belongs to others. Nothing was made by God for man to spoil or destroy. And thus considering the plenty of natural provisions there was a long time in the world, and the few spenders, and to how small a part of that provision the industry of one man could extend itself and engross it to the prejudice of others, especially keeping within the bounds, set by reason, of what might serve for his use, there could be then little room for quarrels or contentions about property so established.

But the chief matter of property being now not the fruits of the earth and the beasts that subsist on it, but the earth itself, as that which takes in and carries with it all the rest, I think it is plain that property in that, too, is acquired as the former. As much land as a man tills, plants, improves, cultivates, and can use the product of, so much is his property. He by his labor does, as it were, enclose it from the common. Nor will it invalidate his right to say everybody else has an equal title to it, and therefore he cannot appropriate, he cannot enclose, without the consent of all his fellow commoners, all mankind. God, when he gave the world in common to all mankind, commanded man also to labor, and the penury of his condition required it of him. God and his reason commanded him to subdue the earth, i.e., improve it for the benefit of life, and therein lay out something upon it that was his own, his labor. He that in obedience to that command of God subdued, tilled, and sowed any part of it, thereby annexed to it something that was his property, which another had no title to, nor could without injury take from him.

Nor was this appropriation of any parcel of land by improving it any prejudice to any other man, since there was still enough and as good left, and more than the yet unprovided could use. So that in effect, there was never the less left for others because of his enclosure for himself. For he that leaves as much as another can make use of, does as good as take nothing at all. Nobody could think himself injured by the drinking of another man, though he took a good draught, who had a whole river of the same water left him to quench his thirst; and the case of land and water, where there is enough for both, is perfectly the same.

God gave the world to men in common; but since he gave it for their benefit, and the greatest conveniences of life they were capable to draw from it, it cannot be supposed he meant it should always remain common and uncultivated. He gave it to the use of the industrious and rational (and labor was to be his title to it) not to the fancy or covetousness of the quarrelsome and contentious. He that had as good left for his improvement as was already taken up needed not complain, ought not to meddle with what was already improved by another's labor; if he did, it is plain he desired the benefit of another's pains, which he had no right to, and not the ground which God had given him in common with others to labor on, and whereof there was as good left as that already possessed, and more than he knew what to do with, or his industry could reach to.

It is true, in land that is common in England, or any other country where there are plenty of people under government who have money and commerce, no one can enclose or appropriate any part without the consent of all his fellow common-ers; because this is left common by compact, i.e., by the law of the land, which is not to be violated. And though it be common in respect of some men, it is not so to all mankind, but is the joint property of this country or this parish. Besides, the remainder after such enclosure would not be as good to the rest of the com-moners as the whole was when they could all make use of the whole; whereas in the beginning and first peopling of the great common of the world it was quite otherwise. The law man was under was rather for appropriating. God commanded, and his wants forced, him to labor. That was his property which could not be taken from him wherever he had fixed it. And hence subduing or cultivating the earth and having dominion, we see are joined together. The one gave title to the other. So that God, by commanding to subdue, gave authority so far to appro-priate; and the condition of human life, which requires labor and material to work on, necessarily introduces private possessions.

Nature has well set the measure of property by the extent of men's labor and the conveniences of life: No man's labor could subdue or appropriate all, nor could his enjoyment consume more than a small part, so that it was impossible for any man, this way, to entrench upon the right of another, or acquire to himself a property to the prejudice of his neighbor, who would still have room for as good and as large a possession (after the other had taken out his) as before it was appropriated. Measure did confine every man's possession to a very moderate proportion, and such as he might appropriate to himself without injury to any-body, in the first ages of the world, when men were more in danger to be lost by wandering from their company in the then vast wilderness of the earth than to be straitened for want of room to plant in. And the same measure may be allowed still without prejudice to anybody, as full as the world seems. For supposing a man or family in the state they were at first peopling of the world by the children of Adam or Noah, let him plant in some inland, vacant places of America; we shall find that the possessions he could make himself, upon the measures we have given, would not be very large, nor, even to this day, prejudice the rest of mankind, or give them reason to complain or think themselves injured by this man's en-croachment, though the race of men have now spread themselves to all the corners of the world and do infinitely exceed the small number [which] was at the beginning. Nay, the extent of ground is of so little value without labor that I have heard it affirmed that in Spain itself a man may be permitted to plough, sow, or reap, without being disturbed, upon land he has no other title to but only his making use of it. But, on the contrary, the inhabitants think themselves beholden to him who by his industry on neglected and consequently waste land has increased the stock of corn which they wanted. But be this as it will, which I lay no stress on, this I dare boldly affirm—that the same rule of property, viz., that every man should have as much as he could make use of, would hold still in the world without straitening anybody, since there is land enough in the world to suffice double the inhabitants, had not the invention of money and the tacit agreement of men to put a value on it introduced (by consent) larger possessions and a right to them; which, how it has done, I shall by-and-by show more at large.

This is certain, that in the beginning, before the desire of having more than man needed had altered the intrinsic value of things which depends only on their usefulness to the life of man, or had agreed that a little piece of yellow metal which would keep without wasting or decay should be worth a great piece of flesh or a whole heap of corn, though men had a right to appropriate, by their labor, each one to himself as much of the things of nature as he could use, yet this could not be much, nor to the prejudice of others, where the same plenty was still left to those who would use the same industry. To which let me add that he who appropriates land to himself by his labor does not lessen but increase the common stock of mankind. For the provisions serving to the support of human life produced by one acre of enclosed and cultivated land are (to speak much within compass) ten times more than those which are yielded by an acre of land of an equal richness lying waste in common. And therefore he that encloses land, and has a greater plenty of the conveniences of life from ten acres than he could have from a hundred left to nature, may truly be said to give ninety acres to mankind; for his labor now supplies him with provisions out of ten acres which were by the product of a hundred lying in common. I have here rated the improved land very low in making its product but as ten to one, when it is much nearer a hundred to one; for I ask whether in the wild woods and uncultivated waste of America left to nature without any improvement, tillage, or husbandry, a thousand acres yield the needy and wretched inhabitants as many conveniences of life as ten acres of equally fertile land do in Devonshire, where they are well cultivated.

Before the appropriation of land, he who gathered as much of the wild fruit, killed, caught, or tamed as many of the beasts as he could; he that so employed his pains about any of the spontaneous products of nature as any way to alter them from the state which nature put them in, by placing any of his labor on them, did thereby acquire a propriety in them; but, if they perished in his possession without their due use, if the fruits rotted or the venison putrified before he could spend it, he offended against the common law of nature and was liable to be punished; he invaded his neighbor's share, for he had no right further than his use called for any of them and they might serve to afford him conveniences of life.

The same measures governed the possession of land, too: whatsoever he tilled and reaped, laid up and made use of before it spoiled, that was his peculiar right; whatsoever he enclosed and could feed and make use of, the cattle and product was also his. But if either the grass of his enclosure rotted on the ground, or the fruit of his planting perished without gathering and laying up, this part of the earth, notwithstanding his enclosure, was still to be looked on as waste, and might be the possession of any other. Thus, at the beginning, Cain might take as much ground as he could till and make it his own land, and yet leave enough for Abel's sheep to feed on; a few acres would serve for both their possessions. But as families increased, and industry enlarged their stocks, their possessions enlarged with the need of them; but yet it was commonly without any fixed property to the ground they made use of, till they incorporated, settled themselves together, and built cities; and then, by consent, they came in time to set out the bounds of their distinct territories, and agree on limits between them and their neighbors, and by laws within themselves settled the properties of those of the same society. For we see that in that part of the world which was first inhabited, and therefore like to be best peopled, even as low down as Abraham's time they wandered with their flocks and their herds, which was their substance, freely up and down; and this Abraham did in a country where he was a stranger. Whence it is plain that at least a great part of the land lay in common, that the inhabitants valued it not, nor claimed property in any more than they made use of. But when there was not room enough in the same place for their herds to feed together, they by consent, as Abraham and Lot did (Gen. xiii. 5), separated and enlarged their pasture where it best liked them. And for the same reason Esau went from his father and his brother and planted in Mount Seir (Gen. xxxvi. 6).

And thus, without supposing any private dominion and property in Adam over all the world exclusive of all other men, which can in no way be proven, nor any one's property be made out from it; but supposing the world given as it was to the children of men in common, we see how labor could make men distinct titles to several parcels of it for their private uses, wherein there could be no doubt of right, no room for quarrel.

Nor is it so strange, as perhaps before consideration it may appear, that the property of labor should be able to overbalance the community of land. For it is labor indeed that put the difference of value on everything; and let anyone consider what the difference is between an acre of land planted with tobacco or sugar, sown with wheat or barley, and an acre of the same land lying in common without any husbandry upon it, and he will find that the improvement of labor makes the far greater part of the value. I think it will be but a very modest computation to say that, of the products of the earth useful to the life of man, nine-tenths are the effects of labor; nay, if we will rightly estimate things as they come to our use and cast up the several expenses about them, what in them is purely owing to nature, and what to labor, we shall find that in most of them ninety-nine hundredths are wholly to be put on the account of labor.

There cannot be a clearer demonstration of anything, than several nations of the Americans are of this, who are rich in land and poor in all the comforts of life; whom nature having furnished as liberally as any other people with the materials of plenty, i. e., a fruitful soil, apt to produce in abundance what might serve for food, raiment, and delight, yet for want of improving it by labor have not one-hundredth part of the conveniences we enjoy. And a king of a large and fruitful territory there feeds, lodges, and is clad worse than a day-laborer in England.

To make this a little clear, let us but trace some of the ordinary provisions of life through their several progresses before they come to our use and see how much they receive of their value from human industry. Bread, wine, and cloth are things of daily use and great plenty; yet, notwithstanding, acorns, water, and leaves, or skins must be our bread, drink, and clothing, did not labor furnish us with these more useful commodities. For whatever bread is more worth than acorns, wine than water, and cloth or silk than leaves, skins, or moss, that is wholly owing to labor and industry: the one of these being the food and raiment which unassisted nature furnishes us with; the other, provisions which our industry and pains prepare for us, which how much they exceed the other in value when anyone has computed, he will then see how much labor makes the far greatest part of the value of things we enjoy in this world. And the ground which produces the materials is scarce to be reckoned in as any, or at most but a very small, part of it; so little that even amongst us land that is left wholly to nature that has no improvement of pasturage, tillage, or planting, is called, as indeed it is, 'waste'; and we shall find the benefit of it amount to little more than nothing.

This shows how much numbers of men are to be preferred to largeness of dominions; and that the increase of lands and the right employing of them is the great art of government; and that prince who shall be so wise and godlike as by established laws of liberty to secure protection and encouragement to the honest industry of mankind, against the oppression of power and narrowness of party, will quickly be too hard for his neighbors; but this by the bye.

To return to the argument in hand.

An acre of land that bears here twenty bushels of wheat, and another in America which, with the same husbandry, would do the like, are, without doubt, of the same natural intrinsic value; but yet the benefit mankind receives from the one in a year is worth £5, and from the other possibly not worth a penny if all the profit an Indian received from it were to be valued and sold here; at least, I may truly say, not one-thousandth. It is labor, then, which puts the greatest art of the value upon land, without which it would scarcely be worth anything; it is to that we owe the greatest part of all its useful products; for all that the straw, bran, bread of that acre of wheat is more worth than the product of an acre of as good land which lies waste, is all the effect of labor. For it is not barely the ploughman's pains, the reaper's and thresher's toil, and the baker's sweat [that] is to be counted into the bread we eat; the labor of those who broke the oxen, who digged and wrought the iron and stones, who felled and framed the timber employed about the plough, mill, oven, or any other utensils, which are a vast number requisite to this corn, from its being seed to be sown to its being made bread, must all be charged on the account of labor, and received as an effect of that: nature and the earth furnished only the almost worthless materials as in themselves. It would be a strange "catalogue of things that industry provided and made use of, about every loaf of bread" before it came to our use, if we could trace them: iron, wood, leather, bark, timber, stone, bricks, coals, lime, cloth, dyeing drugs, pitch, tar, masts, ropes, and all the materials made use of in the ship that brought any of the commodities used by any of the workmen to any part of the work; all which it would be almost impossible, at least too long, to reckon up.

From all which it is evident that, though the things of nature are given in common, yet man, by being master of himself and proprietor of his own person and the actions or labor of it, had still in himself the great foundation of property; and that which made up the great part of what he applied to the support or comfort of his being, when invention and arts had improved the conveniences of life, was perfectly his own and did not belong in common to others.

Thus labor, in the beginning gave a right of property, wherever anyone was pleased to employ it upon what was common, which remained a long while the far greater part, and is yet more than mankind makes use of. Men, at first, for the most part contented themselves with what unassisted nature offered to their necessities; and though afterwards, in some parts of the world (where the increase of people and stock, with the use of money, had made land scarce and so of some value) the several communities settled the bounds of their distinct territories and, by laws within themselves, regulated the properties of the private men of their society, and so, by compact and agreement, settled the property which labor and industry began. And the leagues that have been made between several states and kingdoms, either expressly or tacitly disowning all claim and right to the land in the others' possession, have, by common consent, given up their pretenses to their natural common right which originally they had to those countries, and so have, by positive agreement, settled a property amongst themselves in distinct parts and parcels of the earth; yet there are still great tracts of ground to be found which— the inhabitants thereof not having joined with the rest of mankind in the consent of the use of their common money—lie waste, and are more than the people who dwell on it do or can make use of, and so still lie in common; though this can scarce happen amongst that part of mankind that have consented to the use of money.

The greatest part of things really useful to the life of man, and such as the necessity of subsisting made the first commoners of the world look after, as it does the Americans now, are generally things of short duration, such as, if they are not consumed by use, will decay and perish of themselves; gold, silver, and diamonds are things that fancy or agreement has put the value on, more than real use and the necessary support of life. Now of those good things which nature has provided in common, every one had a right, as has been said, to as much as he could use, and property in all that he could effect with his labor; all that his industry could extend to, to alter from the state nature had put it in, was his. He that gathered a hundred bushels of acorns or apples had thereby a property in them; they were his goods as soon as gathered. He was only to look that he used them before they spoiled, else he took more than his share and robbed others. And indeed it was a foolish thing, as well as dishonest, to hoard up more than he could make use of. If he gave away a part to anybody else so that it perished not uselessly in his possession, these he also made use of. And if he also bartered away plums that would have rotted in a week for nuts that would last good for his eating a whole year, he did no injury; he wasted not the common stock, destroyed no part of the portion of goods that belonged to others, so long as nothing perished uselessly in his hands. Again, if he would give his nuts for a piece of metal, pleased with its color, or exchange his sheep for shells, or wool for a sparkling pebble or a diamond, and keep those by him all his life, he invaded not the right of others; he might heap as much of these durable things as he pleased; the exceeding of the bounds of his just property not lying in the largeness of his possession, but the perishing of anything uselessly in it.

And thus came in the use of money, some lasting thing that men might keep without spoiling, and that by mutual consent men would take in exchange for the truly useful but perishable supports of life.

And as different degrees of industry were apt to give men possessions in different proportions, so this invention of money gave them the opportunity to continue and enlarge them. For supposing an island, separate from all possible commerce with the rest of the world, wherein there were but a hundred families, but there were sheep, horses, and cows, with other useful animals, wholesome fruits, and land enough for corn for a hundred thousand times as many, but nothing in the island, either because of its commonness or perishableness, fit to supply the place of money: what reason could anyone have there to enlarge his possessions beyond the use of his family and a plentiful supply to its consumption, either in what their own industry produced or they could barter for like perishable, useful commodities with others? Where there is not something both lasting and scarce, and so valuable to be hoarded up, there men will not be apt to enlarge their possessions of land were it never so rich, never so free for them to take. For, I ask, what would a man value ten thousand or a hundred thousand acres of excellent land, ready cultivated and well stocked, too, with cattle, in the middle of the inland parts of America where he had no hopes of commerce with other parts of the world to draw money to him by the sale of the product? It would not be worth the enclosing, and we should see him give up again to the wild common of nature whatever was more than would supply the conveniences of life to be had there for him and his family.

Thus in the beginning all the world was America, and more so than that is now; for no such thing as money was anywhere known. Find out something that has the use and value of money amongst his neighbors, you shall see the same man will begin presently to enlarge his possessions.

But since gold and silver, being little useful to the life of man in proportion to food, raiment, and carriage, has its value only from the consent of men, whereof labor yet makes, in great part, the measure, it is plain that men have agreed to a disproportionate and unequal possession of the earth, they having, by a tacit and voluntary consent, found out a way how a man may fairly possess more land than he himself can use the product of, by receiving in exchange for the overplus gold and silver which may be hoarded up without injury to any one, these metals not spoiling or decaying in the hands of the possessor. This partage of things in an inequality of private possessions men have made practicable out of the bounds of society, and without compact, only by putting a value on gold and silver, and tacitly agreeing in the use of money. For, in governments, the laws regulate the right of property, and the possession of land is determined by positive constitutions.

And thus, I think, it is very easy to conceive without any difficulty how labor could at first begin a title of property in the common things of nature, and how the spending it upon our uses bound it. So that there could then be no reason of quarreling about title, nor any doubt about the largeness of possession it gave. Right and convenience went together; for as a man had a right to all he could employ his labor upon, so he had no temptation to labor for more than he could make use of. This left no room for controversy about the title, nor for encroachment on the right of others; what portion a man carved to himself was easily seen, and it was useless as well as dishonest to carve himself too much, or take more than he needed.

CHAPTER 6

Economic Productivity, Individual Initiative, and the Common Good

John Locke, a philosopher in the grand style, wrote masterfully on a full range of subjects. His argument for the justice of private property and his exaltation of the "industrious and rational" as a human ideal, though brilliantly argued and quite influential on developing economic opinion in the late seventeenth century, constituted just one topic among many for Locke. In the next century it remained for Adam Smith (1723–1790), often called the "father of economics," to write *The Wealth of Nations*—the economic treatise for the emerging capitalist economic order. In 1848 Karl Marx would write *The Communist Manifesto*; in 1776 Smith published what could have been called "The Capitalist Manifesto."

The Wealth of Nations has all the appearance of a technical scientific treatise on economics. Yet a view of economic justice is clearly present—and not surprisingly, since Smith's intellectual roots lay in moral philosophy (his first work, published in 1759, was entitled *The Theory of Moral Sentiments*). In *The Wealth of Nations*, Smith's moral vision focuses on the paradoxical contention, ever after fascinating to advocates of *laissez faire*, that in economics the public interest emerges from private interest and justice from selfishness—that the common good is best achieved not by the benevolence of an overseeing government but by the impersonal forces of a free market.

The division or specialization of labor figures prominently in Smith's argument. Later viewed by Marx as a great evil to be overcome because of its alleged injury to human self-development, the division of labor, in Smith's account, becomes

69

perhaps the greatest good. As the division of labor develops spontaneously, Smith argues in *The Wealth of Nations,* the productive power of labor increases, with the result that "a general plenty diffuses itself through all the different ranks of society."

The division of labor, of course, entails the need for a system of trade whereby the individuals (or nations), having divided up the labor of producing the goods of life, have need to exchange the products of their labor. With reference to the prices of products, Smith, like Locke, argues for the labor theory of value—that the value of an item depends upon the quantity of the labor needed to produce it. Marx would later use the labor theory in his critique of capitalism. Smith, however, finds no necessary exploitation of workers by capitalists—no inevitable conflict between the demands of justice and the outcomes of *truly* free market forces. Smith envisions a society of individuals, each pursuing his own interest, intending "his own gain, and he is in this, as in many other cases, led by an invisible hand to promote an end which was no part of his own intention. . . . By pursuing his own interest he frequently promotes that of society more effectually than when he really intends to promote it."

Smith's vision knows no boundaries. Interestingly, the famous "invisible hand" passage deals with imports, not domestic manufacture, and occurs in Book IV, Chapter 2, entitled "Of Restraints upon the Importation from Foreign Countries of Such Goods As Can Be Produced at Home." Similarly, Smith's argument for the division of labor, appearing in the context of an argument leading to advocacy of international free trade, applies with equal force for nations as for individuals.

Smith recognized that free market forces will not produce economic equality, but he believed that labor specialization and wage inequality would generate economic success, rendering all individuals better off. Describing the declining prices of goods brought about by higher labor productivity, Smith states that "luxury extends itself even to the lowest ranks of the people, and that the labouring poor will not now be contented with the same food, clothing and lodging which satisfied them in former times."

Smith believed that the unfettered market would lead to overall economic well-being, but in his analysis, "unfettered" applied to both private and public sectors. While he favored government staying its hand to allow the "invisible hand" to work correctly, Smith also condemned businessmen of his day engaged in restraint of trade, fixing prices higher than true market value. Smith saw danger whenever businessmen huddle—"the conversation ends in conspiracy against the public, or in some contrivance to raise prices."

In Smith one finds, in reality if not in name, Locke's ideal, the "industrious and rational." Smith's ideal human type, his labor power multiplied by the division of labor, is driven by self-interest to better himself and in the process benefits others. The market mechanism—free from barriers imposed by government or special interests—works to meet society's needs by directed self-interested persons. Smith's "invisible hand," as if by magic, transforms economic self-interest into economic justice.

The Wealth of Nations

Adam Smith

OF THE DIVISION OF LABOUR

The greatest improvement in the productive powers of labour, and the greater part of the skill, dexterity, and judgment with which it is anywhere directed or applied, seem to have been the effect of the division of labour.

The effects of the division of labour, in the general business of society, will be more easily understood by considering in what manner it operates in some particular manufactures. It is commonly supposed to be carried furthest in some very trifling ones; not perhaps that it really is carried further in them than in others of more importance: but in those trifling manufactures which are destined to supply the small wants of but a small number of people, the whole number of workmen must necessarily be small; and those employed in every different branch of the work can often be collected into the same workhouse, and placed at once under the view of the spectator. In those great manufactures, on the contrary, which are destined to supply the great wants of the great body of the people, every different branch of the work employs so great a number of workmen, that it is impossible to collect them all into the same workhouse. We can seldom see more, at one time, than those employed in one single branch. Though in such manufactures, therefore, the work may really be divided into a much greater number of parts than in those of a more trifling nature, the division is not near so obvious, and has accordingly been much less observed.

To take an example, therefore, from a very trifling manufacture, but one in which the division of labour has been very often taken notice of, the trade of the pin-maker; a workman not educated to this business (which the division of labour has rendered a distinct trade), nor acquainted with the use of the machinery employed in it (to the invention of which the same division of labour has probably given occasion), could scarce, perhaps, with his utmost industry, make one pin in a day, and certainly could not make twenty. But in the way in which this business is now carried on, not only the whole work is a peculiar trade, but it is divided into a number of branches, of which the greater part are likewise peculiar trades. One man draws out the wire, another straights it, a third cuts it, a fourth points it, a fifth grinds it at the top for receiving the head; to make the head requires two or three distinct operations; to put it on is a peculiar business, to whiten the pins is another; it is even a trade by itself to put them into the paper; and the

---

Adam Smith, An Inquiry into the Nature and Causes of the Wealth of Nations, *1776.*

important business of making a pin is, in this manner, divided into about eighteen distinct operations, which in some manufactories are all performed by distinct hands, though in others the same man will sometimes perform two or three of them. I have seen a small manufactory of this kind where ten men only were employed, and where some of them consequently performed two or three distinct operations. But though they were very poor, and therefore but indifferently accommodated with the necessary machinery, they could, when they exerted themselves, make among them about twelve pounds of pins in a day. There are in a pound upwards of four thousand pins of a middling size. Those ten persons, therefore, could make among them upwards of forty-eight thousand pins in a day. Each person, therefore, making a tenth part of forty-eight thousand pins, might be considered as making four thousand eight hundred pins in a day. But if they had all wrought separately and independently, and without any of them having been educated to this peculiar business, they certainly could not each of them have made twenty, perhaps not one pin in a day; that is, certainly, not the two hundred and fortieth, perhaps not the four thousand eight hundredth part of what they are at present capable of performing, in consequence of a proper division and combination of their different operations.

In every other art and manufacture, the effects of the division of labour are similar to what they are in this very trifling one; though in many of them, the labour can neither be so much subdivided, nor reduced to so great a simplicity of operation. The division of labour, however, so far as it can be introduced, occasions, in every art, a proportionable increase of the productive powers of labour. The separation of different trades and employments from one another seems to have taken place in consequence of this advantage. The separation too is generally carried furthest in those countries which enjoy the highest degree of industry and improvement; what is the work of one man in a rude state of society, being generally that of several in an improved one. In every improved society, the farmer is generally nothing but a farmer; the manufacturer, nothing but a manufacturer. The labour too which is necessary to produce any one complete manufacture, is almost always divided among a great number of hands. . . .

This great increase of the quantity of work, which, in consequence of the division of labour, the same number of people are capable of performing, is owing to three different circumstances: first, to the increase of dexterity in every particular workman; secondly, to the saving of the time which is commonly lost in passing from one species of work to another; and lastly, to the invention of a great number of machines which facilitate and abridge labour, and enable one man to do the work of many.

Thirdly, and lastly, everybody must be sensible how much labour is facilitated and abridged by the application of proper machinery. It is unnecessary to give any example. I shall only observe, therefore, that the invention of all those machines by which labour is so much facilitated and abridged, seems to have been originally owing to the division of labour. Men are much more likely to discover easier and readier methods of attaining any object, when the whole attention of their minds is directed towards that single object, than when it is dissipated among a great variety of things. But in consequence of the division of labour, the whole of every man's attention comes naturally to be directed towards some one very simple object. It is naturally to be expected, therefore, that some one or other of those who are employed in each particular branch of labour should soon find out easier and readier methods of performing their own particular work, wherever the nature of it admits of such improvement. A great part of the machines made use of in those manufactures in which labour is most subdivided, were originally the inventions of common workmen, who, being each of them employed in some very simple operation, naturally turned their thoughts towards finding out easier and readier methods of performing it. Whoever has been much accustomed to visit such manufactures, must frequently have been shown very pretty machines, which were the inventions of such workmen, in order to facilitate and quicken their own particular part of the work. In the first fire-engines, a boy was constantly employed to open and shut alternately the communication between the boiler and the cylinder, according as the piston either ascended or descended. One of the boys, who loved to play with his companions, observed that, by tying a string from the handle of the valve which opened this communication to another part of the machine, the valve would open and shut without his assistance, and leave him at liberty to divert himself with his play-fellows. One of the greatest improvements that has been made upon this machine, since it was first invented, was in this manner the discovery of a boy who wanted to save his own labour.

All the improvements in machinery, however, have by no means been the inventions of those who had occasion to use the machines. Many improvements have been made by the ingenuity of the makers of the machines, when to make them became the business of a peculiar trade; and some by that of those who are called philosophers or men of speculation, whose trade is not to do anything, but to observe everything; and who, upon that account, are often capable of combining together the powers of the most distant and dissimilar objects. In the progress of society, philosophy or speculation becomes, like every other employment, the principal or sole trade and occupation of a particular class of citizens. Like every other employment too, it is subdivided into a great number of different branches, each of which affords occupation to a peculiar tribe or class of philosophers; and this subdivision of employment in philosophy, as well as in every other business, improves dexterity, and saves time. Each individual becomes more expert in his own peculiar branch, more work is done upon the whole, and the quantity of science is considerably increased by it.

It is the great multiplication of the productions of all the different arts, in consequence of the division of labour, which occasions, in a well-governed society, that universal opulence which extends itself to the lowest ranks of the people. Every workman has a great quantity of his own work to dispose of beyond what he himself has occasion for; and every other workman being exactly in the same situation, he is enabled to exchange a great quantity of his own goods for a great quantity, or, what comes to the same thing, for the price of a great quantity of theirs. He supplies them abundantly with what they have occasion for, and they accommodate him as amply with what he has occasion for, and a general plenty diffuses itself through all the different ranks of the society.

Observe the accommodation of the most common artificer or day-labourer in a civilised and thriving country, and you will perceive that the number of people of whose industry a part, though but a small part, has been employed in procuring him this accommodation exceeds all computation. The woollen coat, for example, which covers the day-labourer, as coarse and rough as it may appear, is the produce of the joint labour of a great multitude of workmen. The shepherd, the sorter of the wool, the wool-comber or carder, the dyer, the scribbler, the spinner, the weaver, the fuller, the dresser, with many others, must all join their different arts in order to complete even this homely production. How many merchants and carriers, besides, must have been employed in transporting the materials from some of those workmen to others who often live in a very distant part of the country! how much commerce and navigation in particular, how many ship-builders, sailors, sail-makers, rope-makers, must have been employed in order to bring together the different drugs made use of by the dyer, which often come from the remotest corners of the world! What a variety of labour too is necessary in order to produce the tools of the meanest of those workmen!

OF THE PRINCIPLE WHICH GIVES OCCASION TO THE DIVISION OF LABOUR

This division of labour, from which so many advantages are derived, is not originally the effect of any human wisdom, which foresees and intends that general opulence to which it gives occasion. It is the necessary, though very slow and gradual consequence of a certain propensity in human nature which has in view no such extensive utility; the propensity to truck, barter, and exchange one thing for another.

Whether this propensity be one of those original principles in human nature, of which no further account can be given; or whether, as seems more probable, it be the necessary consequence of the faculties of reason and speech, it belongs not to our present subject to inquire. It is common to all men, and to be found in no other race of animals, which seem to know neither this nor any other species of contracts. Two greyhounds, in running down the same hare, have sometimes the appearance of acting in some sort of concert. Each turns her towards his companion, or endeavours to intercept her when his companion turns her towards himself. This, however, is not the effect of any contract, but of the accidental concurrence of their passions in the same object at that particular time. Nobody ever saw a dog make a fair and deliberate exchange of one bone for another with another dog. Nobody ever saw one animal by its gestures and natural cries signify to another, This is mine, that yours; I am willing to give this for that. When an animal wants to obtain something either of a man or of another animal, it has no other means of persuasion but to gain the favour of those whose service it requires. A puppy fawns upon its dam, and a spaniel endeavours by a thousand attractions to engage the attention of its master who is at dinner, when it wants to be fed by him. Man sometimes uses the same arts with his brethren, and when he has no other means of engaging them to act according to his inclinations, endeavours by every servile and fawning attention to obtain their good-will. He has not time, however, to do this upon every occasion. In civilized society he stands at all times in need of the co-operation and assistance of great multitudes, while his whole life is scarce sufficient to gain the friendship of a few persons. In almost every other race of animals each individual, when it is grown up to maturity, is entirely independent, and in its natural state has occasion for the assistance of no other living creature. But man has almost constant occasion for the help of his brethren, and it is in vain for him to expect it from their benevolence only. He will be more likely to prevail if he can interest their self-love in his favour, and show them that it is for their own advantage to do for him what he requires of them. Whoever offers to another a bargain of any kind, proposes to do this. Give me that which I want, and you shall have this which you want, is the meaning of every such offer; and it is in this manner that we obtain from one another the far greater part of those good offices which we stand in need of. It is not from the benevolence of the butcher, the brewer, or the baker, that we expect our dinner, but from their regard to their own interest. We address ourselves, not to our humanity, but to their self-love, and never talk to them of their own necessities but of their advantages. Nobody but a beggar chooses to depend chiefly upon the benevolence of his fellow-citizens. Even a beggar does not depend upon it entirely. The charity of well-disposed people, indeed, supplies him with the whole fund of his subsistence. But though this principle ultimately provides him with all the necessaries of life which he has occasion for, it neither does nor can provide him with them as he has occasion for them. The greater part of his occasional wants are supplied in the same manner as those of other people, by treaty, by barter, and by purchase. With the money which one man gives him he purchases food. The old clothes which another bestows upon him he exchanges for other old clothes which suit him better, or for lodging, or for food, or for money, with which he can buy either food, clothes, or lodging, as he has occasion.

As it is by treaty, by barter, and by purchase, that we obtain from one another the greater part of those mutual good offices which we stand in need of, so it is this same trucking disposition which originally gives occasion to the division of labour. In a tribe of hunters or shepherds a particular person makes bows and arrows, for example, with more readiness and dexterity than any other. He frequently exchanges them for cattle or for venison with his companions; and he finds at last than he can in this manner get more cattle and venison than if he himself went to the field to catch them. From a regard to his own interest, therefore, the making of bows and arrows grows to be his chief business, and he becomes a sort of armourer. Another excels in making the frames and covers of their little huts or moveable houses. He is accustomed to be of use in this way to his neighbours, who reward him in the same manner with cattle and with venison, till at last he finds it his interest to dedicate himself entirely to this employment, and to become a sort of house-carpenter. In the same manner a third becomes a smith or a brazier, a fourth a tanner or dresser of hides or skins, the principal part of the clothing of savages. And thus the certainty of being able to exchange all that surplus part of the produce of his own labour, which is over and above his own consumption, for such parts of the produce of other men's labour as he may have occasion for, encourages every man to apply himself to a particular occupation, and to cultivate and bring to perfection whatever talent or genius he may possess for that particular species of business. . . .

OF THE COMPONENT PARTS OF THE PRICE OF COMMODITIES

In that early and rude state of society which precedes both the accumulation of stock and the appropriation of land, the proportion between the quantities of labour necessary for acquiring different objects seems to be the only circumstance which can afford any rule for exchanging them for one another. If among a nation of hunters, for example, it usually costs twice the labour to kill a beaver which it does to kill a deer, one beaver should naturally exchange for or be worth two deer. It is natural that what is usually the produce of two days' or two hours' labour, should be worth double of what is usually the produce of one day's or one hour's labour.

If the one species of labour should be more severe than the other, some allowance will naturally be made for this superior hardship; and the produce of one hour's labour in the one way may frequently exchange for that of two hours' labour in the other.

Or if the one species of labour requires an uncommon degree of dexterity and ingenuity, the esteem which men have for such talents will naturally give a value to their produce, superior to what would be due to the time employed about it. Such talents can seldom be acquired but in consequence of long application, and the superior value of their produce may frequently be no more than a reasonable compensation for the time and labour which must be spent in acquiring them. In the advanced state of society, allowances of this kind, for superior hardship and superior skill, are commonly made in the wages of labour; and something of the same kind must probably have taken place in its earliest and rudest period.

In this state of things, the whole produce of labour belongs to the labourer; and the quantity of labour commonly employed in acquiring or producing any commodity is the only circumstance which can regulate the quantity of labour which it ought commonly to purchase, command, or exchange for.

As soon as stock has accumulated in the hands of particular persons, some of them will naturally employ it in setting to work industrious people, whom they will supply with materials and subsistence, in order to make a profit by the sale of their work, or by what their labour adds to the value of the materials. In exchanging the complete manufacture either for money, for labour, or for other goods, over and above what may be sufficient to pay the price of the materials and the wages of the workmen, something must be given for the profits of the undertaker of the work who hazards his stock in this adventure. The value which the workmen add to the materials, therefore, resolves itself in this case into two parts of which the one pays their wages, the other the profits of their employer upon the whole stock of materials and wages which has advanced. He could have no interest to employ them, unless he expected from the sale of their work something more than what was sufficient to replace his stock to him; and he could have no interest to employ a great stock rather than a small one, unless his profits were to bear some proportion to the extent of his stock.

The profits of stock, it may perhaps be thought, are only a different name for the wages of a particular sort of labour, the labour of inspection and direction. They are, however, altogether different, are regulated by quite different principles, and bear no proportion to the quantity, the hardship, or the ingenuity of the supposed labour of inspection and direction. They are regulated altogether by the value of the stock employed, and are greater or smaller in proportion to the extent of this stock. Let us suppose for example, that in some particular place, where the common annual profits of manufacturing stock are ten per cent, there are two different manufactures, in each of which twenty workmen are employed at the rate of fifteen pounds a year each, or at the expense of three hundred a year in each manufactory. Let us suppose too, that the coarse materials annually wrought up in the one cost only seven hundred pounds, while the finer materials in the other cost seven thousand. The capital annually employed in the one will in this case amount only to one thousand pounds; whereas that employed in the other will amount to seven thousand three hundred pounds. At the rate of ten per cent, therefore, the undertaker of the one will expect a yearly profit of about one hundred pounds only; while that of the other will expect about seven hundred and thirty pounds. But though their profits are so very different, their labour of inspection and direction may be either altogether or very nearly the same. In many great works, almost the whole labour of this kind is committed to some principal clerk. His wages properly express the value of this labour of inspection and direction. Though in settling them some regard is had commonly, not only to his labour and skill, but to the trust which is reposed in him, yet they never bear any regular proportion to the capital of which he oversees the management; and the owner of this capital, though he is thus discharged of almost all labour, still expects that his profits should bear a regular proportion to his capital. In the price of commodities, therefore, the profits of stock constitute a component part altogether different from the wages of labour and regulated by quite different principles.

In this state of things, the whole produce of labour does not always belong to the labourer. He must in most cases share it with the owner of the stock which employs him. Neither is the quantity of labour commonly employed in acquiring or producing any commodity the only circumstance which can regulate the quantity which it ought commonly to purchase, command, or exchange for. An additional quantity, it is evident, must be due for the profits of the stock which advanced the wages and furnished the materials of that labour.

As soon as the land of any country has all become private property, the landlords, like all other men, love to reap where they never sowed, and demand a rent even for its natural produce. The wood of the forest, the grass of the field, and all the natural fruits of the earth, which, when land was in common, cost the labourer only the trouble of gathering them, come, even to him, to have an additional price fixed upon them. He must then pay for the licence to gather them; and must give up to the landlord a portion of what his labour either collects or produces. This portion, or, what comes to the same thing, the price of this portion, constitutes the rent of land, and in the price of the greater part of commodities makes a third component part.

The real value of all the different component parts of price, it must be observed, is measured by the quantity of labour which they can, each of them, purchase or command. Labour measures the value not only of that part of price which resolves itself into labour, but of that which resolves itself into rent, and of that which resolves itself into profit.

In every society the price of every commodity finally resolves itself into some one or other, or all of those three parts; and in every improved society, all the three enter more or less, as component parts, into the price of the far greater part of commodities.

In the price of corn, for example, one part pays the rent of the landlord, another pays the wages or maintenance of the labourer and labouring cattle employed in producing it, and the third pays the profit of the farmer. These three parts seem either immediately or ultimately to make up the whole price of corn. A fourth part, it may perhaps be thought, is necessary for replacing the stock of the farmer, or for compensating the wear and tear of his labouring cattle and other instruments of husbandry. But it must be considered that the price of any instrument of husbandry, such as a labouring horse, is itself made up of the same three parts; the rent of the land upon which he is reared, the labour of tending and rearing him, and the profits of the farmer who advances both the rent of this land and the wages of this labour. Though the price of the corn, therefore, may pay the price as well as the maintenance of the horse, the whole price still resolves itself either immediately or ultimately into the same three parts of rent, labour, and profit. . . .

Every individual is continually exerting himself to find out the most advantageous employment for whatever capital he can demand. It is his own advantage, indeed, and not that of the society, which he has in view. But the study of his own advantage naturally or rather necessarily, leads him to prefer that employment which is most advantageous to the society.

But the annual revenue of every society is always precisely equal to the exchangeable value of the whole annual produce of its industry, or rather is precisely the same thing with that exchangeable value. As every individual, therefore, endeavours as much as he can both to employ his capital in the support of domestic industry, and so to direct that industry that its produce may be of the greatest value, every individual necessarily labours to render the annual revenue of the society as great as he can. He generally, indeed, neither intends to promote the public interest, nor knows how much he is promoting it. By preferring the support of domestic to that of foreign industry, he intends only his own security; and by directing that industry in such a manner as its produce may be of the greatest value, he intends only his own gain and he is in this, as in many other cases, led by an invisible hand to promote an end which was no part of his intention. Nor is it always the worse for the society that it was no part of it. By pursuing his own interest he frequently promotes that of the society more effectually than when he really intends to promote it. I have never known much good done by those who affected trade for the public good. It is an affectation, indeed, not very common among merchants, and very few words need be employed in dissuading them from it.

What is the species of domestic industry which his capital can employ, and of which the produce is likely to be of the greatest value, every individual, it is evident, can, in his local situation, judge much better than any statesman or lawgiver can do for him. The statesman, who should attempt to direct private people in what manner they ought to employ their capitals, would not only load himself with a most unnecessary attention, but assume an authority which could safely be trusted, not only to no single person, but to no council or senate whatever, and which would nowhere be so dangerous as in the hands of a man who had folly and presumption enough to fancy himself fit to exercise it.

To give the monopoly of the home market to the produce of domestic industry, in any particular art or manufacture, is in some measure to direct private people in what manner they ought to employ their capitals, and must, in almost all cases, be either a useless or a hurtful regulation. If the produce of domestic can be brought there as cheap as that of foreign industry, the regulation is evidently useless. If it cannot, it must generally be hurtful. It is the maxim of every prudent master of a family, never to attempt to make at home what it will cost him more to make than to buy. The tailor does not attempt to make his own shoes, but buys them of the shoemaker. The shoemaker does not attempt to make his own clothes, but employs a tailor. The farmer attempts to make neither the one nor the other, but employs those different artificers. All of them find it for their interest to employ their whole industry in a way in which they have some advantage over their neighbours, and to purchase with a part of its produce, or, what is the same thing, with the price of a part of it, whatever else they have occasion for.

CHAPTER 7

The Federalist Papers

The same year as the publication of Adam Smith's *The Wealth of Nations*, the American Revolution began. But 1776 was not the last year of revolution for the newly independent nation. In the year 1789—the year of the ratification of the United States Constitution—America put into practice what Locke and Smith had preached.

The Federalist Papers were written in 1787–1788 by James Madison, Alexander Hamilton, and John Jay to sway public opinion toward ratification of the Constitution. Federalist No. 10, authored by Madison, especially demonstrates that the Constitution was intended to realize the conception of economic justice fostered by the ideas of John Locke and Adam Smith.

Addressing "factions," or what today would be called "special interests," Madison analyzes strategies for reducing their ill effects. Removing the causes of factionalism would require either destroying the liberty of the people—a remedy worse than the disease—or giving to every person "the same opinions, the same passions, and the same interests"—an impossibility given human nature. It is the nature of man, Madison contends, to have different opinions, passions, and interests; and because men have different faculties, or abilities, different amounts of wealth or property will result. As Locke argued, so does Madison: The protection of these unequal faculties (and the consequent inequality of property) is the first purpose of government.

Having rejected removing the cause of factionalism because of the desire to preserve liberty and the realities of human nature, Madison turns to controlling the effects of factions. Factions inevitably give rise to different interests—owners, workers, debtors, creditors, and so on. The challenge of justice is how to settle disputes or nullify factions without allowing the interested parties to be judge and jury.

The principle of democracy—majority rule—dramatically lessens the chances that minority factions can use government to gain their ends. But what of majority factions? Nothing in the democratic principle per se can prevent injustice by the majority against the minority. As Madison's analysis shows, democracy in fact puts personal security and property subject to confiscation at the whim of the majority. Or, in the language of Locke, the quarrelsome and contentious may use their political power to gain the advantage over the industrious and rational, with resulting long-term loss for all.

In great detail, Madison shows how the largeness and diversity of the republic established by the Constitution (plus such features as separation of powers, checks and balances, and judicial review) lessen the likelihood that majorities will be able to perpetrate injustice. But more important than the political mechanisms analyzed is the moral vision presumed: that economic justice will be served with protection of the moral right to private property, releasing Locke's "industrious and rational" to realize their potential to the benefit of society, and Smith's "invisible hand" to promote the common good.

Is the Madisonian society simply an arena in which self-interested persons, driven by greed, can play out the logic of their passions? Unquestionably pure selfishness is not forbidden and is perhaps even encouraged. Yet it would be a mistake not to consider the moral and religious ideals Madison's political framework fosters. America's constitutional structure has afforded people the opportunity to reap fruits from a life ethic (Protestant or otherwise) of dedication to work as duty—yes, for the sake of making money, but channeled by a system in which achievements of the industrial and rational, solely self-interested or not, have often abounded for the general economic benefit of society.

Federalist No. 10

James Madison

Among the numerous advantages promised by a well-constructed Union, none deserves to be more accurately developed than its tendency to break and control the violence of faction. The friend of popular governments never finds himself so much alarmed for their character and fate, as when he contemplates their propensity to this dangerous vice. He will not fail, therefore, to set a due value on any plan which, without violating the principles to which he is attached, provides a proper cure for it. The instability, injustice, and confusion introduced into the public councils, have, in truth, been the mortal diseases under which popular governments have everywhere perished; as they continue to be the favorite and fruitful topics from which the adversaries to liberty derive their most specious declamations. The valuable improvements made by the American constitutions on the popular models, both ancient and modern, cannot certainly be too much admired; but it would be an unwarrantable partiality, to contend that they have as effectually obviated the danger on this side, as was wished and expected. Complaints are everywhere heard from our most considerate and virtuous citizens, equally the friends of public and private faith, and of public and personal liberty, that our governments are too unstable, that the public good is disregarded in the conflicts of rival parties, and that measures are too often decided, not according to the rules of justice and the rights of the minor party, but by the superior force of an interested and overbearing majority. . . . These must be chiefly, if not wholly, effects of the unsteadiness and injustice with which a factious spirit has tainted our public administrations.

By a faction, I understand a number of citizens, whether amounting to a majority or minority of the whole, who are united and actuated by some common impulse of passion, or of interest, adverse to the rights of other citizens, or to the permanent and aggregate interests of the community. . . .

. . . Liberty is to faction what air is to fire, an aliment without which it instantly expires. But it could not be less folly to abolish liberty, which is essential to political life, because it nourishes faction, than it would be to wish the annihilation of air, which is essential to animal life, because it imparts to fire its destructive agency.

. . . As long as the reason of man continues fallible, and he is at liberty to exercise it, different opinions will be formed. As long as the connection subsists between his reason and his self-love, his opinions and his passions will have a reciprocal influence on each other; and the former will be objects to which the

---

The Federalist Papers, 1787–1788.

latter will attach themselves. The diversity in the faculties of men, from which the rights of property originate, is not less an insuperable obstacle to a uniformity of interests. The protection of these faculties is the first object of government. From the protection of different and unequal faculties of acquiring property, the possession of different degrees and kinds of property immediately results; and from the influence of these on the sentiments and views of the respective proprietors, ensues a division of the society into different interests and parties.

The latent causes of faction are thus sown in the nature of man. . . .

. . . But the most common and durable source of factions has been the various and unequal distribution of property. Those who hold and those who are without property have ever formed distinct interests in society. Those who are creditors, and those who are debtors, fall under a like discrimination. A landed interest, a manufacturing interest, a mercantile interest, a moneyed interest, with many lesser interests, grow up of necessity in civilized nations, and divide them into different classes, actuated by different sentiments and views. The regulation of these various and interfering interests forms the principal task of modern legislation, and involves the spirit of party and faction in the necessary and ordinary operations of the government.

No man is allowed to be a judge in his own cause, because his interest would certainly bias his judgment, and, not improbably, corrupt his integrity. With equal, nay with greater reason, a body of men are unfit to be both judges and parties at the same time; yet what are many of the most important acts of legislation, but so many judicial determinations, not indeed concerning the rights of single persons, but concerning the rights of large bodies of citizens? And what are the different classes of legislators but advocates and parties to the causes which they determine? Is a law proposed concerning private debts? It is a question to which the creditors are parties on one side and the debtors on the other. Justice ought to hold the balance between them. Yet the parties are, and must be, themselves the judges; and the most numerous party, or, in other words, the most powerful faction must be expected to prevail. Shall domestic manufactures be encouraged, and in what degree, by restrictions on foreign manufacturers? are questions which would be differently decided by the landed and the manufacturing classes, and probably by neither with a sole regard to justice and the public good. The apportionment of taxes on the various descriptions of property is an act which seems to require the most exact impartiality; yet there is, perhaps, no legislative act in which greater opportunity and temptation are given to a predominant party to trample on the rules of justice. Every shilling with which they overburden the inferior number, is a shilling saved to their own pockets.

It is in vain to say that enlightened statesmen will be able to adjust these clashing interests, and render them all subservient to the public good. Enlightened statesmen will not always be at the helm. Nor, in many cases, can such an adjustment be made at all without taking into view indirect and remote considerations, which will rarely prevail over the immediate interest which one party may find in disregarding the rights of another or the good of the whole.

If a faction consists of less than a majority, relief is supplied by the republican principle, which enables the majority to defeat its sinister views by regular vote. It may clog the administration, it may convulse the society; but it will be unable to execute and mask its violence under the forms of the Constitution. When a majority is included in a faction, the form of popular government, on the other hand, enables it to sacrifice to its ruling passion or interest both the public good and the rights of other citizens. To secure the public good and private rights against the danger of such a faction, and at the same time to preserve the spirit and the form of popular government, is then the great object to which our inquiries are directed. . . .

. . . If the impulse and the opportunity be suffered to coincide, we well know that neither moral nor religious motives can be relied on as an adequate control. They are not found to be such on the injustice and violence of individuals, and lose their efficacy in proportion to the number combined together, that is, in proportion as their efficacy becomes needful.

From this view of the subject it may be concluded that a pure democracy, by which I mean a society consisting of a small number of citizens, who assemble and administer the government in person, can admit of no cure for the mischiefs of faction. A common passion or interest will, in almost every case, be felt by a majority of the whole; a communication and concert result from the form of government itself; and there is nothing to check the inducements to sacrifice the weaker party or an obnoxious individual. Hence it is that such democracies have ever been spectacles of turbulence and contention; have ever been found incompatible with personal security or the rights of property; and have in general been as short in their lives as they have been violent in their deaths. Theoretic politicians, who have patronized this species of government, have erroneously supposed that by reducing mankind to a perfect equality in their political rights, they would, at the same time, be perfectly equalized and assimilated in their possessions, their opinions, and their passions.

A republic, by which I mean a government in which the scheme of representation takes place, opens a different prospect, and promises the cure for which we are seeking. . . .

The two great points of difference between a democracy and a republic are: first, the delegation of the government, in the latter, to a small number of citizens elected by the rest; secondly, the greater number of citizens, and greater sphere of country, over which the latter may be extended.

The effect of the first difference is, on the one hand, to refine and enlarge the public views, by passing them through the medium of a chosen body of citizens, whose wisdom may best discern the true interest of their country, and whose patriotism and love of justice will be least likely to sacrifice it to temporary or partial considerations.

. . . As each representative will be chosen by a greater number of citizens in the large than in the small republic, it will be more difficult for unworthy candidates to practise with success the vicious arts by which elections are too often carried; and the suffrages of the people being more free, will be more likely to centre in men who possess the most attractive merit and the most diffusive and established characters. . . .

The other point of difference is, the greater number of citizens and extent of territory which may be brought within the compass of republican than of democratic government; and it is this circumstance principally which renders factious combinations less to be dreaded in the former than in the latter. The smaller the society, the fewer probably will be the distinct parties and interests composing it; the fewer the distinct parties and interests, the more frequently will a majority be found of the same party; and the smaller the number of individuals composing a majority, and the smaller the compass within which they are placed, the more easily will they concert and execute their plans of oppression. Extend the sphere and you take in a greater variety of parties and interests; you make it less probable that a majority of the whole will have a common motive to invade the rights of other citizens; or if such a common motive exists, it will be more difficult for all who feel it to discover their own strength, and to act in unison with each other. Besides other impediments, it may be remarked that, where there is a consciousness of unjust or dishonorable purposes, communication is always checked by distrust in proportion to the number whose concurrence is necessary. . . .

The influence of factious leaders may kindle a flame within their particular States, but will be unable to spread a general conflagration through the other States. A religious sect may degenerate into a political faction in a part of the Confederacy; but the variety of sects dispersed over the entire face of it must secure the national councils against any danger from that source. A rage for paper money, for an abolition of debts, for an equal division of property, or for any other improper or wicked project, will be less apt to pervade the whole body of the Union than a particular member of it; in the same proportion as such a malady is more likely to taint a particular county or district, than an entire State.

In the extent and proper structure of the Union, therefore, we behold a republican remedy for the diseases most incident to republican government.

CHAPTER *8*

Kantian Morality

Thought on economic justice in the early modern age culminated in the moral and political philosophy of late eighteenth-century philosopher Immanuel Kant (1724–1804), one of the most influential thinkers of all time. Kant's views on virtually every topic have had to be reckoned with by subsequent philosophers who would claim the right to be taken seriously, and Kantian morality is certainly no exception. While Kant wrote very little on economic justice per se, his general formulation of a philosophy of morality has enormous implications for how we approach the questions of economic justice.

In the capitalist or "bourgeois" society (envisioned by such thinkers as John Locke and Adam Smith, sought after by the perpetrators of the American and French revolutions, and actually established by the framers of the United States Constitution), the "Rights of Man"—rights to life, liberty, property, and pursuit of happiness—constituted the cornerstone. The Rights of Man at once defined the purpose and limits of public intervention in private activity.

The Rights of Man were for Kant, too, the moral foundation of a just political, economic, and social order. Thus, he wrote of his having learned "to respect human beings," confessing that "I should consider myself more useless than the common workingmen if I did not believe that this consideration could give a value to all others by establishing the rights of man."[1]

But earlier thinkers, to the extent that they did not simply take the Rights of Man as self-evident propositions in need of no proof, had tended to ground their moral principles in "human nature." It sometimes seems difficult to distinguish in Locke, for example, a *desire* for life, supposedly a given of human nature, from a *right* to life. Kant, on the other hand, insisted that the basic principles of morality do not derive from experience of human nature, or indeed any empirical information at all.

Kant believed that the foundation of morality and the Rights of Man rests in a purely abstract reason able to derive absolute, unchanging, universal principles. Indeed, Kant anchored the very definition of morality in "universality," as one of his formulations of the "categorical imperative" in *The Metaphysic of Morality* clearly reveals: "Act as if the maxim from which you act were to become through your will a universal law of nature."

A second formulation of the categorical imperative is also revealing: "Act so as to use humanity, whether in your own person or in the person of another, always as an end, never as merely a means." Pierre Hassner has noted that "this formulation of the categorical imperative . . . directly provides the moral basis of the political doctrine of the rights of man." Notes Hassner, "violation of the duty to respect man as end in himself is most conspicuous in attacks on liberty and property, where the intention can only be to treat one's fellow rational beings as mere means or instruments."[2]

In Kant's moral and political philosophy, the rights that undergird a capitalist economic and a republican political order were raised to an unprecedented peak of moral dignity. Indeed, Kant placed bourgeois man, so despised in subsequent socialist thought, at the highest possible level of human excellence.

For Kant, the person who lives out the reciprocal rights and duties in a society flying the flag of the Rights of Man follows the only possible path to freedom. By "freedom," of course, Kant did not mean the subjective freedom of the creature who, driven by desire for pleasure, feels free only when able to do whatever he wants. Rather, he referred to the objective freedom of the truly *human* being who is free when he gladly wills to follow the laws of his own rational soul and the moral order of the cosmos.

Harkening to the religiously rooted new human ideal that undergirded capitalism, Kant anchored his hopes for the actualization of human excellence not in external reform but rather in inner moral revolution: "Becoming not merely a legally but a morally good man . . . cannot be achieved . . . so long as the foundation of the maxims remain impure; rather it must be achieved through a revolution

---

[1] Quoted in Pierre Hassner, "Immanuel Kant," in Leo Strauss and Joseph Cropsey, eds., *History of Political Philosophy,* 2nd ed. (Chicago: Rand McNally & Company, 1972), p. 564.
[2] Ibid.

in the mentality . . . of the man . . . ; and he can become a new man only by a kind of rebirth resembling a new creation, and a change of heart."[3]

Kant's philosophical speculation reminds us that early capitalism justified itself by a moral vision of man as lofty as any before or after articulated by socialists. And unlike the only predicted perfections of socialism, Kant, the philosopher par excellence of the bourgeoisie, projected a way of living that he, like so many millions of others, knew from life lived in the here and now.

[3]Quoted in ibid., p. 587.

The Metaphysic of Morality

Immanuel Kant

Nothing in the whole world, or even outside of the world, can possibly be regarded as good without limitation except a *good will*. No doubt it is a good and desirable thing to have intelligence, sagacity, judgment, and other intellectual gifts, by whatever name they may be called; it is also good and desirable in many respects to possess by nature such qualities as courage, resolution, and perseverance; but all these gifts of nature may be in the highest degree pernicious and hurtful, if the will which directs them, or what is called the *character*, is not itself good. The same thing applies to *gifts of fortune*. Power, wealth, honour, even good health, and that general well-being and contentment with one's lot which we call *happiness*, give rise to pride and not infrequently to insolence, if a man's will is not good; nor can a reflective and impartial spectator ever look with satisfaction upon the unbroken prosperity of a man who is destitute of the ornament of a pure and good will. A good will would therefore seem to be the indispensable condition without which no one is even worthy to be happy.

A man's will is good, not because the consequences which flow from it are good, nor because it is capable of attaining the end which it seeks, but it is good in itself, or because it wills the good....

To bring to clear consciousness the conception of a will which is good in itself, a conception already familiar to the popular mind, let us examine the conception of *duty*.... *Duty is the obligation to act from reverence for law.*

... the only thing which I can reverence or which can lay me under an obligation to act, is the law which is connected with my will, not as a consequence, but as a principle; a principle which is not dependent upon natural inclination, but overmasters it, or at least allows it to have no influence whatever in determining my course of action. Now if an action which is done out of regard for duty sets entirely aside the influence of natural inclination and along with it every object of the will, nothing else is left by which the will can be determined but objectively the *law* itself, and subjectively *pure reverence* for the law as a principle of action. Thus there arises the maxim, to obey the moral law even at the sacrifice of all my natural inclinations.

The supreme good which we call moral can therefore be nothing but the *idea of the law* in itself, in so far as it is this idea which determines the will, and not

Immanuel Kant, The Metaphysic of Morality, *in* The Philosophy of Kant, *selected and translated by John Watson, new edition (Glasgow:James Maclehose & Sons, 1901).*

any consequences that are expected to follow. Only a *rational* being can have such an idea, and hence a man who acts from the idea of the law is already morally good, no matter whether the consequences which he expects from his action follow or not.

Now what must be the nature of a law, the idea of which is to determine the will, even apart from the effects expected to follow, and which is therefore itself entitled to be called good absolutely and without qualification? As the will must not be moved to act from any desire for the results expected to follow from obedience to a certain law, the only principle of the will which remains is that of the conformity of actions to universal law. In all cases I must act in such a way *that I can at the same time will that my maxim should become a universal law....*

May I, for instance, under the pressure of circumstances, make a promise which I have no intention of keeping? The question is not, whether it is prudent to make a false promise, but whether it is morally right. To enable me to answer this question shortly and conclusively, the best way is for me to ask myself whether it would satisfy me that the maxim to extricate myself from embarrassment by giving a false promise should have the force of a universal law, applying to others as well as to myself. And I see at once, that, while I can certainly will the lie, I cannot will that lying should be a universal law. If lying were universal, there would, properly speaking, be no promises whatever. I might say that I intended to do a certain thing at some future time, but nobody would believe me, or if he did at the moment trust to my promise, he would afterwards pay me back in my own coin. My maxim thus proves itself to be self-destructive, so soon as it is taken as a universal law.

CHAPTER 9

Utilitarianism

In the nineteenth century, philosophers who engaged in abstract speculation about ethics and morality—including the themes of economic justice—often fell into one of two camps.

"Idealists" tended to follow in the tradition of Immanuel Kant. Kant, as we have seen, emphasized universal principles of justice, grounded in reason rather than experience and supposedly valid irrespective of effects on human happiness.

"Utilitarians," on the other hand, identified happiness, which they defined in terms of pleasure, with the concept of justice. While utilitarianism had many precursors (some would consider Adam Smith a utilitarian, for example), certainly the most influential systematic formulation of it is found in the writings of English philosopher Jeremy Bentham (1748–1832). That action is right and just, proclaimed Bentham, which promotes happiness (pleasure), while that which promotes unhappiness (pain) is wrong. On the level of society, that which is right and just promotes, to the greatest degree possible, the sum of individual interests—the greatest happiness (pleasure) of the greatest number.

Bentham, basically an individualist, supported a laissez-faire view of governmental intervention in economic activity. He believed that the capitalist system of organizing the production and distribution of wealth would tend to produce the greatest happiness of the greatest number. Yet his approach to morality makes the final determination of what in fact constitutes economic justice for a particular society at a particular time a matter of empirical determination. In principle, a utilitarian could conclude that a socialist arrangement, either in terms of production or distribution or both, is the most just system if it promotes the greatest happiness of the greatest number.

Indeed, utilitarians after Bentham, best represented by English philosopher John Stuart Mill (1806–1873), were receptive to the possibility that socialism is more just than capitalism. In his later years, Mill gravitated toward the position that while in terms of production laissez faire is probably best, a socialist approach to distribution is more just—more likely, that is, to promote the greatest happiness of the greatest number. As William Ebenstein has noted, because Benthamite utilitarianism "was not committed to any dogma of a priori limitations of public action," and because "its ultimate objective was the greatest happiness of the greatest number rather than any particular mechanism to ensure it, it was only a question of time—and changing social and economic circumstances—before [utilitarianism] was directed into the channels of socialism."[1] Nineteenth- and twentieth-century socialists in the British tradition (often labeled "Fabian" socialism) have tended toward a utilitarian approach, arguing that socialism rather than capitalism brings about the greatest good to the greatest number.

Both earlier and later utilitarianism, preoccupied with the assessment of actual outcomes of alternative economic systems, have notably neglected the theme of the ideal human type. Other than Mill's consideration that certain pleasures are "higher" than others, utilitarianism has tended to take the individual driven by the desire for pleasure as normative.

[1]William Ebenstein, *Great Political Thinkers: Plato to the Present* (New York: Holt, Rinehart and Winston, 1951), p. 506.

Principles of Morals and Legislation

Jeremy Bentham

Mankind governed by pain and pleasure. Nature has placed mankind under the governance of two sovereign masters, *pain* and *pleasure*. It is for them alone to point out what we ought to do, as well as to determine what we shall do. On the one hand the standard of right and wrong, on the other the chain of causes and effects, are fastened to their throne. They govern us in all we do, in all we say, in all we think: every effort we can make to throw off our subjection, will serve but to demonstrate and confirm it. In words a man may pretend to abjure their empire: but in reality he will remain subject to it all the while. The *principle of utility* recognises this subjection, and assumes it for the foundation of that system, the object of which is to rear the fabric of felicity by the hands of reason and of law. Systems which attempt to question it, deal in sounds instead of sense, in caprice instead of reason, in darkness instead of light.

By the principle of utility is meant that principle which approves or disapproves of every action whatsoever, according to the tendency which it appears to have to augment or diminish the happiness of the party whose interest is in question: or, what is the same thing in other words, to promote or to oppose that happiness. I say of every action whatsoever; and therefore not only of every action of a private individual, but of every measure of government.

Utility, what. By utility is meant that property in any object, whereby it tends to produce benefit, advantage, pleasure, good, or happiness, (all this in the present case comes to the same thing) or (what comes again to the same thing) to prevent the happening of mischief, pain, evil, or unhappiness to the party whose interest is considered: if that party be the community in general, then the happiness of the community: if a particular individual, then the happiness of that individual.

Interest of the community, what. The interest of the community is one of the most general expressions that can occur in the phraseology of morals: no wonder that the meaning of it is often lost. When it has a meaning, it is this. The community is a fictitious *body*, composed of the individual persons who are considered as constituting as it were its *members*. The interest of the community then is, what?—the sum of the interests of the several members who compose it.

It is in vain to talk of the interest of the community, without understanding what is the interest of the individual. A thing is said to promote the interest, or to be *for* the interest, of an individual, when it tends to add to the sum total of

---

Jeremy Bentham, Introduction to the Principles of Morals and Legislation, *1789, rev. ed. 1823.*

his pleasures: or, what comes to the same thing, to diminish the sum total of his pains.

An action conformable to the principle of utility, what. An action then may be said to be conformable to the principle of utility, or, for shortness sake, to utility, (meaning with respect to the community at large) when the tendency it has to augment the happiness of the community is greater than any it has to diminish it.

A measure of government conformable to the principle of utility, what. A measure of government (which is but a particular kind of action, performed by a particular person or persons) may be said to be conformable to or dictated by the principle of utility, when in like manner the tendency which it has to augment the happiness of the community is greater than any which it has to diminish it. . . .

To prove the rectitude of this principle is at once unnecessary and impossible. Has the rectitude of this principle been ever formally contested? It should seem that it had, by those who have not known what they have been meaning. Is it susceptible of any direct proof? it should seem not: for that which is used to prove every thing else, cannot itself be proved: a chain of proofs must have their commencement somewhere. To give such proof is as impossible as it is needless.

Principles of Political Economy

John Stuart Mill

The laws and conditions of the production of wealth, partake of the character of physical truths. There is nothing optional or arbitrary in them. Whatever mankind produce, must be produced in the modes, and under the conditions, imposed by the constitution of external things, and by the inherent properties of their own bodily and mental structure. Whether they like it or not, their productions will be limited by the amount of their previous accumulation, and, that being given, it will be proportional to their energy, their skill, the perfection of their machinery, and their judicious use of the advantages of combined labour. Whether they like it or not, a double quantity of labour will not raise, on the same land, a double quantity of food, unless some improvement takes place in the processes of cultivation. Whether they like it or not, the unproductive expenditure of individuals will *pro tanto* tend to impoverish the community, and only their productive expenditure will enrich it. The opinions, or the wishes, which may exist on these different matters, do not control the things themselves. We cannot, indeed, foresee to what extent the modes of production may be altered, or the productiveness of labour increased, by future extensions of our knowledge of the laws of nature suggesting new processes of industry of which we have at present no conception. But howsoever we may succeed in making for ourselves more space within the limits set by the constitution of things, we know that there must be limits. We cannot alter the ultimate properties either of matter or mind, but can only employ those properties more or less successfully, to bring about the events in which we are interested.

It is not so with the Distribution of Wealth. That is a matter of human institution solely. The things once there, mankind, individually or collectively, can do with them as they like. They can place them at the disposal of whomsoever they please, and on whatever terms. Further, in the social state, in every state except total solitude, any disposal whatever of them can only take place by the consent of society, or rather of those who dispose of its active force. Even what a person has produced by his individual toil, unaided by any one, he cannot keep, unless by the permission of society. Not only can society take it from him, but individuals could and would take it from him, if society only remained passive; if it did not

---

John Stuart Mill, Principles of Political Economy, *5th ed. (New York: D. Appleton and Company, 1894).*

either interfere *en masse,* or employ and pay people for the purpose of preventing him from being disturbed in the possession. The distribution of wealth, therefore, depends on the laws and customs of society. The rules by which it is determined, are what the opinions and feelings of the ruling portion of the community make them, and are very different in different ages and countries; and might be still more different, if mankind so chose. . . . We have here to consider, not the causes, but the consequences, of the rules according to which wealth may be distributed. Those, at least, are as little arbitrary, and have as much the character of physical laws, as the laws of production. Human beings can control their own acts, but not the consequences of their acts either to themselves or to others. Society can subject the distribution of wealth to whatever rules it thinks best; but what practical results will flow from the operation of those rules, must be discovered, like any other physical or mental truths, by observation and reasoning. . . .

Private property, as an institution, did not owe its origin to any of those considerations of utility, which plead for the maintenance of it when established. Enough is known of rude ages, both from history and from analogous states of society in our own time, to show, that tribunals (which always precede laws) were originally established, not to determine rights, but to repress violence and terminate quarrels. With this object chiefly in view, they naturally enough gave legal effect to first occupancy, by treating as the aggressor the person who first commenced violence, by turning, or attempting to turn, another out of possession. The preservation of the peace, which was the original object of civil government, was thus attained; while by confirming, to those who already possessed it, even what was not the fruit of personal exertion, a guarantee was incidentally given to them and others that they would be protected in what was so.

In considering the institution of property as a question in social philosophy, we must leave out of consideration its actual origin in any of the existing nations of Europe. We may suppose a community unhampered by any previous possession; a body of colonists, occupying for the first time an uninhabited country; bringing nothing with them but what belonged to them in common, and having a clear field for the adoption of the institutions and polity which they judged most expedient; required, therefore, to choose whether they would conduct the work of production on the principle of individual property, or on some system of common ownership and collective agency.

If private property were adopted, we must presume that it would be accompanied by none of the initial inequalities and injustice which obstruct the beneficial operation of the principle in old society. Every full-grown man or woman, we must suppose, would be secured in the unfettered use and disposal of his or her bodily and mental faculties; and the instruments of production, the land and tools, would be divided fairly among them, so that all might start, in respect to outward appliances, on equal terms. It is possible also to conceive that in this original apportionment, compensation might be made for the injuries of nature, and the balance redressed by assigning to the less robust members of the community advantages in the distribution, sufficient to put them on a par with the rest. But the division, once made, would not again be interfered with; individuals would be left to their own exertions and to the ordinary chances, for making an advantageous use of what was assigned to them. If individual property, on the contrary, were excluded, the plan which must be adopted would be to hold the land and all instruments of production as the joint property of the community, and to carry on the operations of industry on the common account. The direction of the labour of the community would devolve upon a magistrate or magistrates, whom we may suppose elected by the suffrages of the community, and whom we must assume to be voluntarily obeyed by them. The division of the produce would in like manner be a public act. The principle might either be that of complete equality, or of apportionment to the necessities or deserts of individuals, in whatever manner might be conformable to the ideas of justice or policy prevailing in the community. . . . In an age like the present, when a general reconsideration of all first principles is felt to be inevitable, and when more than at any former period of history the suffering portions of the community have a voice in the discussion, it was impossible but that ideas of this nature should spread far and wide. The late revolutions in Europe have thrown up a great amount of speculation of this character, and an unusual share of attention has consequently been drawn to the various forms which these ideas have assumed: nor is this attention likely to diminish, but on the contrary, to increase more and more.

The assailants of the principle of individual property may be divided into two classes: those whose scheme implies absolute equality in the distribution of the physical means of life and enjoyment, and those who admit inequality, but grounded on some principle, or supposed principle, of justice or general expediency, and not, like so many of the existing social inequalities, dependent on accident alone.

. . . The characteristic name for this economical system is Communism, a word of continental origin, only of late introduced into this country. The word Socialism, which originated among the English Communists, and was assumed by them as a name to designate their own doctrine, is now, on the Continent, employed in a larger sense; not necessarily implying Communism, or the entire abolition of private property, but applied to any system which requires that the land and the instruments of production should be the property, not of individuals, but of communities or associations, or of the government. . . .

Whatever may be the merits or defects of these various schemes, they cannot be truly said to be impracticable. No reasonable person can doubt that a village community, composed of a few thousand inhabitants cultivating in joint ownership the same extent of land which at present feeds the number of people, and producing by combined labour and the most improved processes the manufactured articles which they required, could raise an amount of productions sufficient to maintain them in comfort; and would find the means of obtaining, and if need be, exacting, the quantity of labour necessary for this purpose, from every member of the association who was capable of work.

The objection ordinarily made to a system of community of property and equal distribution of the produce, that each person would be incessantly occupied in evading his fair share of the work, points, undoubtedly, to a real difficulty. But those who urge this objection, forget to how great an extent the same difficulty exists under the system on which nine-tenths of the business of society is now conducted. The objection supposes, that honest and efficient labour is only to be had from those who are themselves individually to reap the benefit of their own exertions. But how small a part of all the labour performed in England, from the lowest paid to the highest, is done by persons working for their own benefit. From the Irish reaper or hodman to the chief justice or the minister of state, nearly all the work of society is remunerated by day wages or fixed salaries. A factory operative has less personal interest in his work than a member of a Communist association, since he is not, like him, working for a partnership of which he is himself a member. It will no doubt be said, that though the labourers themselves have not, in most cases, a personal interest in their work, they are watched and superintended, and their labour directed, and the mental part of the labour performed, by persons who have. Even this, however, is far from being universally the fact. In all public, and many of the largest and most successful private undertakings, not only the labours of detail but the control and superintendence are entrusted to salaried officers. And though the "master's eye," when the master is vigilant and intelligent, is of proverbial value, it must be remembered that in a Socialist farm or manufactory, each labourer would be under the eye not of one master, but of the whole community. In the extreme case of obstinate perseverance in not performing the due share of work, the community would have the same resources which society now has for compelling conformity to the necessary conditions of the association. Dismissal, the only remedy at present, is no remedy when any other labourer who may be engaged does no better than his predecessor: the power of dismissal only enables an employer to obtain from his workmen the customary amount of labour, but that customary labour may be of any degree of inefficiency. Even the labourer who loses his employment by idleness or negligence, has nothing worse to suffer, in the most unfavourable case, than the discipline of a workhouse, and if the desire to avoid this be a sufficient motive in the one system, it would be sufficient in the other. I am not undervaluing the strength of the incitement given to labour when the whole or a large share of the benefit of extra exertion belongs to the labourer. But under the present system of industry this incitement, in the great majority of cases, does not exist. If Communistic labour might be less vigorous than that of a peasant proprietor, or a workman labouring on his own account, it would probably be more energetic than that of a labourer for hire, who has no personal interest in the matter at all. The neglect by the uneducated classes of labourers for hire, of the duties which they engage to perform, is in the present state of society most flagrant. Now it is an admitted condition of the Communist scheme that all shall be educated: and this being supposed, the duties of the members of the association would doubtless be as diligently performed as those of the generality of salaried officers in the middle or higher classes; who are not supposed to be necessarily unfaithful to their trust, because so long as they are not dismissed, their pay is the same in however lax a manner their duty is fulfilled. Undoubtedly, as a general rule, remuneration by fixed salaries does not in any class of functionaries produce the maximum of zeal: and this is as much as can be reasonably alleged against Communistic labour.

That even this inferiority would necessarily exist, is by no means so certain as is assumed by those who are little used to carry their minds beyond the state of things with which they are familiar. Mankind are capable of a far greater amount of public spirit than the present age is accustomed to suppose possible. History bears witness to the success with which large bodies of human beings may be trained to feel the public interest their own. And no soil could be more favourable to the growth of such a feeling, than a Communist association, since all the ambition, and the bodily and mental activity, which are now exerted in the pursuit of separate and self-regarding interests, would require another sphere of employment, and would naturally find it in the pursuit of the general benefit of the community. The same cause, so often assigned in explanation of the devotion of the Catholic priest or monk to the interest of his order—that he has no interest apart from it—would, under Communism, attach the citizen to the community. And independently of the public motive, every member of the association would be amenable to the most universal, and one of the strongest, of personal motives, that of public opinion. The force of this motive in deterring from any act or omission positively reproved by the community, no one is likely to deny; but the power also of emulation, in exciting to the most strenuous exertions for the sake of the approbation and admiration of others, is borne witness to by experience in every situation in which human beings publicly compete with one another, even if it be in things frivolous, or from which the public derive no benefit. A contest, who can do most for the common good, is not the kind of competition which Socialists repudiate. To what extent, therefore, the energy of labour would be diminished by Communism, or whether in the long run it would be diminished at all, must be considered for the present an undecided question.

Another of the objections to Communism is similar to that, so often urged against poor-laws: that if every member of the community were assured of subsistence for himself and any number of children, on the sole condition of willingness to work, prudential restraint on the multiplication of mankind would be at an end, and population would start forward at a rate which would reduce the community through successive stages of increasing discomfort to actual starvation. There would certainly be much ground for this apprehension if Communism provided no motives of restraint, equivalent to those which it would take away. But Communism is precisely the state of things in which opinion might be expected to declare itself with greatest intensity against this kind of selfish intemperance. An augmentation of numbers which diminished the comfort or increased the toil of the mass, would then cause (which now it does not) immediate and unmistakable inconvenience to every individual in the association; inconvenience which could not then be imputed to the avarice of employers, or the unjust privileges of the rich. In such altered circumstances opinion could not fail to reprobate, and if reprobation did not suffice, to repress by penalties of some description, this or any other culpable self-indulgence at the expense of the community. The Communistic scheme, instead of being peculiarly open to the objection drawn from danger of over-population, has the recommendation of tending in an especial degree to the prevention of that evil.

A more real difficulty is that of fairly apportioning the labour of the community among its members. There are many kinds of work, and by what standard are they to be measured one against another? Who is to judge how much cotton spinning, or distributing goods from the stores, or bricklaying, or chimney sweeping, is equivalent to so much ploughing? The difficulty of making the adjustment between different qualities of labour is so strongly felt by Communist writers, that they have usually thought it necessary to provide that all should work by turns at every description of useful labour: an arrangement which by putting an end to the division of employments, would sacrifice so much of the advantage of co-operative production as greatly to diminish the productiveness of labour. Besides, even in the same kind of work, nominal equality of labour would be so great a real inequality, that the feeling of justice would revolt against its being enforced. All persons are not equally fit for all labour; and the same quantity of labour is an unequal burthen on the weak and the strong, the hardy and the delicate, the quick and the slow, the dull and the intelligent.

But these difficulties, though real, are not necessarily insuperable. The apportionment of work to the strength and capacities of individuals, the mitigation of a general rule to provide for cases in which it would operate harshly, are not problems to which human intelligence, guided by a sense of justice, would be inadequate. And the worst and most unjust arrangement which could be made of these points, under a system aiming at equality, would be so far short of the inequality and injustice with which labour (not to speak of remuneration) is now apportioned, as to be scarcely worth counting in the comparison. We must remember too that Communism, as a system of society, exists only in idea; that its difficulties, at present, are much better understood than its resources; and that the intellect of mankind is only beginning to contrive the means of organizing it in detail, so as to overcome the one and derive the greatest advantage from the other.

If, therefore, the choice were to be made between Communism with all its chances, and the present state of society with all its sufferings and injustices; if the institution of private property necessarily carried with it as a consequence, that the produce of labour should be apportioned as we now see it, almost in an inverse ratio to the labour—the largest portions to those who have never worked at all, the next largest to those whose work is almost nominal, and so in a descending scale, the remuneration dwindles as the work grows harder and more disagreeable, until the most fatiguing and exhausting bodily labour cannot count with certainty on being able to earn even the necessaries of life; if this, or Communism, were the alternative, all the difficulties, great or small, of Communism, would be but as dust in the balance. But to make the comparison applicable, we must compare Communism at its best, with the régime of individual property, not as it is, but as it might be made. The principle of private property has never yet had a fair trial in any country; and less so, perhaps, in this country than in some others. The social arrangements of modern Europe commenced from a distribution of property which was the result, not of just partition, or acquisition by industry, but of conquest and violence: and notwithstanding what industry has been doing for many centuries to modify the work of force, the system still retains many and large traces of its origin. The laws of property have never yet conformed to the principles on which the justification of private property rests. They have made property of things which never ought to be property, and absolute property where only a qualified property ought to exist. They have not held the balance fairly between human beings, but have heaped impediments upon some, to give advantage to others; they have purposely fostered inequalities, and prevented all from starting fair in the race. That all should indeed start on perfectly equal terms, is inconsistent with any law of private property: but if as much pains as has been taken to aggravate the inequality of chances arising from the natural working of the principle, had been taken to temper that inequality by every means not subversive of the principle itself; if the tendency of legislation had been to favour the diffusion, instead of the concentration of wealth—to encourage the subdivision of the large masses, instead of striving to keep them together; the principle of individual property would have been found to have no necessary connexion with the physical and social evils which almost all Socialist writers assume to be inseparable from it.

Private property, in every defence made of it, is supposed to mean, the guarantee to individuals of the fruits of their own labour and abstinence. The guarantee to them of the fruits of the labour and abstinence of others, transmitted to them without any merit or exertion of their own, is not of the essence of the institution, but a mere incidental consequence, which when it reaches a certain height, does not promote, but conflicts with the ends which render private property legitimate. To judge of the final destination of the institution of property, we must suppose everything rectified, which causes the institution to work in a manner opposed to that equitable principle, of proportion between remuneration and exertion, on which in every vindication of it that will bear the light, it is assumed to be grounded. We must also suppose two conditions realized, without which neither Communism nor any other laws or institutions could make the condition of the mass of mankind other than degraded and miserable. One of these conditions is, universal education; the other, a due limitation of the numbers of the community. With these, there could be no poverty even under the present social institutions: and these being supposed, the question of socialism is not, as generally stated by Socialists, a question of flying to the sole refuge against the evils which now bear down humanity; but a mere question of comparative advantages, which futurity must determine. We are too ignorant either of what individual agency in its best form, or Socialism in its best form, can accomplish, to be qualified to decide which of the two will be the ultimate form of human society.

If a conjecture may be hazarded, the decision will probably depend mainly on one consideration, viz. which of the two systems is consistent with the greatest amount of human liberty and spontaneity. After the means of subsistence are assured, the next in strength of the personal wants of human beings is liberty; and (unlike the physical wants, which as civilization advances become more moderate and more amenable to control) it increases instead of diminishing in intensity, as the intelligence and the moral faculties are more developed. The perfection both of social arrangements and of practical morality would be, to secure to all persons complete independence and freedom of action, subject to no restriction but that of not doing injury to others: and the education which taught or the social institutions which required them to exchange the control of their own actions for any amount of comfort or affluence, or to renounce liberty for the sake of equality, would deprive them of one of the most elevated characteristics of human nature. It remains to be discovered how far the preservation of this characteristic would be found compatible with the Communistic organization of society. No doubt, this, like all other objections to the Socialist schemes, is vastly exaggerated. The members of the association need not be required to live together more than they do now, nor need they be controlled in the disposal of their individual share of the produce, and of the probably large amount of leisure which, if they limited their production to things really worth producing, they would possess. Individuals need not be chained to an occupation, or to a particular locality. The restraints of Communism would be freedom in comparison with the present condition of the majority of the human race. The generality of labourers in this and most other countries, have as little choice of occupation or freedom of locomotion, are practically as dependent on fixed rules and on the will of others, as they could be on any system short of actual slavery; to say nothing of the entire domestic subjection of one half the species, to which it is the signal honour of Owenism and most other forms of Socialism that they assign equal rights, in all respects, with those of the hitherto dominant sex. But it is not by comparison with the present bad state of society that the claims of Communism can be estimated; nor is it sufficient that it should promise greater personal and mental freedom than is now enjoyed by those who have not enough of either to deserve the name. The question is, whether there would be any asylum left for individuality of character; whether public opinion would not be a tyrannical yoke; whether the absolute dependence of each on all, and surveillance of each by all, would not grind all down into a tame uniformity of thoughts, feelings, and actions. This is already one of the glaring evils of the existing state of society, notwithstanding a much greater diversity of education and pursuits, and a much less absolute dependence of the individual on the mass, than would exist in the Communistic régime. No society in which eccentricity is a matter of reproach, can be in a wholesome state. It is yet to be ascertained whether the Communistic scheme would be consistent with that multiform development of human nature, those manifold unlikenesses, that diversity of tastes and talents, and variety of intellectual points of view, which not only form a great part of the interest of human life, but by bringing intellects into stimulating collision, and by presenting to each innumerable notions that he would not have conceived of himself, are the mainspring of mental and moral progression.

CHAPTER *10*

Classical Economics and Economic Justice

In contrast to the basically optimistic vision of Adam Smith, the next generation of classical economists in the early nineteenth century painted a much more gloomy picture of the future. Among the most pessimistic prognosticators was the Rev. Thomas Malthus (1766–1834), who inspired Thomas Carlyle to call economics "the Dismal Science." Malthus feared that early marriages, lack of sexual restraint, and higher wages would lead to disaster for a society. While he articulated no explicit theory of justice, his "scientific" predictions projected a truly dismal economic future especially for the lower class.

Population grows geometrically (1,2,4,8,16 . . .) while, Malthus conjectured, food grows arithmetically (1,2,3 . . .). Thus, Malthus believed that the growing population would surpass society's ability to produce food. The result, unless population growth was somehow checked, would be misery, war, or starvation. Malthus criticized the "poor laws" of his day for contributing to this dangerous scenario. The poverty programs helped to support the poor financially and thus gave incentives for marriage and family. An increase in population with no subsequent increase in the ability to produce food would result.

David Ricardo (1772–1823) developed similar pessimistic views. By trading in the stock market, in a few years Ricardo gained a fortune large enough to allow him to retire from business life, enter Parliament, and write on economics. Ironically, the classical capitalist economist Ricardo laid a foundation upon which so-cialist Karl Marx would later build.

In the view of the classical economists, "rent" has a different meaning than it does in common usage today. To the classical economist, rent arises from the superior productivity of a resource. The farmer owning a particularly fertile piece of ground earns rent by producing more bushels per acre than a farmer with less fertile property. Population pressures force less productive land into farm use. The price of crops must be sufficiently high to compensate the landowner and laborers, as the marginal land would not otherwise be farmed. Owners of more productive land, by receiving the same price per bushel as those farming the poor land, reap rents, since an acre of their land could produce more bushels. Rising rents, rather than causing high food prices, result from high food prices brought about by a growing population and the use of less arable land for farming.

Wages, in the Ricardian view, are set to the subsistence level. Workers receive enough wages to permit them to live and procreate. This "Iron Law of Wages" later helped fuel Marx's thinking about the exploitation of labor.

But Ricardo did qualify the Iron Law. He recognized that additional capital or technological improvements would lead to rising wages. As long as capital growth and technological growth outpaced population growth, the workers would enjoy a rising standard of living.

Profits accrue to the owner of capital. Capital or machinery is embodied labor. The value of an item is determined by the value of direct and indirect (embodied) labor used to produce it. Profit is a payment for this past, indirect labor.

Ricardo's explanation of profits, in the eyes of Marx, pointed to worker exploita-tion. If profits were due to the efforts of workers embodied in the capital, the profits rightfully belonged to labor. Rather than being received by the workers, however, profits went to the capitalist.

Ricardo, finding what he thought were mistakes in the writings of Smith, wrote as a classical economist to try to correct economic theory. Though he did a master-ful job in explaining some parts of economics, he muddied the waters in other aspects. The next great economic theorist was Karl Marx, who upon reading Smith and Ricardo sought to refine economic theory once again. Ricardo, like Malthus, had painted a dismal picture for the laboring class that would be grist for Marx's mill as he ground out his critique of capitalism.

The Principles of Political Economy and Taxation
David Ricardo

ON WAGES

Labour, like all other things which are purchased and sold, and which may be increased or diminished in quantity, has its natural and its market price. The natural price of labour is that price which is necessary to enable the labourers, one with another, to subsist and to perpetuate their race, without either increase or diminution.

The power of the labourer to support himself, and the family which may be necessary to keep up the number of labourers, does not depend on the quantity of money which he may receive for wages, but on the quantity of food, necessaries, and conveniences become essential to him from habit which that money will purchase. The natural price of labour, therefore, depends on the price of the food, necessaries, and conveniences required for the support of the labourer and his family. With a rise in the price of food and necessaries, the natural price of labour will rise; with the fall in their price, the natural price of labour will fall.

With the progress of society the natural price of labour has always a tendency to rise, because one of the principal commodities by which its natural price is regulated has a tendency to become dearer from the greater difficulty of producing it. As, however, the improvements in agriculture, the discovery of new markets, whence provisions may be imported, may for a time counteract the tendency to a rise in the price of necessaries, and may even occasion their natural price to fall, so will the same causes produce the correspondent effects on the natural price of labour.

The natural price of all commodities, excepting raw produce and labour, has a tendency to fall in the progress of wealth and population; for though, on one hand, they are enhanced in real value, from the rise in the natural price of the raw material of which they are made, this is more than counterbalanced by the improvements in machinery, by the better division and distribution of labour, and by the increasing skill, both in science and art, of the producers.

The market price of labour is the price which is really paid for it, from the natural operation of the proportion of the supply to the demand; labour is dear when it is scarce and cheap when it is plentiful. However much the market price of labour may deviate from its natural price, it has, like commodities, a tendency to conform to it.

David Ricardo, The Principles of Political Economy and Taxation *(London: J. M. Dent & Sons Ltd., 1911).*

It is when the market price of labour exceeds its natural price that the condition of the labourer is flourishing and happy, that he has it in his power to command a greater proportion of the necessaries and enjoyments of life, and therefore to rear a healthy and numerous family. When, however, by the encouragement which high wages give to the increase of population, the number of labourers is increased, wages again fall to their natural price, and indeed from a reaction sometimes fall below it.

When the market price of labour is below its natural price, the condition of the labourers is most wretched: then poverty deprives them of those comforts which custom renders absolute necessaries. It is only after their privations have reduced their number, or the demand for labour has increased, that the market price of labour will rise to its natural price, and that the labourer will have the moderate comforts which the natural rate of wages will afford.

Notwithstanding the tendency of wages to conform to their natural rate, their market rate may, in an improving society, for an indefinite period, be constantly above it; for no sooner may the impulse which an increased capital gives to a new demand for labour be obeyed, than another increase of capital may produce the same effect; and thus, if the increase of capital be gradual and constant, the demand for labour may give a continued stimulus to an increase of people.

Capital is that part of the wealth of a country which is employed in production, and consists of food, clothing, tools, raw materials, machinery, etc., necessary to give effect to labour.

Capital may increase in quantity at the same time that its value rises. An addition may be made to the food and clothing of a country at the same time that more labour may be required to produce the additional quantity than before; in that case not only the quantity but the value of capital will rise.

Or capital may increase without its value increasing, and even while its value is actually diminishing; not only may an addition be made to the food and clothing of a country, but the addition may be made by the aid of machinery, without any increase, and even with an absolute diminution in the proportional quantity of labour required to produce them. The quantity of capital may increase, while neither the whole together, nor any part of it singly, will have a greater value than before, but may actually have a less.

In the first case, the natural price of labour, which always depends on the price of food, clothing, and other necessaries, will rise; in the second, it will remain stationary or fall; but in both cases the market rate of wages will rise, for in proportion to the increase of capital will be the increase in the demand for labour; in proportion to the work to be done will be the demand for those who are to do it.

In both cases, too, the market price of labour will rise above its natural price; and in both cases it will have a tendency to conform to its natural price, but in the first case this agreement will be most speedily effected. The situation of the labourer will be improved, but not much improved; for the increased price of food and necessaries will absorb a large portion of his increased wages; consequently a small supply of labour, or a trifling increase in the population, will soon reduce the market price to the then increased natural price of labour.

In the second case, the condition of the labourer will be very greatly improved; he will receive increased money wages without having to pay any increased price, and perhaps even a diminished price for the commodities which he and his family consume; and it will not be till after a great addition has been made to the population that the market price of labour will again sink to its then low and reduced natural price.

Thus, then, with every improvement of society, with every increase in its capital, the market wages of labour will rise; but the permanence of their rise will depend on the question whether the natural price of labour has also risen; and this again will depend on the rise in the natural price of those necessaries on which the wages of labour are expended.

It is not to be understood that the natural price of labour, estimated even in food and necessaries, is absolutely fixed and constant. It varies at different times in the same country, and very materially differs in different countries. It essentially depends on the habits and customs of the people. An English labourer would consider his wages under their natural rate, and too scanty to support a family, if they enabled him to purchase no other food than potatoes, and to live in no better habitation than a mud cabin; yet these moderate demands of nature are often deemed sufficient in countries where "man's life is cheap" and his wants easily satisfied. Many of the conveniences now enjoyed in an English cottage would have been thought luxuries at an earlier period of our history....

With a population pressing against the means of subsistence, the only remedies are either a reduction of people or a more rapid accumulation of capital. In rich countries, where all the fertile land is already cultivated, the latter remedy is neither very practicable nor very desirable, because its effect would be, if pushed very far, to render all classes equally poor. But in poor countries, where there are abundant means of production in store, from fertile land not yet brought into cultivation, it is the only safe and efficacious means of removing the evil, particularly as its effect would be to elevate all classes of the people.

The friends of humanity cannot but wish that in all countries the labouring classes should have a taste for comforts and enjoyments, and that they should be stimulated by all legal means in their exertions to procure them. There cannot be a better security against a superabundant population. In those countries where the labouring classes have the fewest wants, and are contented with the cheapest food, the people are exposed to the greatest vicissitudes and miseries. They have no place of refuge from calamity; they cannot seek safety in a lower station; they are already so low that they can fall no lower. On any deficiency of the chief article of their subsistence there are few substitutes of which they can avail themselves and dearth to them is attended with almost all the evils of famine.

In the natural advance of society, the wages of labour will have a tendency to fall, as far as they are regulated by supply and demand; for the supply of labourers will continue to increase at the same rate, whilst the demand for them will increase at a slower rate. If, for instance, wages were regulated by a yearly increase of capital at the rate of 2 per cent., they would fall when it accumulated only at the rate of 1½ per cent. They would fall still lower when it increased only at the rate of 1 or ½ per cent., and would continue to do so until the capital became stationary, when wages also would become stationary, and be only sufficient to keep up the numbers of the actual population. I say that, under these circumstances, wages would fall if they were regulated only by the supply and demand of labourers; but we must not forget that wages are also regulated by the prices of the commodities on which they are expended.

As population increases, these necessaries will be constantly rising in price, because more labour will be necessary to produce them. If, then, the money wages of labour should fall, whilst every commodity on which the wages of labour were expended rose, the labourer would be doubly affected, and would be soon totally deprived of subsistence. Instead, therefore, of the money wages of labour falling, they would rise; but they would not rise sufficiently to enable the labourer to purchase as many comforts and necessaries as he did before the rise in the price of those commodities. If his annual wages were before £24, or six quarters of corn when the price was £4 per quarter, he would probably receive only the value of five quarters when corn rose to £5 per quarter. But five quarters would cost £25; he would, therefore, receive an addition in his money wages, though with that addition he would be unable to furnish himself with the same quantity of corn and other commodities which he had before consumed in his family.

Notwithstanding, then, that the labourer would be really worse paid, yet this increase in his wages would necessarily diminish the profits of the manufacturer; for his goods would sell at no higher price, and yet the expense of producing them would be increased. This, however, will be considered in our examination into the principles which regulate profits.

It appears, then, that the same cause which raises rent, namely, the increasing difficulty of providing an additional quantity of food with the same proportional quantity of labour, will also raise wages; and therefore, if money be of an unvarying value, both rent and wages will have a tendency to rise with the progress of wealth and population. . . .

These, then, are the laws by which wages are regulated, and by which the happiness of far the greatest part of every community is governed. Like all other contracts, wages should be left to the fair and free competition of the market, and should never be controlled by the interference of the legislature.

The clear and direct tendency of the poor laws is in direct opposition to these obvious principles: it is not, as the legislature benevolently intended, to amend the condition of the poor, but to deteriorate the condition of both poor and rich; instead of making the poor rich, they are calculated to make the rich poor; and whilst the present laws are in force, it is quite in the natural order of things that the fund for the maintenance of the poor should progressively increase till it has absorbed all the net revenue of the country, or at least so much of it as the state shall leave to us, after satisfying its own never-failing demands for the public expenditure.

This pernicious tendency of these laws is no longer a mystery, since it has been fully developed by the able hand of Mr. Malthus; and every friend to the poor must ardently wish for their abolition. Unfortunately, however, they have been so long established, and the habits of the poor have been so formed upon their operation, that to eradicate them with safety from our political system requires the most cautious and skilful management. It is agreed by all who are most friendly to a repeal of these laws that, if it be desirable to prevent the most overwhelming distress to those for whose benefit they were erroneously enacted, their abolition should be effected by the most gradual steps.

It is a truth which admits not a doubt that the comforts and well-being of the poor cannot be permanently secured without some regard on their part, or some effort on the part of the legislature, to regulate the increase of their numbers, and to render less frequent among them early and improvident marriages. The operation of the system of poor laws has been directly contrary to this. They have rendered restraint superfluous, and have invited imprudence, by offering it a portion of the wages of prudence and industry.

The nature of the evil points out the remedy. By gradually contracting the sphere of the poor laws; by impressing on the poor the value of independence, by teaching them that they must look not to systematic or casual charity, but to their own exertions for support, that prudence and forethought are neither unnecessary nor unprofitable virtues, we shall by degrees approach a sounder and more healthful state.

CHAPTER *11*

Scientific Socialism: Karl Marx on Capitalism and Communism

Karl Marx (1818–1883), capitalism's greatest critic and the leading father of scientific socialism, was not just an economist as the term is used today, but a philosopher with a comprehensive teaching about all things—all aspects of man, all of nature, the world as a whole, the cosmos. True, he would deny that he had a teaching about "justice," for he believed that all moral conceptions are tied to particular historical epochs, with morals, politics, art, religion, indeed every cultural dimension, a function of economics. Be that as it may, Marx clearly incorporated ethical or moral matters in his thought when he alleged "exploitation" of workers under capitalism and predicted a "new man" as the final outcome of history.[1]

Marx philosophized at a time when the philosophy of Georg Wilhelm Friedrich Hegel prevailed as perhaps no system of any philosopher had since Aristotle's reign during the Middle Ages. For present purposes, the following passage from Hegel's *Lectures on the Philosophy of History* contains the relevant aspect of Hegel's world view: "The nature of God of being pure spirit is *revealed to man in*

---

[1]See Allen E. Buchanan, *Marx and Justice: The Radical Critique of Liberalism* (Totowa, N.J.: Rowman & Allanheld, 1982); also see Bertell Ollman, *Alienation: Marx's Conception of Man in Capitalist Society* (Cambridge: Cambridge University Press, 1971), pp. 43–51.

the Christian religion. And what is the spirit? He is the One, the infinite consistent within himself, the pure identity."[2]

The Hegel we have identified differs greatly from this century's prevailing interpretation. Propounded by Alexandre Kojeve,[3] the "God is dead" theologians, and others, the common view pictures Hegel as incipient atheist and somehow responsible for Marx and Nietzsche—in spite of the fact that they, primarily because of their adoption of atheism as primary premise, explicitly rejected Hegel! On the other hand, by taking seriously what Hegel actually said as opposed to what he "really meant," we discover a philosopher who "was and wanted to be a Christian philosopher," who "to the end of his life maintained that he considered himself a Lutheran," who "rejected . . . those interpretations of his thought which put them in a pantheistic framework," who "believed in a personal God whose spirit, the Holy Ghost of Christian doctrine, was at work shaping the destiny of man."[4] It was *that* Hegel who affirmed that "the nature of God of being pure spirit is *revealed to man in the Christian religion,*"[5] who warmly responded to the efforts of Karl Friedrich Goschel "to interpret the philosopher's theory of the relation between the form of thought peculiar to the religious consciousness and pure thought or knowledge in such a way as not to imply that religion is inferior to philosophy."[6] Soon after Hegel's death, "Goschel published writings designed to show that Hegelianism was compatible with the doctrines of a personal God and of personal immortality."[7] Certainly, it is difficult to deny that Christianity, *at least as Hegel understood it*—whether "orthodox" or not—constituted the core of his system of ideas.

As is clear from the *Lectures on the Philosophy of History,* Hegel considered God "the Infinite," maintaining that God would not truly be infinite were He not in some sense the totality of reality. Yet Hegel, if he was a pantheist, was a most complex one. He viewed history as the reconciliation of God to a world that had of necessity become alienated from Him—the necessary process by which God achieves self-consciousness: "The history of the world with all the changing scenes which its annals present, is . . . [the] process and development of realization of Spirit."[8]

Hegel also considered history a *rational* process aiming at a goal, a final end, in the form of the "rational state." The "rational state" is the civilization that appears

---

[2]Quoted in C. J. Friedrich, "Introduction to Dover Edition," Georg Wilhelm Friedrich Hegel, *The Philosophy of History,* trans. J. Sibree (New York: Dover Publications, 1956), no page number.

[3]See Alexandre Kojeve, *Introduction to the Reading of Hegel,* ed. Allan Bloom, James H. Nichols, Jr. [trans.] (New York: Basic Books, 1969); also see Alexandre Kojeve, "Tyranny and Wisdom," in Leo Strauss, *On Tyranny,* revised and enlarged (New York: The Free Press of Glencoe, 1963), pp. 143–188.

[4]Friedrich, "Introduction," no page number.

[5]Ibid.

[6]Frederick Copleston, *A History of Philosophy,* Vol. 7, Part 1 (Garden City, N.Y.: Image Books, 1965), p. 292.

[7]Ibid.

[8]Hegel, *The Philosophy of History,* p. 457.

when Christianity has expressed itself fully and is embodied in institutions after the Protestant Reformation, when at last men may know complete self-fulfillment or "self-consciousness."

For Hegel, self-consciousness comes from (1) commitment to the ethical life of the family (spouse and offspring reflecting back one's self); (2)dedicated work in a calling, 'a la Weber's "Protestant ethic" (the product of one's activity reflecting back one's self); (3) citizenship in a rational state through obedience to laws that rational men give themselves (the state and its laws reflecting back one's self); and (4) worship of God in truth and Spirit (the Godhead reflecting back one's self via the reconciliation of man and God through Christ).

The latter source of satisfaction points to an absolute, total fulfillment in a future life—personal immortality and eternal communion with the Godhead; whether Hegel *really* believed in this as Goschel argued is less important than the fact that bourgeois man believed it and lived its logic. Moreover, family, work, and the state are satisfying only because, in Hegel's view, all are divine—no wall separates the sacred and the secular. Hence the importance of the Protestant Reformation to Hegel; Luther had elevated state, family, and work above the mere mundane and sensuous to Spirit and participation in the Divine:

> It is now perceived that Morality and Justice in the State are also divine and commanded by God, and that in point of substance there is nothing higher or more sacred. One inference is that *Marriage* is no longer deemed less holy than *Celibacy*. . . . Moreover the repudiation of work no longer earned the reputation of sanctity; it was acknowledged to be more commendable for men to rise from a state of *activity*, intelligence, and industry, and make themselves independent. It is more consonant with justice that he who has money should spend it even in luxuries, than that he should give it away to idlers and beggars; for he bestows it upon an equal number of persons by so doing, and these must at any rate have worked diligently for it. Industry, crafts and trades now have their moral validity recognized, and the obstacles to their prosperity which originated with the [medieval] Church, have vanished.[9]

After Hegel, philosophers who called themselves Hegelians split over how to interpret the master's statement, "The rational is the real and the real is the rational."

In contrast to the reactionary Right or Old Hegelians who sanctified the status quo, the revolutionary Left or Young Hegelians essentially said, "If it's not rational yet we observe it in the world, then it's not really real." In other words, according to the Left Hegelians, anything that is not "rational" is ripe for abolition and overthrow. The Left Hegelians became, as Marx later described them, "critical critics," rejecting all that could not stand before the bar of reason.

As the Left Hegelians followed out what they considered to be the logic of their position, they became, surprisingly enough, atheists. They began to deny what Hegel had explicitly affirmed repeatedly, namely, the truth of Christianity.

[9]Ibid., pp. 422–423.

Religion, specifically the Christian religion, became the main subject of critical attack. Rather than God and the belief in God constituting man's highest satisfaction, out of Left Hegelianism emerged the idea that the denial of God necessarily preconditions further human fulfillment—the emergence of "true humanity."

Much is given up with belief in God—immortality . . . eternal communion with the Infinite. Gone is the grand prospect of complete and total satisfaction in the next life, of course, if there is no next life. But additionally, satisfaction possible through family, work, and state necessarily seemed dramatically diminished—quite literally, de-divinized.

From the perspective of this history of ideas after Hegel, it appears that once Western man had given serious consideration to immortality, communion with the Infinite, and total satisfaction in a future life, contentment with the comparatively limited rewards conventionally thought possible in this life becomes difficult. Post-Christian, post-Hegelian atheistic thought, therefore, has tended to raise expectations this side of eternity. Once it headed down the road of atheism, German philosophy, perhaps inevitably, elevated natural man—man in *this* life—to the (former) status of God.

After what we may call atheistic Hegelianism, atheistic materialism constituted the next link between Hegel and Marx's anthropological conceptions.

Hegel had been an idealist, believing that ideas, spirit, mind, or reason, all names for the same reality, is the ultimate substance of all things: "Reason is the *substance* of the Universe; viz, that by which and in which all reality has its being and subsistence. . . . It is the *Infinite Energy* of the universe. . . . It is the *infinite complex of things*, their entire Essence and Truth."[10]

Ludwig Feuerbach added materialism to the atheism that developed out of Left Hegelianism. Feuerbach argued that "the secret of theology is anthropology" (*The Essence of Christianity, 1841*).[11] As Feuerbach's position has been described, "everything men have said about God is an expression in mystified terms of their knowledge about themselves."[12] In religion, argued Feuerbach, a person projects his own ideal human characteristics onto an imaginary divine being, and in the process alienates his very human essence from himself. The task of the "critical critic" is to preach the gospel of atheism and convert the masses to a new religion of humanity. And as a materialist, Feuerbach assumed that this life, material nature, is the only reality.

Marx, as an atheist and a materialist, went the next step beyond Feuerbach. We should not simply preach atheism, argued Marx, but instead find the reason that men feel the need to create God. A quotation from Marx's article, "Toward the Critique of Hegel's Philosophy of Law," written in 1844, reveals his basic strategy: "The criticism of religion ends with the doctrine that man is the highest

---

[10]Ibid., p. 9; see also p. 10.

[11] Quoted in Leszek Kolakowski, *Main Currents of Marxism: Vol 1, The Founders,* trans. P. S. Falla (Oxford: Oxford University Press, 1978).

[12]Ibid.

being for man, hence, with a categorical imperative to overthrow all conditions in which man is a degraded, enslaved, abandoned, contemptible being."[13]

Marx's question then is this: What makes a person religious? Why does someone create God through the imaginary projection of his ideal human characteristics onto an imaginary divine being? Marx contended that a person will always do so as long as he is unsatisfied in this life. Alienation through religion occurs only because alienation already exists in this life. Marx's task was to find the cure for religion—how to overcome alienation in this life so that an individual would no longer alienate his human essence to God.[14]

As Marx analyzed it in *The Economic and Philosophic Manuscripts of 1844*, alienation is essentially a split within an identity.[15] He traced the root cause of alienation—deeper than the division of labor as a factor producing alienation[16]—to the split between man as a conscious laboring being and man as an animal with physical, bodily needs. For Marx, man is the animal who engages in conscious laboring or production,[17] but man alienates his very essence, his conscious laboring production, by subordinating it to his existence as an animal. There is a split within the self between essence and existence, with the essentially human enslaved to bodily needs not essentially different from those of beasts.

Marx solved the problem of alienation by imagining a society in which people would no longer work out of necessity. Marx proposed nothing less than this: Alienation will be overcome only when man regards work as an end in itself, apart from the economic product as an object of consumption and apart from satisfying the animal passions. Such is the "new man" that Marx predicted as the goal or end of history—an ideal human type radically different from anything hitherto suggested by any philosopher or economist and from anything yet seen in actuality.

After 1844, Marx the philosopher began to focus on economics as the root area of alienation. An economic analysis then became central to his theory of man and

[13]*The Essential Marx: The Non-Economic Writings*, ed. Saul K. Padover [trans.] (New York: Mentor Books, 1978), p. 287.

[14]On this sort of understanding of Marx's attitude toward religion, see Norman Birnbaum, "Beyond Marx in the Sociology of Religion?" in *Beyond the Classics? Essays in the Scientific Study of Religion*, ed. Charles Y. Glock and Phillip E. Hammond (New York: Harper & Row, 1973), pp. 3–69.

[15]See Karl Marx, *The Economic and Philosophic Manuscripts of 1844*, in Karl Marx, *Early Writings*, ed. T. B. Bottomore [trans.] (New York: McGraw-Hill, 1963), especially pp. 123–131. On aspects of alienation, or more precisely, "estrangement," see Isodore Wallimann, *Estrangement: Marx's Conception of Human Nature and the Division of Labor* (Westport, Conn.: Greenwood Press, 1981), pp. 31–37; also Ollman, *Alienation*, pp. 131–157.

[16]For analysis of division of labor as the cause of alienation, see Wallimann, *Estrangement*, pp. 89–97; and Ollman, *Alienation*, pp. 158–167. For a rejection of division of labor as cause, see Paul Craig Roberts *Alienation and the Soviet Economy: Toward a General Theory of Marxian Alienation, Organizational Principles, and the Soviet Economy* (Albuquerque: University of New Mexico Press, 1971), pp. 109–113.

[17]See Marx, *The Economic and Philosophic Manuscripts of 1844*, p. 127; also Karl Marx, *Capital: A Critique of Political Economy*, trans. Samuel Moore and Edward Aveling (New York: Modern Library, 1906), pp. 197–198.

the cosmos. Marx, from this point on—from about 1844—became an economist. But broad philosophical questions remained at the root of his economics.

Marx the economist turned to an examination of the dominant economic system of his time, which was capitalism. He developed a critique of capitalism that falls into three main parts: dialectical materialism, the theory of surplus value, and predictions for the future.

1. Dialectical Materialism.   Marx argued that in any given historical epoch, there are dominant forces of production—that is, technology—that differ from era to era. Given a certain state of the *forces* of production, certain *relations* of production—basically having to do with property arrangements—come into existence. A match develops between a particular state of the forces of production with a certain form of relations of production.

It became Marx's view that economics is the infrastructure, the determining dimension, of human civilization. Arising above the infrastructure—the forces and relations of production—is a "superstructure," with everything in this superstructure determined by the infrastructure.

What kinds of things are in the superstructure? The family is part of it, the state is part of it, activities such as art and philosophy are part of it, and foremost of all, religion is part of it. Marx claimed to have turned Hegel "on his head." Hegel considered religion the independent variable and believed everything else in a civilization is determined by religion. Marx, on the other hand, contended that economics is primary and everything else, including religion, is a function of prevailing economic arrangements. This emphasis is part and parcel of Marx's "materialism."

Marx, however, believed not in materialism simply but in *dialectical* materialism. *Dialectic* is a term that Marx took over from Hegel's theory of logic. In Hegel's formulation, thinking essentially is the positing of a *thesis* that gives rise to a contrasting or opposing idea, an *antithesis*. The next step is the production of a synthesis, which incorporates whatever truth remains in the thesis and the antithesis. Essentially what Marx did was to say that we can be materialists and yet retain the Hegelian logic.

Marx argued that a dialectical tension produces new syntheses. As there are changes in the forces of production new relations of production will emerge, because the existing ones have become contradictory to and "fetters" upon the new forces of production. And as the forces of production, followed by the relations of production, change, then everything else—the superstructure—will change to become consistent with the new forces and relations of production. Marx contended that in the capitalist economic system prevailing in his time, the forces of production and the relations of production were in dialectical tension. The inevitable result, he thought, would be revolution.

2. Surplus Value.   Marx's theory of surplus value explains why there is going to be a revolution, an overthrow of capitalism, and the replacement of capitalism with a new economic system.

In his theory of value, Marx focused on exchange value. *Use* value refers to the intrinsic value of the object in using it. *Exchange* value refers to what it can be exchanged for in the marketplace. In an exchange, there must be something in common between different things that permits their comparison and exchange. What is the fundamental quality that all products of human labor have in common that permits them to be exchanged? To answer this question, Marx employed the labor theory of value, which he took over from classical economists (including John Locke, Adam Smith, and David Ricardo). The labor theory of value explains how people can compare objects and exchange them. An object is exchanged for another object that is equal in the amount of labor time socially necessary to produce each of them. This common denominator of labor, said Marx, is the basis of exchange.

According to Marx, in a capitalist economy human labor itself is exchanged as a commodity. The workers, whom Marx called collectively the "proletariat," own no property and must sell their labor power to the capitalists who own the means of production. When a worker freely contracts with a capitalist to work for him, he sells his labor *power*. The capitalist pays the prevailing standard of exchange value for all commodities in the capitalist economy. What he pays is an amount of money equivalent to the amount of labor to produce the goods required to sustain the life of the worker and his family.

Here lies the great economic injustice of capitalism, the source of what Marx contends is its fundamental exploitation of the proletariat. The worker sells his labor power for the amount of time each day that the capitalist, who enjoys the advantage, can wrestle away from the laborer. But suppose the laborer after six hours work puts out as much labor as needed to produce the goods to sustain his life and those of his family. The contract between the worker and the capitalist, however, is for a full workday, not for six hours only. The amount of production created the worker has worked enough time to equal the labor power needed to sustain him and his family is *surplus value*. That surplus value is the source of profit—another name, according to Marx, for exploitation.

3. Marx's Predictions.   Marx's predictions about the future of capitalism were all based upon the foregoing concepts. Marx predicted increasing monopoly, with more and more wealth falling into fewer and fewer hands. And as that wealth fell into fewer and fewer hands, more and more people would be cast down into the growing proletariat. Marx predicted that this growing proletariat would increase in misery. The workers would not necessarily—and would not in fact—suffer a reduction in wages, for under the capitalist rule of exchange they would always be paid the amount of money equal to the labor time necessary to reproduce that life, that is, the labor needed to produce the goals to sustain the workers and their families. But the work itself would become increasingly miserable as each person became merely more and more an appendage of a machine; every advance in mechanization would result in the further dehumanizing effect of work. And the mechanization would result in the further dehumanizing effect of work. And the mechanization, predicted Marx, would throw more and more of the proletariat into the ranks of the unemployed.

In addition to increasing misery and increasing unemployment for the proletariat, Marx predicted worse and worse crises of production, or rather, of nonproduction—economic depressions. Things would finally reach the point, predicted Marx, that the proletariat would rise up, throw off capitalism, and set up a new order of things—socialism, which is the public ownership of the means of production.

History failed to verify Marx's predictions about capitalism. With so many falsified predictions, why would anyone remain a "Marxist"? Perhaps the answer lies in Marx's first premises, particularly his atheism, and certain consequences that follow.

In rejecting belief in God, Marx had to rule out ultimate satisfactions enjoyable only in a future life. He expected the withering away of the state and perhaps transcendence of the traditional family. Marx thus put all his eggs in one basket. For Hegel's bourgeois man, work had been but one source of satisfaction. For Marx's socialist man, work becomes the sole source of satisfaction.

Marx believed that, with the overthrow of a capitalistic economy through a proletarian revolution and the establishment of public ownership of the means of production, the productive forces allegedly "fettered" under capitalism would be released. Marx predicted that these new forces of production, once unleashed, would lead to the transformation of the division of labor—the main obstacle to work becoming an end in itself. As Marx wrote in *Capital*:

> Modern Industry . . . through its catastrophes imposes the necessity of recognizing, as a fundamental law of production, variation of work, consequently fitness of the labourer for varied work, consequently the greatest possible development of his varied aptitudes. It becomes a question of life and death for society to adapt the mode of production to the normal functioning of this law. Modern industry, indeed, compels society, under penalty of death, to replace the detail-worker of today, crippled by lifelong repetition of one and the same trivial operation, and thus reduced to a mere fragment of a man, by the fully developed individual, fit for a variety of labors, ready to face any change of production, and to whom the different social functions he performs are but so many modes of giving free scope to his own natural and acquired powers.[18]

Thus, in his most mature writings, Marx echoed the utopian tone of the famous passage from *The German Ideology*, written in the mid-1840s:

> As soon as labour is distributed, each man has a particular, exclusive sphere of activity, which is forced upon him and from which he cannot escape. He is a hunter, a fisherman, a shepherd, or a critical critic, and must remain so if he does not want to lose his means of livelihood; while in communist society, where nobody has one exclusive sphere of activity but each can become accom-

---

[18]Marx, *Capital*, p. 445.

plished in any branch he wishes, society regulates the general production and thus makes it possible for me to do one thing to-day and another to-morrow, to hunt in the morning, fish in the afternoon, criticize after dinner, just as I have a mind, without ever becoming hunter, fisherman, shepherd or critic.[19]

Marx expected that in the new order of things, with the productive forces unleashed and the division of labor transformed, people will find work so satisfying that they will pursue it as an end in itself. Society can make transition to the production-distribution principle, "From each according to his ability, to each according to his needs." All sources of social disharmony will cease, and people can enjoy a complete total fulfillment unlike anything ever expected hitherto in this life.

It has been argued that merely a voluntary division of labor rather than the absolute end of division of labor was all that Marx expected.[20] However, it would seem that *anything* standing in the way of people doing *whatever* they had a mind to do would have to disappear in the Marxist millennium. If a person wanted to write poetry but utterly lacked poetic ability, would not this be a source of discontent? Note that in *The German Ideology* Marx predicted a time when "each can become *accomplished* in any branch [of work] he wishes." That prediction implies a condition of absolute and universal equality of ability—certainly far more than mere equality of opportunity, as difficult as that may be to achieve absolutely in practice. Genetic engineering would seem to be required for Marx's agenda for the future. And what of the physical distinctions between the sexes? That is surely a form of the division of labor,[21] and one that seems to stand in the way of any person doing whatever he or she wants. Men cannot have babies, and the best woman cannot beat the best man in tennis. Again, genetic engineering looms on the horizon.

All this, like Marx's prediction of the demise of capitalism, remains a Marxist prediction that history, has not yet seen fit to fulfill. But only by coming to grips with the ideal human types of socialism and capitalism can one begin to understand the contemporary appeal of "socialist man" and the failure of capitalism's contemporary defenders to contest radical socialism for the moral high ground. At the deepest level, the quarrel between socialism and capitalism is a disagreement over what kind of human being is desirable, for with each goes an ideal human type—a "state of soul," as Plato would have said.

In a post-Christian atheistic society, it is probably inevitable that something like Marx's secular apocalyptic vision will enchant many. In one of the great ironies of the history of ideas, it was Marx the materialist who drew a model of man far more "ideal" than what Hegel the philosophical idealist described.

---

[19]Karl Marx and Friedrich Engels, *The German Ideology*, ed. R. Pascal (New York: International Publishers, 1947), p. 22.

[20]Wallimann, *Estrangement*, pp. 99–123.

[21]See Ollman, *Alienation*, p. 160.

Manifesto of the Communist Party

Karl Marx and Friedrich Engels

BOURGEOIS AND PROLETARIANS

The history of all hitherto-existing society is the history of class struggles.

Freeman and slave, patrician and plebeian, lord and serf, guild-master and journeyman, in a word, oppressor and oppressed, stood in constant opposition to one another, carried on an uninterrupted, now hidden, now open fight, a fight that each time ended, either in a revolutionary re-constitution of society at large, or in the common ruin of the contending classes.

In the earlier epochs of history, we find almost everywhere a complicated arrangement of society into various orders, a manifold gradation of social rank. In ancient Rome we have patricians, knights, plebeians, slaves; in the Middle Ages, feudal lords, vassals, guild-masters, journeymen, apprentices, serfs; in almost all of these classes, again, subordinate gradations.

The modern bourgeois society that has sprouted from the ruins of feudal society has not done away with class antagonisms. It has but established new classes, new conditions of oppression, new forms of struggle in place of the old ones.

Our epoch, the epoch of the bourgeoisie, possesses, however, this distinctive feature: it has simplified the class antagonisms. Society as a whole is more and more splitting up into two great hostile camps, into two great classes directly facing each other: Bourgeoisie and Proletariat.

From the serfs of the Middle Ages sprang the chartered burghers of the earliest towns. From these burgesses the first elements of the bourgeoisie were developed.

The discovery of America, the rounding of the Cape, opened up fresh ground for the rising bourgeoisie. The East-Indian and Chinese markets, the colonization of America, trade with the colonies, the increase in the means of exchange and in commodities generally, gave to commerce, to navigation, to industry, an impulse never before known, and thereby, to the revolutionary element in the tottering feudal society, a rapid development.

The feudal system of industry, under which industrial production was monopolised by closed guilds, now no longer sufficed for the growing wants of the new markets. The manufacturing system took its place. The guild-masters were pushed on one side by the manufacturing middle class; division of labour between the different corporate guilds vanished in the face of division of labour in each single workshop.

1848, English edition of 1888, edited by Engels

Meantime the markets kept ever growing, the demand ever rising. Even manufacture no longer sufficed. Thereupon, steam and machinery revolutionized industrial production. The place of manufacture was taken by the giant, Modern Industry, the place of the industrial middle class, by industrial millionaires, the leaders of whole industrial armies, the modern bourgeois.

Modern industry has established the world-market, for which the discovery of America paved the way. This market has given an immense development to commerce, to navigation, to communication by land. This development has, in its turn, reacted on the extension of industry; and in proportion as industry, commerce, navigation, railways extended, in the same proportion the bourgeoisie developed, increased its capital, and pushed into the background every class handed down from the Middle-Ages.

We see, therefore, how the modern bourgeoisie is itself the product of a long course of development, of a series of revolutions in the modes of production and of exchange.

Each step in the development of the bourgeoisie was accompanied by a corresponding political advance of that class. An oppressed class under the sway of the feudal nobility, an armed and self-governing association in the mediaeval commune; here independent urban republic (as in Italy and Germany), there taxable "third estate" of the monarchy (as in France), afterwards, in the period of manufacture proper, serving either the semi-feudal or the absolute monarchy as a counterpoise against the nobility, and, in fact, corner stone of the great monarchies in general, the bourgeoisie has at last, since the establishment of Modern Industry and of the world market, conquered for itself, in the modern representative State, exclusive political sway. The executive of the modern State is but a committee for managing the common affairs of the whole bourgeoisie.

The bourgeoisie, historically, has played a most revolutionary part.

The bourgeoisie, wherever it has got the upper hand, has put an end to all feudal, patriarchal, idyllic relations. It has pitilessly torn asunder the motley feudal ties that bound man to his "natural superiors," and has left remaining no other nexus between man and man than naked self-interest, than callous "cash payment." It has drowned the most heavenly ecstasies of religious fervour, of chivalrous enthusiasm, of philistine sentimentalism, in the icy water of egotistical calculation. It has resolved personal worth into exchange value, and in place of the numberless indefeasible chartered freedoms, has set up that single, unconscionable freedom—Free Trade. In one word, for exploitation, veiled by religious and political illusions, it has substituted naked, shameless, direct, brutal exploitation.

The bourgeoisie has stripped of its halo every occupation hitherto honoured and looked up to with reverent awe. It has converted the physician, the lawyer, the priest, the poet, the man of science, into its paid wage-labourers.

The bourgeoisie has torn away from the family its sentimental veil, and has reduced the family relation to a mere money relation.

The bourgeoisie has disclosed how it came to pass that the brutal display of vigour in the Middle Ages, which Reactionists so much admire, found its fitting complement in the most slothful indolence. It has been the first to shew what man's activity can bring about. It has accomplished wonders far surpassing Egyptian pyramids, Roman aqueducts, and Gothic cathedrals; it has conducted expeditions that put in the shade all former Exoduses of nations and crusades.

The bourgeoisie cannot exist without constantly revolutionising the instruments of production, and thereby the relations of production, and with them the whole relations of society. Conservation of the old modes of production in unaltered form, was, on the contrary, the first condition of existence for all earlier industrial classes. Constant revolutionising of production, uninterrupted disturbance of all social conditions, everlasting uncertainty and agitation distinguish the bourgeois epoch from all earlier ones. All fixed, fast-frozen relations, with their train of ancient and venerable prejudices and opinions, are swept away, all new-formed ones become antiquated before they can ossify. All that is solid melts into air, all that is holy is profaned, and man is at last compelled to face with sober senses, his real conditions of life, and his relations with his kind.

The need of a constantly expanding market for its products chases the bourgeoisie over the whole surface of the globe. It must nestle everywhere, settle everywhere, establish connexions everywhere.

The bourgeoisie has through its exploitation of the world-market given a cosmopolitan character to production and consumption in every country. To the great chagrin of Reactionists, it has drawn from under the feet of industry the national ground on which it stood. All old-established national industries have been destroyed or are daily being destroyed. They are dislodged by new industries, whose introduction becomes a life and death question for all civilised nations, by industries that no longer work up indigenous raw material, but raw material drawn from the remotest zones; industries whose products are consumed, not only at home, but in every quarter of the globe. In place of the old wants, satisfied by the productions of the country, we find new wants, requiring for their satisfaction the products of distant lands and climes. In place of the old local and national seclusion and self-sufficiency, we have intercourse in every direction, universal interdependence of nations. And as in material, so also in intellectual production. The intellectual creations of individual nations become common property. National one-sidedness and narrow-mindedness become more and more impossible, and from the numerous national and local literatures, there arises a world-literature.

The bourgeoisie, by the rapid improvement of all instruments of production, by the immensely facilitated means of communication, draws all, even the most barbarian, nations into civilisation. The cheap prices of its commodities are the heavy artillery with which it batters down all Chinese walls, with which it forces the barbarians' intensely obstinate hatred of foreigners to capitulate. It compels all nations, on pain of extinction, to adopt the bourgeois mode of production; it compels them to introduce what it calls civilisation into their midst, i.e., to become bourgeois themselves. In one word, it creates a world after its own image.

The bourgeoisie has subjected the country to the rule of the towns. It has created enormous cities, has greatly increased the urban population as compared with the rural, and has thus rescued a considerable part of the population from the idiocy of rural life. Just as it has made the country dependent on the towns, so it has made barbarian and semi-barbarian countries dependent on the civilised ones, nations of peasants on nations of bourgeois, the East on the West.

The bourgeoisie keeps more and more doing away with the scattered state of the population, of the means of production, and of property. It has agglomerated population, centralised means of production, and has concentrated property in a few hands. The necessary consequence of this was political centralisation. Independent, or but loosely connected provinces, with separate interests, laws, governments and systems of taxation, became lumped together into one nation, with one government, one code of laws, one national class-interest, one frontier and one customs-tariff.

The bourgeoisie, during its rule of scarce one hundred years, has created more massive and more colossal productive forces than have all preceding generations together. Subjection of Nature's forces to man, machinery, application of chemistry to industry and agriculture, steam-navigation, railways, electric telegraphs, clearing of whole continents for cultivation, canalisation of rivers, whole populations conjured out of the ground—what earlier century had even a presentiment that such productive forces slumbered in the lap of social labour?

We see then: the means of production and of exchange, on whose foundation the bourgeoisie built itself up, were generated in feudal society. At a certain stage in the development of these means of production and of exchange, the conditions under which feudal society produced and exchanged, the feudal organisation of agriculture and manufacturing industry, in one word, the feudal relations of property became no longer compatible with the already developed productive forces; they became so many fetters. They had to be burst asunder; they were burst asunder.

Into their place stepped free competition, accompanied by a social and political constitution adapted to it, and by the economical and political sway of the bourgeois class.

A similar movement is going on before our own eyes. Modern bourgeois society with its relations of production, of exchange and of property, a society that has conjured up such gigantic means of production and of exchange, is like the sorcerer, who is no longer able to control the powers of the nether world whom he has called up by his spells. For many a decade past the history of industry and commerce is but the history of the revolt of modern productive forces against modern conditions of production, against the property relations that are the conditions of production, against the property relations that are the conditions for the existence of the bourgeoisie and of its rule. It is enough to mention the commercial crises that by their periodical return put on its trial, each time more threateningly, the existence of the entire bourgeois society. In these crises a great part not only of the existing products, but also of the previously created productive forces, are periodically destroyed. In these crises there breaks out an epidemic that, in all earlier epochs, would have seemed an absurdity—the epidemic of over-production. Society suddenly finds itself put back into a state of momentary barbarism; it appears as if a famine, a universal war of devastation had cut off the supply of every means of subsistence; industry and commerce seem to be destroyed; and why? Because there is too much civilisation, too much means of subsistence, too much industry, too much commerce. The productive forces at the disposal of society no longer tend to further the development of the conditions of bourgeois property; on the contrary, they have become too powerful for these conditions, by which they are fettered, and so soon as they overcome these fetters, they bring disorder into the whole of bourgeois society, endanger the existence of bourgeois property. The conditions of bourgeois society are too narrow to comprise the wealth created by them. And how does the bourgeoisie get over these crises? On the one hand by enforced destruction of a mass of productive forces; on the other, by the conquest of new markets, and by the more thorough exploitation of the old ones. That is to say, by paving the way for more extensive and more destructive crises, and by diminishing the means whereby crises are prevented.

The weapons with which the bourgeoisie felled feudalism to the ground are now turned against the bourgeoisie itself.

But not only has the bourgeoisie forged the weapons that bring death to itself; it has also called into existence the men who are to wield those weapons—the modern working class—the proletarians.

In proportion as the bourgeoisie, *i.e.*, capital, is developed, in the same proportion is the proletariat, the modern working class, developed—a class of labourers, who live only so long as they find work, and who find work only so long as their labour increases capital. These labourers, who must sell themselves piecemeal, are a commodity, like every other article of commerce, and are consequently exposed to all the vicissitudes of competition, to all the fluctuations of the market.

Owing to the extensive use of machinery and to division of labour, the work of the proletarians has lost all individual character, and, consequently, all charm for the workman. He becomes an appendage of the machine, and it is only the most simple, most monotonous, and most easily acquired knack, that is required of him. Hence, the cost of production of a workman is restricted, almost entirely, to the means of subsistence that he requires for his maintenance, and for the propagation of his race. But the price of a commodity, and therefore also of labour is equal to its cost of production. In proportion, therefore, as the repulsiveness of the work increases, the wage decreases. Nay more, in proportion as the use of machinery and division of labour increases, in the same proportion the burden of toil also increases, whether by prolongation of the working hours, by increase of the work exacted in a given time or by increased speed of the machinery, etc.

Modern industry has converted the little workshop of the patriarchal master into the great factory of the industrial capitalist. Masses of labourers, crowded into the factory, are organised like soldiers. As privates of the industrial army they are placed under the command of a perfect hierarchy of officers and sergeants. Not only are they slaves of the bourgeois class, and of the bourgeois State; they are daily and hourly enslaved by the machine, by the over-looker, and, above all, by the individual bourgeois manufacturer himself. The more openly this despotism proclaims gain to be its end and aim, the more petty, the more hateful and the more embittering it is.

The less the skill and exertion of strength implied in manual labour, in other words, the more modern industry becomes developed, the more is the labour of men superseded by that of women. Differences of age and sex have no longer any distinctive social validity for the working class. All are instruments of labour, more or less expensive to use, according to their age and sex.

No sooner is the exploitation of the labourer by the manufacturer, so far, at an end, that he receives his wages in cash, than he is set upon by the other portions of the bourgeoisie, the landlord, the shopkeeper, the pawnbroker, etc.

The lower strata of the middle class—the small tradespeople, shopkeepers, and retired tradesmen generally, the handicraftsmen and peasants—all these sink gradually into the proletariat, partly because their diminutive capital does not suffice for the scale on which Modern Industry is carried on, and is swamped in the competition with the large capitalists, partly because their specialised skill is rendered worthless by new methods of production. Thus the proletariat is recruited from all classes of the population.

The proletariat goes through various stages of development. With its birth begins its struggle with the bourgeoisie. At first the contest is carried on by individual labourers, then by the work-people of a factory, then by the operatives of one trade, in one locality, against the individual bourgeois who directly exploits them. They direct their attacks not against the bourgeois conditions of production, but against the instruments of production themselves; they destroy imported wares that compete with their labour, they smash to pieces machinery, they set factories ablaze, they seek to restore by force the vanished status of the workman of the Middle Ages.

At this stage the labourers still form an incoherent mass scattered over the whole country, and broken up by their mutual competition. If anywhere they unite to form more compact bodies, this is not yet the consequence of their own active union, but of the union of the bourgeoisie, which class, in order to attain its own political ends, is compelled to set the whole proletariat in motion, and is moreover yet, for a time, able to do so. At this stage, therefore, the proletarians do not fight their enemies, but the enemies of their enemies, the remnants of absolute monarchy, the landowners, the non-industrial bourgeois, the petty bourgeoisie. Thus the whole historical movement is concentrated in the hands of the bourgeoisie; every victory so obtained is a victory for the bourgeoisie.

But with the development of industry the proletariat not only increases in number; it becomes concentrated in greater masses, its strength grows, and it feels that strength more. The various interests and conditions of life within the ranks of the proletariat are more and more equalised, in proportion as machinery obliterates all distinctions of labour, and nearly everywhere reduces wages to the same low level. The growing competition among the bourgeois, and the resulting commercial crises, make the wages of the workers ever more fluctuating. The unceasing improvement of machinery, ever more rapidly developing, makes their livelihood more and more precarious; the collisions between individual workmen and individual bourgeois take more and more the character of collisions between two classes. Thereupon the workers begin to form combinations (Trades' Unions) against the bourgeois; they club together in order to keep up the rate of wages; they found permanent associations in order to make provision beforehand for these occasional revolts. Here and there the contest breaks out into riots.

Now and then the workers are victorious, but only for a time. The real fruit of their battles lies, not in the immediate result, but in the ever-expanding union of the workers. This union is helped on by the improved means of communication that are created by modern industry and that place the workers of different localities in contact with one another. It was just this contact that was needed to centralise the numerous local struggles, all of the same character, into one national struggle between classes. But every class struggle is a political struggle. And that union, to attain which the burghers of the Middle Ages, with their miserable highways, required centuries, the modern proletarians, thanks to railways, achieve in a few years.

This organisation of the proletarians into a class, and consequently into a political party, is continually being upset again by the competition between the workers themselves. But it ever rises up again, stronger, firmer, mightier. It compels legislative recognition of particular interests of the workers, by taking advantage of the divisions among the bourgeoisie itself. Thus the ten-hours' bill in England was carried.

Altogether collisions between the classes of the old society further, in many ways, the course of development of the proletariat. The bourgeoisie finds itself involved in a constant battle. At first with the aristocracy; later on, with those portions of the bourgeoisie itself, whose interests have become antagonistic to the progress of industry; at all times, with the bourgeoisie of foreign countries. In all these battles it sees itself compelled to appeal to the proletariat, to ask for its help, and thus, to drag it into the political arena. The bourgeoisie itself, therefore, supplies the proletariat with its own elements of political and general education, in other words, it furnishes the proletariat with weapons for fighting the bourgeoisie.

Further, as we have already seen, entire sections of the ruling classes are, by the advance of industry, precipitated into the proletariat, or are at least threatened in their conditions of existence. These also supply the proletariat with fresh elements of enlightenment and progress.

Finally, in times when the class-struggle nears the decisive hour, the process of dissolution going on within the ruling-class, in fact within the whole range of old society, assumes such a violent, glaring character, that a small section of the ruling class cuts itself adrift, and joins the revolutionary class, the class that holds the future in its hands. Just as, therefore, at an earlier period, a section of the nobility went over to the bourgeoisie, so now a portion of the bourgeoisie goes over to the proletariat, and in particular, a portion of the bourgeois ideologists, who have raised themselves to the level of comprehending theoretically the historical movement as a whole.

Of all the classes that stand face to face with the bourgeoisie today, the proletariat alone is a really revolutionary class. The other classes decay and finally disappear in the face of modern industry; the proletariat is its special and essential product.

The lower middle class, the small manufacturer, the shopkeeper, the artisan, the peasant, all these fight against the bourgeoisie, to save from extinction their existence as fractions of the middle class. They are therefore not revolutionary, but conservative. Nay more, they are reactionary, for they try to roll back the wheel of history. If by chance they are revolutionary, they are so only in view of their impending transfer into the proletariat, they thus defend not their present, but their future interests, they desert their own standpoint to place themselves at that of the proletariat.

The "dangerous class," the social scum, that passively rotting mass thrown off by the lowest layers of old society, may, here and there, be swept into the movement by a proletarian revolution; its conditions of life, however, prepare it far more for the part of a bribed tool of reactionary intrigue.

In the conditions of the proletariat, those of old society at large are already virtually swamped. The proletarian is without property; his relation to his wife and children has no longer anything in common with the bourgeois family-relations; modern industrial labour, modern subjection to capital, the same in England as in France, in America as in Germany, has stripped him of every trace of national character. Law, morality, religion, are to him so many bourgeois prejudices, behind which lurk in ambush just as many bourgeois interests.

All the preceding classes that got the upper hand, sought to fortify their already acquired status by subjecting society at large to their conditions of appropriation. The proletarians cannot become masters of the productive forces of society, except by abolishing their own previous mode of appropriation, and thereby also every other previous mode of appropriation. They have nothing of their own to secure and to fortify; their mission is to destroy all previous securities for, and insurances of, individual property.

All previous historical movements were movements of minorities, or in the interest of minorities. The proletarian movement is the self-conscious, independent movement of the immense majority, in the interest of the immense majority. The proletariat, the lowest stratum of our present society, cannot stir, cannot raise itself up, without the whole superincumbent strata of official society being sprung into the air.

Though not in substance, yet in form, the struggle of the proletariat with the bourgeoisie is at first a national struggle. The proletariat of each country must, of course, first of all settle matters with its own bourgeoisie.

In depicting the most general phases of the development of the proletariat, we traced the more or less veiled civil war, raging within existing society, up to the point where that war breaks out into open revolution, and where the violent overthrow of the bourgeoisie, lays the foundation for the sway of the proletariat.

Hitherto, every form of society has been based, as we have already seen, on the antagonism of oppressing and oppressed classes. But in order to oppress a class, certain conditions must be assured to it under which it can, at least, continue its slavish existence. The serf, in the period of serfdom, raised himself to membership in the commune, just as the petty bourgeois, under the yoke of feudal absolutism, managed to develop into a bourgeois. The modern labourer, on the contrary, instead of rising with the progress of industry, sinks deeper and deeper below the conditions of existence of his own class. He becomes a pauper, and pauperism develops more rapidly than population and wealth. And here it becomes evident, that the bourgeoisie is unfit any longer to be the ruling class in society, and to impose its conditions of existence upon society as an over-riding law. It is unfit to rule because it is incompetent to assure an existence to its slave within his slavery, because it cannot help letting him sink into such a state, that it has to feed him, instead of being fed by him. Society can no longer live under this bourgeoisie, in other words, its existence is no longer compatible with society.

The essential condition for the existence, and for the sway of the bourgeois class, is the formation and augmentation of capital; the condition for capital is wage-labour. Wage-labour rests exclusively on competition between the labourers. The advance of industry, whose involuntary promoter is the bourgeoisie, replaces the isolation of the labourers, due to competition, by their revolutionary combination, due to association. The development of Modern Industry, therefore, cuts from under its feet the very foundation on which the bourgeoisie produces and appropriates products. What the bourgeoisie, therefore, produces, above all, are its own grave-diggers. Its fall and the victory of the proletariat are equally inevitable.

PROLETARIANS AND COMMUNISTS

In what relation do the Communists stand to the proletarians as a whole?

The Communists do not form a separate party opposed to other working-class parties.

They have no interests separate and apart from those of the proletariat as a whole.

They do not set up any sectarian principles of their own, by which to shape and mould the proletarian movement.

The Communists are distinguished from the other working-class parties by this only: 1. In the national struggles of the proletarians of the different countries, they point out and bring to the front the common interests of the entire-proletariat, independently of all nationality. 2. In the various stages of development which the struggle of the working class against the bourgeoisie has to pass through, they always and everywhere represent the interests of the movement as a whole.

The Communists, therefore, are on the one hand, practically, the most advanced and resolute section of the working-class parties of every country, that section which pushes forward all others; on the other hand, theoretically, they have over the great mass of the proletariat the advantage of clearly understanding the line of march, the conditions, and the ultimate general results of the proletarian movement.

The immediate aim of the Communists is the same as that of all the other proletarian parties: formation of the proletariat into a class, overthrow of the bourgeois supremacy, conquest of political power by the proletariat.

The theoretical conclusions of the Communists are in no way based on ideas or principles that have been invented, or discovered, by this or that would-be universal reformer.

They merely express, in general terms, actual relations springing from an existing class struggle, from a historical movement going on under our very eyes. The abolition of existing property-relations is not at all a distinctive feature of Communism.

All property-relations in the past have continually been subject to historical change consequent upon the change in historical conditions.

The French Revolution, for example, abolished feudal property in favour of bourgeois property.

The distinguishing feature of Communism is not the abolition of property generally, but the abolition of bourgeois property. But modern bourgeois private property is the final and most complete expression of the system of producing and appropriating products, that is based on class antagonisms, on the exploitation of the many by the few.

In this sense, the theory of the Communists may be summed up in the single sentence: Abolition of private property.

We Communists have been reproached with the desire of abolishing the right of personally acquiring property as the fruit of a man's own labour, which property is alleged to be the ground work of all personal freedom, activity and independence.

Hard-won, self-acquired, self-earned property! Do you mean the property of the petty artizan and of the small peasant, a form of property that preceded the bourgeois form? There is no need to abolish that; the development of industry has to a great extent already destroyed it, and is still destroying it daily.

Or do you mean modern bourgeois private property?

But does wage-labour create any property for the labourer? Not a bit. It creates capital, *i.e.*, that kind of property which exploits wage-labour, and which cannot increase except upon condition of begetting a new supply of wage-labour for fresh exploitation. Property, in its present form, is based on the antagonism of capital and wage-labour. Let us examine both sides of this antagonism.

To be a capitalist, is to have not only a purely personal, but a social *status* in production. Capital is a collective product, and only by the united action of many members, nay, in the last resort, only by the united action of all members of society, can it be set in motion.

Capital is, therefore, not a personal, it is a social power.

When, therefore, capital is converted into common property, into the property of all members of society, personal property is not thereby transformed into social property. It is only the social character of the property that is changed. It loses its class-character.

Let us now take wage-labour.

The average price of wage-labour is the minimum wage, *i.e.*, that quantum of the means of subsistence, which is absolutely requisite to keep the labourer in bare existence as a labourer. What, therefore, the wage-labourer appropriates by means of his labour, merely suffices to prolong and reproduce a bare existence. We by no means intend to abolish this personal appropriation of the products of labour, an appropriation that is made for the maintenance and reproduction of human life, and that leaves no surplus wherewith to command the labour of others. All that we want to do away with, is the miserable character of this appropriation, under which the labourer lives merely to increase capital, and is allowed to live only in so far as the interest of the ruling class requires it.

In bourgeois society, living labour is but a means to increase accumulated labour. In Communist society, accumulated labour is but a means to widen, to enrich, to promote the existence of the labourer.

In bourgeois society, therefore, the past dominates the present; in Communist society, the present dominates the past. In bourgeois society capital is independent and has individuality, while the living person is dependent and has no individuality.

And the abolition of this state of things is called by the bourgeois, abolition of individuality and freedom! And rightly so. The abolition of bourgeois individuality, bourgeois independence, and bourgeois freedom is undoubtedly aimed at.

By freedom is meant, under the present bourgeois conditions of production, free trade, free selling and buying.

But if selling and buying disappears, free selling and buying disappears also. This talk about free selling and buying, and all the other "brave words" of our bourgeoisie about freedom in general, have a meaning, if any, only in contrast with restricted selling and buying, with the fettered traders of the Middle Ages, but have no meaning when opposed to the Communistic abolition of buying and selling, of the bourgeois conditions of production, and of the bourgeoisie itself.

You are horrified at our intending to do away with private property. But in your existing society, private property is already done away with for nine-tenths of the population; its existence for the few is solely due to its non-existence in the hands of those nine-tenths. You reproach us, therefore, with intending to do away with a form of property, the necessary condition for whose existence is, the non-existence of any property for the immense majority of society.

In one word, you reproach us with intending to do away with your property. Precisely so; that is just what we intend.

From the moment when labour can no longer be converted into capital, money, or rent, into a social power capable of being monopolised, *i.e.*, from the moment when individual property can no longer be transformed into bourgeois property, into capital, from that moment, you say, individuality vanishes.

You must, therefore, confess that by "individual" you mean no other person than the bourgeois, than the middle-class owner of property. This person must, indeed, be swept out of the way, and made impossible.

Communism deprives no man of the power to appropriate the products of society; all that it does is to deprive him of the power to subjugate the labour of others by means of such appropriation.

It has been objected that upon the abolition of private property all work will cease, and universal laziness will overtake us.

According to this, bourgeois society ought long ago to have gone to the dogs through sheer idleness; for those of its members who work, acquire nothing, and those who acquire anything, do not work. The whole of this objection is but another expression of the tautology: that there can no longer be any wage-labour when there is no longer any capital.

All objections urged against the Communistic mode of producing and appropriating material products, have, in the same way, been urged against the Communistic modes of producing and appropriating intellectual products. Just as, to the bourgeois, the disappearance of class property is the disappearance of production itself, so the disappearance of class culture is to him identical with the disappearance of all culture.

That culture, the loss of which he laments, is, for the enormous majority, a mere training to act as a machine.

But don't wrangle with us so long as you apply, to our intended abolition of bourgeois property, the standard of your bourgeois notions of freedom, culture, law, &c. Your very ideas are but the outgrowth of the conditions of your bourgeois production and bourgeois property, just as your jurisprudence is but the will of your class made into a law for all, a will, whose essential character and direction are determined by the economical conditions of existence of your class.

The selfish misconception that induces you to transform into eternal laws of nature and of reason, the social forms springing from your present mode of production and form of property—historical relations that rise and disappear in the progress of production—this misconception you share with every ruling class that has preceded you. What you see clearly in the case of ancient property, what you admit in the case of feudal property, you are of course forbidden to admit in the case of your own bourgeois form of property.

Abolition of the family! Even the most radical flare up at this infamous proposal of the Communists.

On what foundation is the present family, the bourgeois family, based? On capital, on private gain. In its completely developed form this family exists only among the bourgeoisie. But this state of things finds its complement in the practical absence of the family among the proletarians, and in public prostitution.

The bourgeois family will vanish as a matter of course when its complement vanishes, and both will vanish with the vanishing of capital.

Do you charge us with wanting to stop the exploitation of children by their parents? To this crime we plead guilty.

But, you will say, we destroy the most hallowed of relations, when we replace home education by social.

And your education! Is not that also social, and determined by the social conditions under which you educate, by the intervention, direct or indirect, of society, by means of schools, &c.? The Communists have not invented the intervention of society in education; they do but seek to alter the character of that intervention, and to rescue education from the influence of the ruling class.

The bourgeois clap-trap about the family and education, about the hallowed co-relation of parent and child, becomes all the more disgusting, the more, by the action of Modern Industry, all family ties among the proletarians are torn asunder, and their children transformed into simple articles of commerce and instruments of labour.

But you Communists would introduce community of women, screams the whole bourgeoisie in chorus.

The bourgeois sees in his wife a mere instrument of production. He hears that the instruments of production are to be exploited in common, and, naturally, can come to no other conclusion than that the lot of being common to all will likewise fall to the women.

He has not even a suspicion that the real point aimed at is to do away with the status of women as mere instruments of production.

For the rest, nothing is more ridiculous than the virtuous indignation of our bourgeois at the community of women which, they pretend, is to be openly and officially established by the Communists. The Communists have no need to introduce community of women; it has existed almost from time immemorial.

Our bourgeois, not content with having the wives and daughters of their proletarians at their disposal, not to speak of common prostitutes, take the greatest pleasure in seducing each others' wives.

Bourgeois marriage is in reality a system of wives in common and thus, at the most, what the Communists might possibly be reproached with, is that they desire to introduce, in substitution for a hypocritically concealed, an openly legalised community of women. For the rest, it is self-evident that the abolition of the present system of production must bring with it the abolition of the community of women springing from that system, *i.e.*, of prostitution both public and private.

The Communists are further reproached with desiring to abolish countries and nationality.

The working men have no country. We cannot take from them what they have not got. Since the proletariat must first of all acquire political supremacy, must rise to be the leading class of the nation, must constitute itself *the* nation, it is, so far, itself national, though not in the bourgeois sense of the word.

National differences, and antagonisms between peoples are daily more and more vanishing, owing to the development of the bourgeoisie, to freedom of commerce, to the world-market, to uniformity in the mode of production and in the conditions of life corresponding thereto.

The supremacy of the proletariat will cause them to vanish still faster. United action, of the leading civilised countries at least, is one of the first conditions for the emancipation of the proletariat.

In proportion as the exploitation of one individual by another is put an end to, the exploitation of one nation by another will also be put an end to. In proportion as the antagonism between classes within the nation vanishes, the hostility of one nation to another will come to an end.

The charges against Communism made from a religious, a philosophical, and, generally, from an ideological standpoint, are not deserving of serious examination.

Does it require deep intuition to comprehend that man's ideas, views and conceptions, in one word, man's consciousness, changes with every change in the conditions of his material existence, in his social relations and in his social life?

What else does the history of ideas prove, than that intellectual production changes its character in proportion as material production is changed? The ruling ideas of each age have ever been the ideas of its ruling class.

When people speak of ideas that revolutionise society, they do but express the fact, that within the old society, the elements of a new one have been created, and that the dissolution of the old ideas keeps even pace with the dissolution of the old conditions of existence.

When the ancient world was in its last throes, the ancient religions were overcome by Christianity. When Christian ideas succumbed in the 18th century to rationalist ideas, feudal society fought its death battle with the then revolutionary bourgeoisie. The ideas of religious liberty and freedom of conscience, merely gave expression to the sway of free competition within the domain of knowledge.

"Undoubtedly," it will be said, "religious, moral, philosophical and juridical ideas have been modified in the course of historical development. But religion, morality, philosophy, political science, and law, constantly survived this change."

"There are, besides, eternal truths, such as Freedom, Justice, etc., that are common to all states of society. But Communism abolishes eternal truths, it abolishes all religion, and all morality, instead of constituting them on a new basis; it therefore acts in contradiction to all past historical experience."

What does this accusation reduce itself to? The history of all past society has consisted in the development of class antagonisms, antagonisms that assumed different forms at different epochs:

But whatever form they may have taken, one fact is common to all past ages, *viz.*, the exploitation of one part of society by the other. No wonder, then, that the social consciousness of past ages, despite all the multiplicity and variety it displays, moves within certain common forms, or general ideas, which cannot completely vanish except with the total disappearance of class antagonisms.

The Communist revolution is the most radical rupture with traditional property relations; no wonder that its development involves the most radical rupture with traditional ideas.

But let us have done with the bourgeois objections to Communism.

We have seen above, that the first step in the revolution by the working class, is to raise the proletariat to the position of ruling class, to win the battle of democracy.

The proletariat will use its political supremacy to wrest, by degrees, all capital from the bourgeoisie, to centralise all instruments of production in the hands of the State, *i.e.*, of the proletariat organised as the ruling class; and to increase the total of productive forces as rapidly as possible.

Of course, in the beginning, this cannot be effected except by means of despotic inroads on the rights of property, and on the conditions of bourgeois production; by means of measures, therefore, which appear economically insufficient and untenable, but which, in the course of the movement, outstrip themselves, necessitate further inroads upon the old social order, and are unavoidable as a means of entirely revolutionising the mode of production.

These measures will of course be different in different countries.

Nevertheless in the most advanced countries, the following will be pretty generally applicable.

1. Abolition of property in land and application of all rents of land to public purposes.
2. A heavy progressive or graduated income tax.
3. Abolition of all right of inheritance.
4. Confiscation of the property of all emigrants and rebels.
5. Centralisation of credit in the hands of the State, by means of a national bank with State capital and an exclusive monopoly.
6. Centralisation of the means of communication and transport in the hands of the State.
7. Extension of factories and instruments of production owned by the State; the bringing into cultivation of waste-lands, and the improvement of the soil generally in accordance with a common plan.
8. Equal liability of all to labour. Establishment of industrial armies, especially for agriculture.
9. Combination of agriculture with manufacturing industries; gradual abolition of the distinction between town and country, by a more equable distribution of the population over the country.
10. Free education for all children in public schools. Abolition of children's factory labour in its present form. Combination of education with industrial production, &c., &c.

When, in the course of development, class distinctions have disappeared, and all production has been concentrated in the hands of a vast association of the whole nation, the public power will lose its political character. Political power, properly so called, is merely the organised power of one class for oppressing another. If the proletariat during its contest with the bourgeoisie is compelled, by the force of circumstances, to organise itself as a class, if, by means of a revolution, it makes itself the ruling class, and , as such, sweeps away by force the old conditions of production, then it will, along with these conditions, have swept away the conditions for the existence of class antagonisms and of classes generally, and will thereby have abolished its own supremacy as a class.

In place of the old bourgeois society, with its classes and class antagonisms, we shall have an association, in which the free development of each is the condition for the free development of all. . . .

The Communists disdain to conceal their views and aims. They openly declare that their ends can be attained only by the forcible overthrow of all existing social conditions. Let the ruling classes tremble at a Communistic revolution. The proletarians have nothing to lose but their chains. They have a world to win.

Working men of all countries, unite!

CHAPTER *12*

Social Darwinism

The publication in 1859 of Darwin's *Origin of the Species*, in addition to its enormous impact on the science of biology, also had an effect on the science of sociology.

Among the leading proponents of Social Darwinism was William Graham Sumner. Sumner believed that just as the laws of physical nature are fixed and immutable, so are the laws of social order. In Darwin's biological world, the present state of nature is due to the struggle for survival and the survival of the fittest. Sumner's philosophy held that the same is true in society.

Wealth and material success, said Sumner, are the natural and just result of talent, ability, and merit; poverty is the just reward of the lazy or unfit. Thus, differences in personal abilities, opportunities, and talent, according to Sumner, justify the state of income and wealth distribution between the separate classes. In Sumner's world, the consequences of the lack of ability, laziness, or the unfortunate luck of the fathers are visited upon the sons and grandsons. Any attempt to change the present social order and move toward equality would violate the laws of nature and the natural Social Darwinian process. In Sumner's philosophy, justice, by definition, is what results from the Darwinian process in society.

For Sumner, the social process is natural and amoral. "Might makes a right, whether that right is or is not rightful, just, fair, good, seemly, or proper, is quite another matter, for it involves a moral judgment."[1] Sumner had no moral philosophy, other than the thought that the present condition of society is just and best left to natural sociological processes.

Sociological evolution, like its biological counterpart, occurs slowly and imperceptibly over time. The current mode of production, the result of that evolution, is therefore the best and most just. Potential reformers work against natural sociological laws and therefore seek a society and economy that is unjust. The ideal human type of Social Darwinism is the person possessing the drive, talent, and/or ability to work within the evolved system to generate wealth. The biological counterpart of this evolution would be the thought that man is the premier species in the biological world today.

Steel magnate Andrew Carnegie agreed that inequality of wealth is necessary. In fact, it is a sign of progress from the days when little economic difference existed between the Indian chief and the brave, the master and the apprentice. But because of industrial progress and the resulting inequalities of wealth, the poor today enjoy what the rich in days past could not. Human society loses homogeneity with such change, as class distinctions evolve between the employer of thousands and the thousands themselves. But the result is "cheap comforts and luxuries." The law of competition is severe; it may be tough at times on the individual, but the survival of the fittest creates greater well-being for society.

All progress that has occurred up to the present time is due to the movement of society away from communism. Any movement toward communism would not be "evolution but revolution"; it would necessitate the changing of human nature.

Carnegie's ideal human type differs greatly from that of other Social Darwinists such as Sumner. Carnegie's "man of wealth" is not to flaunt his wealth, but to use it wisely to meet his needs and the needs of his dependents. After taking care of his family, the man of wealth should "consider all surplus revenues . . . as trust funds, which he is called upon to administer . . . to produce the most beneficial results for the community." The wealthy, because they have won the struggle for survival, are to be generous and assist the less fortunate as their "agent and trustee."

Although Carnegie was an ardent antisocialist, his men of wealth in fact constitute a type of ruling socialist elite. By directing investment and capital to meet those social needs that they perceive to be the most urgent, the man of wealth becomes a Big Brother to his "poorer brethren." By directing his wealth toward the needs of the poor, the man of wealth assists the poor better than the poor "could or would have done" for themselves.

---

[1]William Graham Sumner and Albert Galloway Keller, *The Science of Society*, Vol. I (New Haven: Yale University Press, 1927), p. 591.

Wealth

Andrew Carnegie

The problem of our age is the proper administration of wealth, so that the ties of brotherhood may still bind together the rich and poor in harmonious relationship. The conditions of human life have not only been changed, but revolutionized, within the past few hundred years. In former days there was little difference between the dwelling, dress, food, and environment of the chief and those of his retainers. The Indians are to-day where civilized man then was. When visiting the Sioux, I was led to the wigwam of the chief. It was just like the others in external appearance, and even within the difference was trifling between it and those of the poorest of his braves. The contrast between the palace of the millionaire and the cottage of the laborer with us to-day measures the change which has come with civilization.

This change, however, is not to be deplored, but welcomed as highly beneficial. It is well, nay, essential for the progress of the race, that the houses of some should be homes for all that is highest and best in literature and the arts, and for all the refinements of civilization, rather than that none should be so. Much better this great irregularity than universal squalor. Without wealth there can be no Maecenas. The "good old times" were not good old times. Neither master nor servant was as well situated then as today. A relapse to old conditions would be disastrous to both—not the least so to him who serves—and would sweep away civilization with it. But whether the change be for good or ill, it is upon us, beyond our power to alter, and therefore to be accepted and made the best of. It is a waste of time to criticise the inevitable.

It is easy to see how the change has come. One illustration will serve for almost every phase of the cause. In the manufacture of products we have the whole story. It applies to all combinations of human industry, as stimulated and enlarged by the inventions of this scientific age. Formerly articles were manufactured at the domestic hearth or in small shops which formed part of the household. The master and his apprentices worked side by side, the latter living with the master, and therefore subject to the same conditions. When these apprentices rose to be masters, there was little or no change in their mode of life, and they, in turn, educated in the same routine succeeding apprentices. There was, substantially, social equality, and even political equality, for those engaged in industrial pursuits had then little or no political voice in the State.

But the inevitable result of such a mode of manufacture was crude articles at

North American Review, Vol. 148 (June 1889), pp. 653–664.

high prices. To-day the world obtains commodities of excellent quality at prices which even the generation preceding this would have deemed incredible. In the commercial world similar causes have produced similar results, and the race is benefited thereby. The poor enjoy what the rich could not before afford. What were the luxuries have become the necessaries of life. The laborer has now more comforts than the farmer had a few generations ago. The farmer has more luxuries than the landlord had, and is more richly clad and better housed. The landlord has books and pictures rarer, and appointments more artistic, than the King could then obtain.

The price we pay for this salutary change is, no doubt, great. We assemble thousands of operatives in the factory, in the mine, and in the counting-house, of whom the employer can know little or nothing, and to whom the employer is little better than a myth. All intercourse between them is at an end. Rigid Castes are formed, and, as usual, mutual ignorance breeds mutual distrust. Each Caste is without sympathy for the other, and ready to credit anything disparaging in regard to it. Under the law of competition, the employer of thousands is forced into the strictest economies, among which the rates paid to labor figure prominently, and often there is friction between the employer and the employed, between capital and labor, between rich and poor. Human society loses homogeneity.

The price which society pays for the law of competition, like the price it pays for cheap comforts and luxuries, is also great; but the advantages of this law are also greater still, for it is to this law that we owe our wonderful material development, which brings improved conditions in its train. But, whether the law be benign or not, we must say of it, as we say of the change in the conditions of men to which we have referred: It is here; we cannot evade it; no substitutes for it have been found; and while the law may be sometimes hard for the individual, it is best for the race, because it insures the survival of the fittest in every department. We accept and welcome, therefore, as conditions to which we must accommodate ourselves, great inequality of environment, the concentration of business, industrial and commercial, in the hands of a few, and the law of competition between these, as being not only beneficial, but essential for the future progress of the race. Having accepted these, it follows that there must be great scope for the exercise of special ability in the merchant and in the manufacturer who has to conduct affairs upon a great scale. That this talent for organization and management is rare among men is proved by the fact that it invariably secures for its possessor enormous rewards, no matter where or under what laws or conditions. The experienced in affairs always rate the MAN whose services can be obtained as a partner as not only the first consideration, but such as to render the question of his capital scarcely worth considering, for such men soon create capital; while, without the special talent required, capital soon takes wings. Such men become interested in firms or corporations using millions; and estimating only simple interest to be made upon the capital invested., it is inevitable that their income must exceed their expenditures, and that they must accumulate wealth. Nor is there any middle ground which such men can occupy, because the great manufacturing or commercial concern which does not earn at least interest upon its capital soon becomes bankrupt. It must either go forward or fall behind: to stand still is impossible. It is a condition essential for its successful operation that it should be thus far profitable, and even that, in addition to interest on capital, it should make profit. It is a law, as certain as any of the others named, that men possessed of this peculiar talent for affairs, under the free play of economic forces, must, of necessity, soon be in receipt of more revenue than can be judiciously expended upon themselves; and this law is as beneficial for the race as the others.

Objections to the foundations upon which society is based are not in order, because the condition of the race is better with these than it has been with any others which have been tried. Of the effect of any new substitutes proposed we cannot be sure. The Socialist or Anarchist who seeks to overturn present conditions is to be regarded as attacking the foundation upon which civilization itself rests, for civilization took its start from the day that the capable, industrious workman said to his incompetent and lazy fellow, "If thou dost not sow, thou shalt not reap," and thus ended primitive Communism by separating the drones from the bees. One who studies this subject will soon be brought face to face with the conclusion that upon the sacredness of property civilization itself depends—the right of the laborer to his hundred dollars in the savings bank, and equally the legal right of the millionaire to his millions. To those who propose to substitute Communism for this intense Individualism the answer, therefore, is: The race has tried that. All progress from that barbarous day to the present time has resulted from its displacement. Not evil, but good, has come to the race from the accumulation of wealth by those who have the ability and energy that produce it. But even if we admit for a moment that it might be better for the race to discard its present foundation, Individualism,—that it is a nobler ideal that man should labor, not for himself alone, but in and for a brotherhood of his fellows, and share with them all in common, realizing Swedenborg's idea of Heaven, where, as he says, the angels derive their happiness, not from laboring for self, but for each other,—even admit all this, and a sufficient answer is, This is not evolution, but revolution. It necessitates the changing of human nature itself—a work of aeons, even if it were good to change it, which we cannot know. It is not practicable in our day or in our age. Even if desirable theoretically, it belongs to another and long-succeeding sociological stratum. Our duty is with what is practicable now; with the next step possible in our day and generation. It is criminal to waste our energies in endeavoring to uproot, when all we can profitably or possibly accomplish is to bend the universal tree of humanity a little in the direction most favorable to the production of good fruit under existing circumstances. We might as well urge the destruction of the highest existing type of man because he failed to reach our ideal as to favor the destruction of Individualism, Private Property, the Law of Accumulation of Wealth, and the Law of Competition; for these are the highest results of human experience, the soil in which society so far has produced the best fruit. Unequally or unjustly, perhaps, as these laws sometimes operate, and imperfect as they appear to the Idealist, they are, nevertheless, like the highest type of man, the best and most valuable of all that humanity has yet accomplished.

We start, then, with a condition of affairs under which the best interests of the race are promoted, but which inevitably gives wealth to the few. Thus far, accepting conditions as they exist, the situation can be surveyed and pronounced good. The question then arises,—and, if the foregoing be correct, it is the only question with which we have to deal,—What is the proper mode of administering wealth after the laws upon which civilization is founded have thrown it into the hands of the few? And it is of this great question that I believe I offer the true solution. It will be understood that *fortunes* are here spoken of, not moderate sums saved by many years of effort, the returns from which are required for the comfortable maintenance and education of families. This is not *wealth*, but only *competence*, which it should be the aim of all to acquire.

There are but three modes in which surplus wealth can be disposed of. It can be left to the families of the decedents; or it can be bequeathed for public purposes; or, finally, it can be administered during their lives by its possessors. Under the first and second modes most of the wealth of the world that has reached the few has hitherto been applied. Let us in turn consider each of these modes. The first is the most injudicious. In monarchical countries, the estates and the greatest portion of the wealth are left to the first son, that the vanity of the parent may be gratified by the thought that his name and title are to descend to succeeding generations unimpaired. The condition of this class in Europe to-day teaches the futility of such hopes or ambitions. The successors have become impoverished through their follies or from the fall in the value of land. Even in Great Britain the strict law of entail has been found inadequate to maintain the status of an hereditary class. Its soil is rapidly passing into the hands of the stranger. Under republican institutions the division of property among the children is much fairer, but the question which forces itself upon thoughtful men in all lands is: Why should men leave great fortunes to their children? If this is done from affection, is it not misguided affection? Observation teaches that, generally speaking, it is not well for the children that they should be so burdened. Neither is it well for the state. Beyond providing for the wife and daughters moderate sources of income, and very moderate allowances indeed, if any, for the sons, men may well hesitate, for it is no longer questionable that great sums bequeathed oftener work more for the injury than for the good of the recipients. Wise men will soon conclude that, for the best interests of the members of their families and of the state, such bequests are an improper use of their means.

It is not suggested that men who have failed to educate their sons to earn a livelihood shall cast them adrift in poverty. If any man has seen fit to rear his sons with a view to their living idle lives, or, what is highly commendable, has instilled in them the sentiment that they are in a position to labor for public ends without reference to pecuniary considerations, then, of course, the duty of the parent is to see that such are provided for *in moderation*. There are instances of millionaires' sons unspoiled by wealth, who, being rich, still perform great services in the community. Such are the very salt of the earth, as valuable as, unfortunately, they are rare; still it is not the exception, but the rule, that men must regard, and, looking at the usual result of enormous sums conferred upon legatees, the thoughtful man must shortly say, "I would as soon leave to my son a curse as the almighty dollar," and admit to himself that it is not the welfare of the children, but family pride, which inspires these enormous legacies.

As to the second mode, that of leaving wealth at death for public uses, it may be said that this is only a means for the disposal of wealth, provided a man is content to wait until he is dead before it becomes of much good in the world. Knowledge of the results of legacies bequeathed is not calculated to inspire the brightest hopes of much posthumous good being accomplished. The cases are not few in which the real object sought by the testator is not attained, nor are they few in which his real wishes are thwarted. In many cases the bequests are so used as to become only monuments of his folly. It is well to remember that it requires the exercise of not less ability than that which acquired the wealth to use it so as to be really beneficial to the community. Besides this, it may fairly be said that no man is to be extolled for doing what he cannot help doing, nor is he to be thanked by the community to which he only leaves wealth at death. Men who leave vast sums in this way may fairly be thought men who would not have left it at all, had they been able to take it with them. The memories of such cannot be held in grateful remembrance, for there is no grace in their gifts. It is not to be wondered at that such bequests seem so generally to lack the blessing.

The growing disposition to tax more and more heavily large estates left at death is a cheering indication of the growth of a salutary change in public opinion. The State of Pennsylvania now takes—subject to some exceptions—one-tenth of the property left by its citizens. The budget presented in the British Parliament the other day proposes to increase the death-duties; and, most significant of all, the new tax is to be a graduated one. Of all forms of taxation, this seems the wisest. Men who continue hoarding great sums all their lives, the proper use of which for public ends would work good to the community, should be made to feel that the community, in the form of the state, cannot thus be deprived of its proper share. By taxing estates heavily at death the state marks its condemnation of the selfish millionaire's unworthy life.

It is desirable that nations should go much further in this direction. Indeed, it is difficult to set bounds to the share of a rich man's estate which should go at his death to the public through the agency of the state, and by all means such taxes should be graduated, beginning at nothing upon moderate sums to dependents, and increasing rapidly as the amounts swell, until of the millionaire's hoard, as of Shylock's, at least

> "——The other half
> Comes to the privy coffer of the state."

This policy would work powerfully to induce the rich man to attend to the administration of wealth during his life, which is the end that society should always have in view, as being that by far most fruitful for the people. Nor need it be feared that this policy would sap the root of enterprise and render men less anxious to accumulate, for to the class whose ambition it is to leave great fortunes and be talked about after their death, it will attract even more attention, and, indeed, be a somewhat nobler ambition to have enormous sums paid over to the state from their fortunes.

There remains, then, only one mode of using great fortunes; but in this we have the true antidote for the temporary unequal distribution of wealth, the reconciliation of the rich and the poor—a reign of harmony—another ideal, differing, indeed, from that of the Communist in requiring only the further evolution of existing conditions, not the total overthrow of our civilization. It is founded upon the present most intense individualism, and the race is prepared to put it in practice by degrees whenever it pleases. Under its sway we shall have an ideal state, in which the surplus wealth of the few will become, in the best sense, the property of the many, because administered for the common good, and this wealth, passing through the hands of the few, can be made a much more potent force for the elevation of our race than if it had been distributed in small sums to the people themselves. Even the poorest can be made to see this, and to agree that great sums gathered by some of their fellow-citizens and spent for public purposes, from which the masses reap the principal benefit, are more valuable to them than if scattered among them through the course of many years in trifling amounts.

If we consider what results flow from the Cooper Institute, for instance, to the best portion of the race in New York not possessed of means, and compare these with those which would have arisen for the good of the masses from an equal sum distributed by Mr. Cooper in his lifetime in the form of wages, which is the highest form of distribution, being for work done and not for charity, we can form some estimate of the possibilities for the improvement of the race which lie embedded in the present law of the accumulation of wealth. Much of this sum, if distributed in small quantities among the people, would have been wasted in the indulgence of appetite, some of it in excess, and it may be doubted whether even the part put to the best use, that of adding to the comforts of the home, would have yielded results for the race, as a race, at all comparable to those which are flowing and are to flow from the Cooper Institute from generation to generation. Let the advocate of violent or radical change ponder well this thought.

We might even go so far as to take another instance, that of Mr. Tilden's bequest of five millions of dollars for a free library in the city of New York, but in referring to this one cannot help saying involuntarily. How much better if Mr. Tilden had devoted the last years of his own life to the proper administration of this immense sum; in which case neither legal contest nor any other cause of delay could have interfered with his aims. But let us assume that Mr. Tilden's millions finally became the means of giving to this city a noble public library, where the treasures of the world contained in books will be open to all forever, without money and without price. Considering the good of that part of the race which congregates in and around Manhattan Island, would its permanent benefit have been better promoted had these millions been allowed to circulate in small sums through the hands of the masses? Even the most strenuous advocate of Communism must entertain a doubt upon this subject. Most of those who think will probably entertain no doubt whatever.

Poor and restricted are our opportunities in this life; narrow our horizon; our best work most imperfect; but rich men should be thankful for one inestimable boon. They have it in their power during their lives to busy themselves in organizing benefactions from which the masses of their fellows will derive lasting advantage, and thus dignify their own lives. The highest life is probably to be reached, not by such imitation of the life of Christ as Count Tolstoï gives us, but, while animated by Christ's spirit, by recognizing the changed conditions of this age, and adopting modes of expressing this spirit suitable to the changed conditions under which we live; still laboring for the good of our fellows, which was the essence of his life and teaching, but laboring in a different manner.

This, then, is held to be the duty of the man of Wealth: First, to set an example of modest, unostentatious living, shunning display or extravagance; to provide moderately for the legitimate wants of those dependent upon him; and after doing so to consider all surplus revenues which come to him simply as trust funds, which he is called upon to administer, and strictly bound as a matter of duty to administer in the manner which, in his judgment, is best calculated to produce the most beneficial results for the community—the man of wealth thus becoming the mere agent and trustee for his poorer brethren, bringing to their service his superior wisdom, experience, and ability to administer, doing for them better than they would or could do for themselves. . . .

Thus is the problem of Rich and Poor to be solved. The laws of accumulation will be left free; the laws of distribution free. Individualism will continue, but the millionaire will be but a trustee for the poor; intrusted for a season with a great part of the increased wealth of the community, but administering it for the community far better than it could or would have done for itself. The best minds will thus have reached a stage in the development of the race in which it is clearly seen that there is no mode of disposing of surplus wealth creditable to thoughtful and earnest men into whose hands it flows save by using it year by year for the general good. This day already dawns. But a little while, and although, without incurring the pity of their fellows, men may die sharers in great business enterprises from which their capital cannot be or has not been withdrawn, and is left chiefly at death for public uses, yet the man who dies leaving behind him millions of available wealth, which was his to administer during life, will pass away "unwept, unhonored, and unsung," no matter to what uses he leaves the dross which he cannot take with him. Of such as these the public verdict will then be: "The man who dies thus rich dies disgraced."

Such, in my opinion, is the true Gospel concerning Wealth, obedience to which is destined some day to solve the problem of the Rich and the Poor, and to bring "Peace on earth, among men Good-Will."

CHAPTER 13

Amelioration of American Capitalism

Marx was wrong; the capitalist system has not collapsed in a struggle between the proletariat and bourgeoisie. Business run solely for profit and greed has been replaced by a business community that is also concerned with morality and society. Main Street is a more powerful economic force than Wall Street. American capitalism is a *popular* capitalism because it has popular support and because the people, not just the elite, can participate in it.

Such is the message of the writers of the excerpt below. Basic morality and indignation over injustice initiated the transformation of greed-driven unbridled capitalism to a moral and responsible capitalism. The American people, once informed of an injustice, will rise up collectively to correct it. The existence of a free press, writers, intellectuals, social reformers, and politicians help to inform the public and voice opinions about the current state of affairs. Action by the public follows, remedying injustices and restraining future reoccurrences.

Management has changed. For a person to have a successful business and management career, such battles as "management vs. labor," "management vs. shareholders," and "management vs. society" are all losing propositions. Management is a profession. A manager holds a job because he or she is good at it. The manager realizes that to guide the firm and seek a profit today and to prepare to make profits in the future the firm must conduct business responsibly and not alienate any of its constituencies—shareholders, bondholders, customers, employees, creditors, and society.

Due to their skill and ability, society has given business managers a position of importance. Business must therefore be aware of social concerns as business is conducted. The arrival of a benevolent, moral, responsible capitalism, tempered and disciplined by the democratic political system, has saved capitalism from a Marxist revolution.

U.S.A.: The Permanent Revolution

The Editors of Fortune *and R. W. Davenport*

... Fifty years ago American capitalism seemed to be what Marx predicted it would be and what all the muckrakers said it was—the inhuman offspring of greed and irresponsibility, committed by its master, Wall Street, to a long life of monopoly. It seemed to provide overwhelming proof of the theory that private ownership could honor no obligation except the obligation to pile up profits. It was, indeed, close to the capitalism that Andrei Vishinsky today keeps on denouncing so laboriously and humorlessly. And it was the capitalism that millions of people abroad and many even at home, to the immense aid and comfort of the Communists, still think American capitalism is.

But American capitalism today is actually nothing of the kind. There has occurred a great transformation, of which the world as a whole is as yet unaware, the speed of which has outstripped the perception of the historians, the commentators, the writers of business books—even many businessmen themselves. No important progress whatever can be made in the understanding of America unless the nature of this transformation is grasped and the obsolete intellectual stereotypes discarded.

Many evidences of the transformation are at hand, though they have never yet been drawn together into what is very urgently needed—a restatement of capitalistic theory in modern American terms. Take, for example, the all-pervasive character of American capitalism, as stressed in The American Way of Life. There has been a vast dispersion of ownership and initiative, so that the capitalist system has become intimately bound in with the political system and takes nourishment from its democratic roots. What might be called the influence of Main Street has become vastly more important than the control of Wall Street. U.S. capitalism is *popular* capitalism, not only in the sense that it has popular support, but in the deeper sense that the people as a whole participate in it and use it.

But perhaps the transformation can best be understood by looking at what has happened to "Big Business," which once was supposed to have controlled the economy from its headquarters in Wall Street. The fact is that Wall Street no longer wields much power over Big Business, which in turn is far from being the most powerful sector of the economy. For economic power boils down to the

---

ability to decide who makes what and who gets what and in what proportions, and business alone no longer decides this. "The class struggle in America," writes Professor Clair Wilcox in the *Harvard Business Review*, "is not a struggle between the proletariat and the bourgeoisie. It is a struggle between functional groups possessing concentrated power—a struggle to control the products of industry." These groups, as Professor Wilcox describes them, are Big Labor, Big Agriculture, Big Little Business, and Big Business. Of them all, Big Business, if only because it is subject to the most pressure, exercises its power with a strong and growing sense of responsibility. It has led the way to the formation of a kind of capitalism that neither Karl Marx nor Adam Smith ever dreamed of.

At the bottom of the change is simple morality, which has concerned the U.S. throughout its history, sometimes to the point of fanaticism. "The American," H. L. Mencken once said, "save in moments of conscious and swiftly lamented deviltry, casts up all ponderable values, including the value even of beauty, in terms of right and wrong." Like the European who described moral indignation as suppressed envy, Mencken scorned it as the mark of the peasant; and the American's capacity for moral indignation *has* resulted in many "uncivilized" excesses like prohibition. But it has also made him the most omnivorous reformer in history. Karl Marx based his philosophy on the fatalistic assumption that what he described as the inherent defects of capitalism are above the will of men to affect them. It has remained for the history of U.S. capitalism, beginning as early as the 1870's, to show that the moral convictions of men can change the course of capitalistic development.

And it would have been strange if a nation that had only recently fought a terrible war over the question of slavery had *not* got indignant about the excesses of its "robber barons." People, of course, do not necessarily rise up voluntarily and act on moral indignation. What is essential is their capacity for it; given a free, lively press and plenty of politicians, the action follows. Action followed in the U.S. because a whole school of commentators, from novelists to reporters, from historians to cartoonists, rose up to expose the financial and industrial scandals of the day. There were the Ida Tarbells and Henry Demarest Lloyds, the Upton Sinclairs and Frederick Oppers, backed by the Hearsts, McClures, and Munseys. Some were hypocritical and others wholly sincere, but all operated on the effective principle that the public could be fetched by an earnest appeal to its moral standards.

In their zeal the muckrakers paid little attention to the great economic role played by "robber barons" in forming the capital to lay the rails, erect the factories, build the machinery for a new and expanding economy. Naturally the muckrakers were concerned not with amoral economics but with immoral practices. Their pictures of the American economic brigandage of the late nineteenth and early twentieth centuries became stereotypes all over the world—Daniel Drew feeding his cattle salt to make them drink heavily the day before market; Cornelius Vanderbilt bragging how "we busted the hull damn legislature"; foxy Jay Gould, whom Vanderbilt called the smartest man in America, cornering the national gold-coin

supply through his White House connections, and systematically and openly rob-
bing the Erie; gelid old John D. Rockefeller perfecting the trust system and eliminating competitors like clay pigeons. Here was the principle of property ownership
carried to its absurd conclusion, capitalism gone berserk. But here also was the
moral indignation of the American people. Fanned by lurid accounts in the press
and by politicians and publicists of almost every persuasion, from Populists to
Republicans,it started the transformation of American capitalism.

. . . The American's moral indignation, naturally enough, did not burn with a
steady flame. In good times he tended to overlook violations of his basic notions;
in bad times he looked for something to blame things on, and demanded that
something be done about them. During the 1920's popular demand for reform
was almost nonexistent. For one thing, the scorn of some of the nation's most
effective writers made preoccupation with moral issues unfashionable if not ludi-
crous. For another, business seemed to be doing fine, and seemed to deserve not
reform but praise. As the immensely popular *Saturday Evening Post* demonstrated
in almost every issue, as Herbert Hoover himself phrased it, "The slogan of progress is changing from the full dinner pail to the full garage."

The catastrophe of depression blasted this dream. The shocked and angry people, seeing their livelihood disappear, put the Right to Life above the other rights.
Their natural tendency to blame the bust on those who only yesterday were taking
credit for having started an eternal boom was strengthened by revelations such as
those of the Pecora congressional investigation into Wall Street financial practices.
So they embraced the latter-day Populism of the New Deal, and demanded that
something be done. Writers and intellectuals took up the cudgels. Some were
merely inclined to condemn what they had for so long contemned, but many tried
to find out how and why it had happened, and how to keep it from happening
again.

Many of the ensuing reforms survived. Immediately after the Pecora investigation, Congress passed a law divorcing investment banking from deposit banking.
And a year later it passed the well-intentioned Securities Exchange Act, which
put the Stock Exchange under federal regulation, gave the Federal Reserve Board
authority to limit speculative margins, required all officers and stockholders of big
companies to report their dealings in their companies' securities, and created the
Securities and Exchange Commission to watch over the investment market.

Other attempts at reform were less successful. NRA, for example, went to a
well-deserved death. As for the famed Temporary National Economic Committee,
much of what it investigated was beside the point by the time it was in print—
and not only because of the impending war. Even while the committee was mull-
ing over the power of big business, and the intellectuals were in full cry on the
trail of finance capitalism, business initiative had been dispersed among hundreds
of enterprises; business power in the aggregate found itself confronted by the
rising power of the unions on the one hand, the farmers on the other; and Wall
Street had ceased to be a valid symbol of great tyranny.

The decline of Wall Street actually began long before the reforms of the New Deal. It began when corporations grew rich and independent. The rights to their profits, of course, were by traditional economics vested in the stockholders. But their managers saw no point in paying, say, $20 a share in dividends on their stock, when $10 was enough to sustain the company's credit rating. They also reasoned that it was *they*, and not the stockholders, who were directly responsible for the profits. So they began to hold back on the stockholders and put the money into corporate reserves. As early as 1905 the Santa Fe, under Edward Ripley, adopted the policy of a dollar for the stockholder, a dollar for the property. Owen Young of G.E. and others, some years later, further developed the idea of self-capitalization, arguing that the money plowed back would in the long run enhance the stockholder's equity. Whether it did or not, it enabled a large part of business to do its own banking.

The cataclysm of the depression, which forever broke apart the old business universe, also heaved up the bright new stars of the unions and the farmers. With between 14 and 16 million members in labor unions, labor leaders now enjoy tremendous industrial power. This power is exercised through the familiar method of tying up an entire industry in order to win certain gains for the workers, whether these gains be "economic" or not. In the face of such power, industry is impotent; and since the national welfare is often enough at stake, the White House itself becomes directly involved. The danger of such power is obvious, and was recently accented by John L. Lewis, who put his miners on a three-day week, not merely to enforce a wage demand, but to keep the price of coal up by creating a scarcity. Here, indeed, is a problem that the permanent revolution has not yet solved, although certain solutions are beginning to emerge.... The point to note here is that the power of Wall Street, which has declined in any case, has been met, and sometimes over-matched, by the power of modern labor; a development that has played an enormous role in the transformation of American capitalism.

The power of the farmer, if less direct than that of labor, is likewise formidable. Represented in Congress out of proportion to his numbers, the farmer has been championed by legislators and bureaucrats who have effectively insulated him from the law of supply and demand. By restricting output, fixing prices, and storing up surpluses at government expense, they have done for agriculture what a watertight cartel would do for a group of manufacturers of widely varying efficiency. They have not only saddled the public with high prices, they have, of course, tended to prevent American farming from becoming as efficient as it ought to be and can be. For they have spread a price umbrella over the farmers that has enabled the worst of them to do all right and the best of them to make fantastic and undeserved profits without necessarily encouraging any of them to become more efficient. The $23-billion farm industry, furthermore, is hardly comparable to any one industry, it is more comparable to all industry—to all industry cartelized, subsidized, and rigidified. In terms of deciding who makes what and who gets what, it is one of the most powerful blocs in American history. . . .

One of the two chief characteristics of big modern enterprise is that it is run by hired management. As Berle and Means put it, the power inherent in the control of the "active property"—the plant, organization and good will—has superseded the power inherent in "passive property"—the stocks and bonds. Even companies whose owners are managers may be described as management-run. The Ford company, for example, behaves not as an organization solely dedicated to earning the maximum number of dollars for the Ford family, but as an organization dedicated first of all to its own perpetuation and growth.

The other chief characteristic of the big modern enterprise is that management is becoming a profession. This means, to begin with, that a professional manager holds his job primarily because he is good at it. . . .

More important, the manager is becoming a professional in the sense that like all professional men he has a responsibility to society as a whole. This is not to say that he no longer needs good, old-fashioned business sense. He does, and more than ever. The manager is responsible primarily to his company as a profit-earning mechanism, and current talk about the corporation as a non-profit institution is more than a little naïve. . . .

But the great happy paradox of the profit motive in the American system is that management, precisely because it is in business to make money years on end, cannot concentrate exclusively on making money here and now. To keep on making money years on end, it must, in the words of Frank Abrams, Chairman of the Standard Oil Co. of New Jersey, "conduct the affairs of the enterprise in such a way as to maintain an *equitable and working balance* among the claims of the various directly interested groups—stockholders, employees, customers, and the public at large." . . .

. . . Almost any good manager can honestly argue that the growing importance of the hired management and its policy of self-capitalization have been to the benefit of the stockholder. Above all, he can argue that the stockholder's long-term interests lie in letting competent, responsible management build up the company and deal justly with employees, customers, and the public.

But modern management exhibits also a sense of responsibility toward its employees, not only to prevent or anticipate the demands of labor unions (though this motive has often been strong) but for the simple, obvious, and honest reason that a satisfied, loyal group of employees is at least as much of an asset as a modern plant or a vital piece of machinery. The trend toward more enlightened employment policies has been growing for years, and while there is still a great distance to go, an old-style capitalist would be appalled by the wide variety of benefits that modern corporations offer those who work for them. There is a growing tendency on the part of blue-chip management to regard a job in the company as a kind of employment package, complete with pensions, savings plan, and numerous "fringe" benefits such as severance pay, maternity leave, hospitalization and medical insurance. . . .

But material benefits, as Elton Mayo and others have demonstrated, are often not as important as job satisfaction—the feeling of having done a good job, and of having it recognized by people who know what a good job is. Related and equally important is the question of real participation in the company's affairs. The problem involved here is tremendous, and it cannot be solved merely by the resolution to do something about it. In one of the Standard Oil affiliates, for example, management was stumped by a case of group dissatisfaction until the president of the company began to talk to the men informally about some of the problems that were plaguing him and his board. "The men showed an immediate and extraordinary interest, and that gradually revealed the source of their dissatisfaction," recalls Frank Abrams. "They had been 'left out of things.'" The point to be noted here is that not every president could have done that. This president obviously had the "something" it takes to put a man across with his employees. And the gradual cultivation of that something is one of the unfinished tasks ahead of management.

This fundamental point is met, and is combined with material incentives, by the "participation" school, which is growing, and whose most promising development is that fostered by Joseph Scanlon of M.I.T. The Scanlon approach actually brings the worker into the enterprise system by giving him a share in productivity decisions and a cut in productivity profits. Since January, 1950, at least a dozen firms, including Stromberg-Carlson of Rochester, New York, have adopted the Scanlon system, and many more are preparing for it. This approach can hardly fail to revolutionize American industrial relations and thus carry further the great transformation in which American capitalism is engaged.

How well American management has actually done by its employees is a question that leads to inevitable debate. The fact is incontestable, however, that it has done better than management anywhere else—and, for that matter, better than management ever dreamed it could, under the old form of capitalism. The problem, indeed, may be to prevent management from becoming overgenerous. For when a company distributes employee benefits that are not compensated by rising productivity, it must in the long run pass the cost increase on to the consumer. Obviously a company *can* be tempted to win employee cooperation easily; a few producers and a single union can combine to gang up on the public.

One of the most pressing concerns of almost every large company today is what people are going to think about it. Board meetings often turn into self-examination sessions, with managers defending or explaining their actions as if before accusing judges. At a recent board meeting of a large consumer-goods company, the president rose up and remarked that the foremen had in effect built up a block between management and labor, and that management was mostly at fault. Fully two hours were devoted to soul-searching and discussion. There was also the matter of closing an old mill in a small town. Not only was the specific situation explored thoroughly, but the history of other similar cases was brought up. This problem was solved, after a full hour's discussion, by the decision to move a storage plant into the town and thus absorb nearly all the displaced employees. As one executive remarked, "At least half our time is taken up with discussing the repercussions of what we propose to do. And this is what the boys who write the books call the managerial revolution."

Nothing perhaps is more indicative of the corporation's awareness of its responsibilities than the growth of public-relations activities. Upwards of 4,000 companies now go in for public-relations "programs." Although many of them are hardly more than publicity campaigns, more and more managers understand tolerably well that good business public relations is good performance publicly appreciated, because adequately communicated. Now the mere comprehension of a moral axiom, as all parents know, does not guarantee its observance. But its constant iteration does make the subject more and more acutely aware of its importance, and thus eventually influences his behavior. As Paul Garrett of G.M. has been saying for years, "Our program is finding out what people like, doing more of it; finding out what people don't like, doing less of it."

All of which should not be interpreted to mean that business is already rolling us down the six-lane, highspeed highway to economic paradise. We have concerned ourselves here with the pace-setters of American management, and do not presume to imply that all managers and all other companies are doing as well.

What counts, however, is that certain business leaders *are* setting the pace, and *are* being followed. What counts is that the old concept that the owner has a right to use his property just the way he pleases has evolved into the belief that ownership carries social obligations, and that a manager is a trustee not only for the owner but for society as a whole. Such is the Transformation of American Capitalism. In all the world there is no more hopeful economic phenomenon.

CHAPTER 14

The Catholic Social Tradition

In the twentieth century, Roman Catholics have played a major role in developing a philosophy of economic justice based upon a nearly 2000-year collection of Catholic social teaching.

In 1980, the National Conference of Catholic Bishops appointed a committee, chaired by Archbishop Rembert Weakland of Milwaukee, to draft a pastoral letter on the American economy. After several drafts were presented and discussed, both in secular and religious circles, a final draft was approved in November 1986.

The pastoral letter has several themes that continually surface. First is the "fundamental option for the poor" that is needed in the American economy. It is a moral and social scandal, wrote the bishops, that one in every seven Americans is poor. The bishops state that the basis upon which all economic decisions, private or public, must be judged is what they do to and for the poor. The bishops assert the primary purpose of the economy is to meet the basic needs of the poor. Private initiatives to help the poor are insufficient. Government action is needed.

A second theme is that human dignity is all-important. This theme is closely related to the first, in that their human dignity requires that the poor receive special assistance. To examine justice, the bishops used the standard that what the system or institution does to people and for people is of primary concern.

This concept of dignity, based upon the biblical teaching that man is created in the image of God, is a standard that condemns exploitation of persons for selfish gain. It also entails a standard of giving: One must willingly and liberally give to meet the true economic needs of another person.

A third theme of the letter is that the community is to work to meet the needs of the poor and to maintain human dignity. The bishops stressed that the foundation of community must be a stable, healthy family unit, but that outside the family, the broader community must also help the poor and maintain human dignity. Even though the bishops stated their support for free enterprise and private property, their discussions rely heavily upon government action and intervention.

For the bishops, an economic system is just if it provides a safety net for all. Those on the lower economic strata deserve extra assistance and consideration; this is the "preferential option for the poor" stressed by the bishops—sharing of wealth and skills to meet the needs of the poor.

The bishops condemned the inequity of the present distribution of wealth. Though concurring that some inequality of wealth is necessary, they considered extreme inequality of wealth undesirable. A free market distribution of wealth does not necessarily create a just distribution of wealth; therefore, a system that will guarantee "minimum conditions of human dignity" is needed.

Trade is discussed and placed on a moral plane by the bishops. Output by business firms must fulfill the needs of people while providing jobs, eliminating discrimination, and maintaining environmental quality. The bishops deplored conspicuous consumption of luxury goods as long as the basic needs of some individuals are not met. Firms driven by profit must reorder their priorities so that basic human needs and workers' rights become primary. The guiding light of business should be the common good rather than the maximization of profits.

When the bishops' final draft was approved and released, the Lay Commission on Catholic Social Teaching released its own comments and thoughts on the bishops' letter. The Lay Commission is a group of lay Catholics who had written and spoken critically of the bishops' pastoral letter during its drafting. Though pleased by the moderation of the final draft as compared to earlier ones, the Lay Commission disagreed with several portions of the letter which criticized certain aspects of the United States economy. For example, the Lay Commission states:

> Despite the many improvements that the bishops have made in their letter since 1984, we still find in the final draft several serious intellectual defects. Among these are: a failure to grasp what makes poor nations into developed nations; deficient understandings of *political economy* (the relative roles of government and the free economy); excessive trust in the state and its officials; an inadequate grasp of crucial concepts such as enterprise, markets, and profits; significant confusions about economic rights; fateful confusions between de-

fense spending and spending on weapons; a preference for "solidarity" over pluralism; and an inadequate exposition of "liberty."[1]

The Lay Commission's main point of contention with the pastoral letter concerns the morality and positive results of free enterprise in the United States. It pointed out that the 60 to 70 million new jobs that Latin America will need to generate between now and the year 2000 will have to come from free enterprise, through the exercise of individual liberty and the striking down of social and government bureaucracy and custom. The national economic success story of the Pacific Rim countries—Japan, Taiwan, and Hong Kong, among others—occurred due to free enterprise there.

The Lay Commission does not support an unfettered free market. It recognizes that government has a legitimate role to play, but its authors assert, that role is less than the pastoral letter advocates. Government must facilitate the access of the underprivileged to the free market by removing the restrictive barriers that tend to perpetuate a privileged class due to position rather than ability. But as long as no group monopolizes political or economic power, the free market will provide the means for the poor, through work, to lift themselves out of their poverty.

One purpose of the state should be to reduce barriers that prevent the profit motive (Adam Smith's "invisible hand") from working correctly. Welfare systems that subsidize nonparticipation in the work force and tax systems that penalize saving and investment are two examples of government policy that hinder economic growth and expansion of opportunities, jobs, and liberty for all. The Lay Commission points out that in the United States the wealthy of one generation are usually different from those who followed them in later generations. The free enterprise system allows for "churning" or changeover between the families in the various income groups from generation to generation.

The ideal human type implicitly envisioned by the Lay Commission is more in line with the spirit of capitalist bourgeois man than that envisioned by the bishops. Liberty allows the work ethic to function, rewarding initiative, talent, insight, and self-reliance, whereas government programs, by reducing personal initiative, can hurt the poor or underprivileged person more than they help. Economic improvement, according to the Lay Commission, is best achieved by a "bottom-up approach" giving the poor a safety net and entry into the economic system, rather than by a "top-down approach" with the government extending special privileges and seeking statist solutions to income inequality.

---

[1]W. Simon and M. Novak, cochairmen, Lay Commission on Catholic Social Teaching and the U.S. Economy, "Liberty and Justice for All," *Crisis Magazine*, November 1986.

Economic Justice for All

U.S. Catholic Bishops

PRINCIPAL THEMES OF THE PASTORAL LETTER

The pastoral letter is not a blueprint for the American economy. It does not embrace any particular theory of how the economy works, nor does it attempt to resolve the disputes between different schools of economic thought. Instead, our letter turns to Scripture and to the social teachings of the Church. There, we discover what our economic life must serve, what standards it must meet. Let us examine some of these basic moral principles.

Every economic decision and institution must be judged in light of whether it protects or undermines the dignity of the human person. The pastoral letter begins with the human person. We believe the person is sacred—the clearest reflection of God among us. Human dignity comes from God, not from nationality, race, sex, economic status, or any human accomplishment. We judge any economic system by what it does *for* and *to* people and by how it permits all to *participate* in it. The economy should serve people, not the other way around.

Human dignity can be realized and protected only in community. In our teaching, the human person is not only sacred but also social. How we organize our society—in economics and politics, in law and policy—directly affects human dignity and the capacity of individuals to grow in community. The obligation to "love our neighbor" has an individual dimension, but it also requires a broader social commitment to the common good. We have many partial ways to measure and debate the health of our economy: Gross National Product, per capita income, stock market prices, and so forth. The Christian vision of economic life looks beyond them all and asks, Does economic life enhance or threaten our life together as a community?

All people have a right to participate in the economic life of society. Basic justice demands that people be assured a minimum level of participation in the economy. It is wrong for a person or group to be excluded unfairly or to be unable to participate or contribute to the economy. For example, people who are both able and willing, but cannot get a job are deprived of the participation that is so vital to human development. For, it is through employment that most individuals and

---

Selections from Economic Justice for All: Pastoral Letter on Catholic Social Teaching and the U.S. Economy, *Washington, D.C.:* © *1986 United States Catholic Conference, Used by permission.*

families meet their material needs, exercise their talents, and have an opportunity to contribute to the larger community. Such participation has a special significance in our tradition because we believe that it is a means by which we join in carrying forward God's creative activity.

All members of society have a special obligation to the poor and vulnerable. From the Scriptures and church teaching, we learn that the justice of a society is tested by the treatment of the poor. The justice that was the sign of God's covenant with Israel was measured by how the poor and unprotected—the widow, the orphan, and the stranger—were treated. The kingdom that Jesus proclaimed in his word and ministry excludes no one. Throughout Israel's history and in early Christianity, the poor are agents of God's transforming power. "The Spirit of the Lord is upon me, therefore he has anointed me. He has sent me to bring glad tidings to the poor" (Lk 4:18). This was Jesus' first public utterance. Jesus takes the side of those most in need. In the Last Judgment, so dramatically described in St. Matthew's Gospel, we are told that we will be judged according to how we respond to the hungry, the thirsty, the naked, the stranger. As followers of Christ, we are challenged to make a fundamental "option for the poor"—to speak for the voiceless, to defend the defenseless, to assess life styles, policies, and social institutions in terms of their impact on the poor. This "option for the poor" does not mean pitting one group against another, but rather, strengthening the whole community by assisting those who are most vulnerable. As Christians, we are called to respond to the needs of *all* our brothers and sisters, but those with the greatest needs require the greatest response.

Human rights are the minimum conditions for life in community. In Catholic teaching, human rights include not only civil and political rights but also economic rights. As Pope John XXIII declared, "all people have a right to life, food, clothing, shelter, rest, medical care, education, and employment." This means that when people are without a chance to earn a living, and must go hungry and homeless, they are being denied basic rights. Society must ensure that these rights are protected. In this way, we will ensure that the minimum conditions of economic justice are met for all our sisters and brothers.

Society as a whole, acting through public and private institutions, has the moral responsibility to enhance human dignity and protect human rights. In addition to the clear responsibility of private institutions, government has an essential responsibility in this area. This does not mean that government has the primary or exclusive role, but it does have a positive moral responsibility in safeguarding human rights and ensuring that the minimum conditions of human dignity are met for all. In a democracy, government is a means by which we can act together to protect what is important to us and to promote our common values.

These six moral principles are not the only ones presented in the pastoral letter, but they give an overview of the moral vision that we are trying to share. This vision of economic life cannot exist in a vacuum; it must be translated into concrete measures. Our pastoral letter spells out some specific applications of Catholic moral principles. We call for a new national commitment to full employment.

We say it is a social and moral scandal that one of every seven Americans is poor, and we call for concerted efforts to eradicate poverty. The fulfillment of the basic needs of the poor is of the highest priority. We urge that all economic policies be evaluated in light of their impact on the life and stability of the family. We support measures to halt the loss of family farms and to resist the growing concentration in the ownership of agricultural resources. We specify ways in which the United States can do far more to relieve the plight of poor nations and assist in their development. We also reaffirm church teaching on the rights of workers, collective bargaining, private property, subsidiarity, and equal opportunity.

We believe that the recommendations in our letter are reasonable and balanced. In analyzing the economy, we reject ideological extremes and start from the fact that ours is a "mixed" economy, the product of a long history of reform and adjustment. We know that some of our specific recommendations are controversial. As bishops, we do not claim to make these prudential judgments with the same kind of authority that marks our declarations of principle. But, we feel obliged to teach-by example how Christians can undertake concrete analysis and make specific judgments on economic issues. The Church's teachings cannot be left at the level of appealing generalities.

In the pastoral letter, we suggest that the time has come for a "New American Experiment"—to implement economic rights, to broaden the sharing of economic power, and to make economic decisions more accountable to the common good. This experiment can create new structures of economic partnership and participation within firms at the regional level, for the whole nation, and across borders.

Of course, there are many aspects of the economy the letter does not touch, and there are basic questions it leaves to further exploration. There are also many specific points on which men and women of good will may disagree. We look for a fruitful exchange among differing viewpoints. We pray only that all will take to heart the urgency of our concerns; that together we will test our views by the Gospel and the Church's teaching; and that we will listen to other voices in a spirit of mutual respect and open dialogue.

THE CHURCH AND THE FUTURE OF THE U.S. ECONOMY

Every perspective on economic life that is human, moral, and Christian must be shaped by three questions: What does the economy do *for* people? What does it do *to* people? And how do people *participate* in it? The economy is a human reality: men and women working together to develop and care for the whole of God's creation. All this work must serve the material and spiritual well-being of people. It influences what people hope for themselves and their loved ones. It affects the way they act together in society. It influences their very faith in God.[a]

---

[a]Vatican Council II, *The Pastoral Constitution on the Church in the Modern World,* 33. [Note: This

URGENT PROBLEMS OF TODAY

The preeminent role of the United States in an increasingly interdependent global economy is a central sign of our times.[b] The United States is still the world's economic giant. Decisions made here have immediate effects in other countries; decisions made abroad have immediate consequences for steelworkers in Pittsburgh, oil company employees in Houston, and farmers in Iowa. U.S. economic growth is vitally dependent on resources from other countries and on their purchases of our goods and services. Many jobs in U.S. industry and agriculture depend on our ability to export manufactured goods and food.

In some industries the mobility of capital and technology makes wages the main variable in the cost of production. Overseas competitors with the same technology but with wage rates as low as one-tenth of ours put enormous pressure on U.S. firms to cut wages, relocate abroad, or close. U.S. workers and their communities should not be expected to bear these burdens alone.

All people on this globe share a common ecological environment that is under increasing pressure. Depletion of soil, water, and other natural resources endangers the future. Pollution of air and water threatens the delicate balance of the biosphere on which future generations will depend.[c] The resources of the earth have been created by God for the benefit of all, and we who are alive today hold them in trust. This is a challenge to develop a new ecological ethic that will help shape a future that is both just and sustainable.

In short, nations separated by geography, culture, and ideology are linked in a complex commercial, financial, technological, and environmental network. These links have two direct consequences. First, they create hope for a new form of community among all peoples, one built on dignity, solidarity, and justice. Second, this rising global awareness calls for greater attention to the stark inequities across countries in the standards of living and control of resources. We must not look at the welfare of U.S. citizens as the only good to be sought. Nor may we overlook the disparities of power in the relationships between this nation and the developing countries. The United States is the major supplier of food to other countries, a major source of arms sales to developing nations, and a powerful influence in multilateral institutions such as the International Monetary Fund, the World Bank, and the United Nations. What Americans see as a growing interdependence is regarded by many in the less developed countries as a pattern of domination and dependence.

Within this larger international setting, there are also a number of challenges to the domestic economy that call for creativity and courage. The promise of the

pastoral letter frequently refers to documents of the Second Vatican Council, papal encyclicals, and other official teachings of the Roman Catholic Church. Most of these texts have been published by the United States Catholic Conference Office of Publishing and Promotion Services; many are available in collections, though no single collection is comprehensive.

[b]Pope John XXIII, *Peace on Earth* (1963), 130–131.

[c]Synod of Bishops, *Justice in the World* (1971), 8; Pope John Paul II, *Redeemer of Man* (1979), 15.

"American dream"—freedom for all persons to develop their God-given talents to the full—remains unfulfilled for millions in the United States today.

Several areas of U.S. economic life demand special attention. Unemployment is the most basic. Despite the large number of new jobs the U.S. economy has generated in the past decade, approximately 8 million people seeking work in this country are unable to find it, and many more are so discouraged they have stopped looking.[d] Over the past two decades the nation has come to tolerate an increasing level of unemployment. The 6 to 7 percent rate deemed acceptable today would have been intolerable twenty years ago. Among the unemployed are a disproportionate number of blacks, Hispanics, young people, or women who are the sole support of their families.[e] Some cities and states have many more unemployed persons than others as a result of economic forces that have little to do with people's desire to work. Unemployment is a tragedy no matter whom it strikes, but the tragedy is compounded by the unequal and unfair way it is distributed in our society.

Harsh poverty plagues our country despite its great wealth. More than 33 million Americans are poor; by any reasonable standard another 20 to 30 million are needy. Poverty is increasing in the United States, not decreasing.[f] For a people who believe in "progress," this should be cause for alarm. These burdens fall most heavily on blacks, Hispanics, and Native Americans. Even more disturbing is the large increase in the number of women and children living in poverty. Today children are the largest single group among the poor. This tragic fact seriously threatens the nation's future. That so many people are poor in a nation as rich as ours is a social and moral scandal that we cannot ignore.

Many working people and middle-class Americans live dangerously close to poverty. A rising number of families must rely on the wages of two or even three members just to get by. From 1968 to 1978 nearly a quarter of the U.S. population was in poverty part of the time and received welfare benefits in at least one year.[g] The loss of a job, illness, or the breakup of a marriage may be all it takes to push people into poverty.

The lack of a mutually supportive relation between family life and economic life is one of the most serious problems facing the United States today.[h] The

---

[d]U.S. Department of Labor, Bureau of Labor Statistics, *The Employment Situation: August 1985* (September 1985), Table A-1.

[e]Ibid.

[f]U.S. Bureau of the Census, Current Population Reports, Series P-60, 145, *Money Income and Poverty Status of Families and Persons in the United States: 1983* (Washington, D.C.: U.S. Government Printing Office, 1984), 20.

[g]Greg H. Duncan, *Years of Poverty, Years of Plenty: The Changing Economic Fortunes of American Workers and Their Families* (Ann Arbor, Mich.: Institute for Social Research, University of Michigan, 1984).

[h]See Pope John Paul II, *Familiaris Consortio* (1981), 46.

economic and cultural strength of the nation is directly linked to the stability and health of its families.ⁱ When families thrive, spouses contribute to the common good through their work at home, in the community, and in their jobs; and children develop a sense of their own worth and of their responsibility to serve others. When families are weak or break down entirely, the dignity of parents and children is threatened. High cultural and economic costs are inflicted on society at large. . . .

The quality of the national discussion about our economic future will affect the poor most of all, in this country and throughout the world. The life and dignity of millions of men, women, and children hang in the balance. Decisions must be judged in light of what they do *for* the poor, what they do *to* the poor, and what they enable the poor to do *for themselves*. The fundamental moral criterion for all economic decisions, policies, and institutions is this: They must be at the service of *all people, especially the poor*. . . .

THE CHRISTIAN VISION OF ECONOMIC LIFE

The basis for all that the Church believes about the moral dimensions of economic life is its vision of the transcendent worth—the sacredness—of human beings. *The dignity of the human person, realized in community with others, is the criterion against which all aspects of economic life must be measured.*ⁱ All human beings, therefore, are ends to be served by the institutions that make up the economy, not means to be exploited for more narrowly defined goals. Human personhood must be respected with a reverence that is religious. When we deal with each other, we should do so with the sense of awe that arises in the presence of something holy and sacred. For that is what human beings are: we are created in the image of God (Gn 1:27). Similarly, all economic institutions must support the bonds of community and solidarity that are essential to the dignity of persons. Wherever our economic arrangements fail to conform to the demands of human dignity lived in community, they must be questioned and transformed. These convictions have a biblical basis. They are also supported by a long tradition of theological and philosophical reflection and through the reasoned analysis of human experience by contemporary men and women. . . .

The biblical vision of creation has provided one of the most enduring legacies of Church teaching. To stand before God as the creator is to respect God's creation, both the world of nature and of human history. *From the patristic period to the present, the Church has affirmed that misuse of the world's resources or appropri-*

ⁱ*Pastoral Constitution*, 47.

ⁱ*Mater et Magistra*, 219–220. See *Pastoral Constitution*, 63.

ation of them by a minority of the world's population betrays the gift of creation since "whatever belongs to God belongs' to all."[k] . . .

Human life is life in community. Catholic social teaching proposes several complementary perspectives that show how moral responsibilities and duties in the economic sphere are rooted in this call to community. . . .

MORAL PRIORITIES FOR THE NATION

The common good demands justice for all, the protection of the human rights of all.[l] Making cultural and economic institutions more supportive of the freedom, power, and security of individuals and families must be a central, long-range objective for the nation. Every person has a duty to contribute to building up the commonweal. All have a responsibility to develop their talents through education. Adults must contribute to society through their individual vocations and talents. Parents are called to guide their children to the maturity of Christian adulthood and responsible citizenship. Everyone has special duties toward the poor and the marginalized. Living up to these responsibilities, however, is often made difficult by the social and economic patterns of society. Schools and educational policies both public and private often serve the privileged exceedingly well, while the children of the poor are effectively abandoned as second-class citizens. Great stresses are created in family life by the way work is organized and scheduled, and by the social and cultural values communicated on TV. Many in the lower middle class are barely getting by and fear becoming victims of economic forces over which they have no control.

The obligation to provide justice for all means that the poor have the single most urgent economic claim on the conscience of the nation. Poverty can take many forms, spiritual as well as material. All people face struggles of the spirit as they ask deep questions about their purpose in life. Many have serious problems in marriage and family life at some time in their lives, and all of us face the certain reality of sickness and death. The Gospel of Christ proclaims that God's love is stronger than all these forms of diminishment. Material deprivation, however, seriously compounds such sufferings of the spirit and heart. To see a loved one sick is bad enough, but to have no possibility of obtaining health care is worse. To face family problems, such as the death of a spouse or a divorce, can be devastating, but to have these lead to the loss of one's home and end with living on the streets is something no one should have to endure in a country as rich as

---

[k]St. Cyprian, *On Works and Almsgiving*, 25, trans. R.J. Deferrari, *St. Cyprian: Treatises*, 36 (New York: Fathers of the Church, 1958), 251. Original text in Migne, *Patrologia Latina*, vol. 4, 620. On the Patristic teaching, see C. Avila, *Ownership: Early Christian Teaching* (Maryknoll, N.Y.: Orbis Books, 1983). Collection of original texts and translations.

[l]*Mater et Magistra*, 65.

ours. In developing countries these human problems are even more greatly intensified by extreme material deprivation. This form of human suffering can be reduced if our own country, so rich in resources, chooses to increase its assistance.

As individuals and as a nation, therefore, we are called to make a fundamental "option for the poor."[m] The obligation to evaluate social and economic activity from the viewpoint of the poor and the powerless arises from the radical command to love one's neighbor as one's self. Those who are marginalized and whose rights are denied have privileged claims if society is to provide justice for *all*. This obligation is deeply rooted in Christian belief. As Paul VI stated:

> In teaching us charity, the Gospel instructs us in the preferential respect due to the poor and the special situation they have in society: the more fortunate should renounce some of their rights so as to place their goods more generously at the service of others.[n]

John Paul II has described this special obligation to the poor as "a call to have a special openness with the small and the weak, those that suffer and weep, those that are humiliated and left on the margin of society, so as to help them win their dignity as human persons and children of God."[o]

The prime purpose of this special commitment to the poor is to enable them to become active participants in the life of society. It is to enable *all* persons to share in and contribute to the common good.[p] The "option for the poor," therefore, is not an adversarial slogan that pits one group or class against another. Rather it states that the deprivation and powerlessness of the poor wounds the whole community. The extent of their suffering is a measure of how far we are from being a true community of persons. These wounds will be healed only by greater solidarity with the poor and among the poor themselves.

In summary, the norms of love, basic justice, and human rights imply that personal decisions, social policies, and economic institutions should be governed by several key priorities. These priorities do not specify everything that must be considered in economic decision making. They do indicate the most fundamental and urgent objectives.

---

[m]On the recent use of this term see: Congregation for the Doctrine of the Faith, *Instruction on Christian Freedom and Liberation*, 46–50, 66–68; *Evangelization in Latin America's Present and Future*, Final Document of the Third General Conference of the Latin American Episcopate (Puebla, Mexico, January 27–February 13, 1979), esp. part VI, ch. 1, "A Preferential Option for the Poor," in J. Eagleson and P. Scharper, eds., *Puebla and Beyond* (Maryknoll: Orbis Books, 1979), 264–267; Donal Dorr, *Option for the Poor: A Hundred Years of Vatican Social Teaching* (Dublin: Gill and Macmillan/Maryknoll, N.Y.: Orbis Books, 1983).

[n]*Octogesima Adveniens*, 23.

[o]Address to Bishops of Brazil, 6, 9, *Origins* 10:9 (July 31, 1980): 135.

[p]Pope John Paul II, Address to Workers at Sao Paulo, 4, *Origins*, 10:9 (July 31, 1980): 138; Congregation for the Doctrine of the Faith, *Instruction on Christian Freedom and Liberation*, 66–68.

a. *The fulfillment of the basic needs of the poor is of the highest priority.* Personal decisions, policies of private and public bodies, and power relationships must all be evaluated by their effects on those who lack the minimum necessities of nutrition, housing, education, and health care. In particular, this principle recognizes that meeting fundamental human needs must come before the fulfillment of desires for luxury consumer goods, for profits not conducive to the common good, and for unnecessary military hardware.

b. *Increasing active participation in economic life by those who are presently excluded or vulnerable is a high social priority.* The human dignity of all is realized when people gain the power to work together to improve their lives, strengthen their families, and contribute to society. Basic justice calls for more than providing help to the poor and other vulnerable members of society. It recognizes the priority of policies and programs that support family life and enhance economic participation through employment and widespread ownership of property. It challenges privileged economic power in favor of the well-being of all. It points to the need to improve the present situation of those unjustly discriminated against in the past. And it has very important implications for both the domestic and the international distribution of power.

c. *The investment of wealth, talent, and human energy should be specially directed to benefit those who are poor or economically insecure.* Achieving a more just economy in the United States and the world depends in part on increasing economic resources and productivity. In addition, the ways these resources are invested and managed must be scrutinized in light of their effects on non-monetary values. Investment and management decisions have crucial moral dimensions: they create jobs or eliminate them; they can push vulnerable families over the edge into poverty or give them new hope for the future; they help or hinder the building of a more equitable society. Indeed they can have either positive or negative influence on the fairness of the global economy. Therefore, this priority presents a strong moral challenge to policies that put large amounts of talent and capital into the production of luxury consumer goods and military technology while failing to invest sufficiently in education, health, the basic infrastructure of our society, and economic sectors that produce urgently needed jobs, goods, and services.

d. *Economic and social policies as well as the organization of the work world should be continually evaluated in light of their impact on the strength and stability of family life.* The long-range future of this nation is intimately linked with the well-being of families, for the family is the most basic form of human community.[q] Efficiency and competition in the marketplace must be moderated by greater concern for the way work schedules and compensation support or threaten the bonds between spouses and between parents and children. Health, education, and

---

[q]*Pastoral Constitution*, 47.

social service programs should be scrutinized in light of how well they ensure both individual dignity and family integrity.

These priorities are not policies. They are norms that should guide the economic choices of all and shape economic institutions. They can help the United States move forward to fulfill the duties of justice and protect economic rights. They were strongly affirmed as implications of Catholic social teaching by Pope John Paul II during his visit to Canada in 1984: "The needs of the poor take priority over the desires of the rich; the rights of workers over the maximization of profits; the preservation of the environment over uncontrolled industrial expansion; production to meet social needs over production for military purposes."[r] There will undoubtedly be disputes about the concrete applications of these priorities in our complex world. We do not seek to foreclose discussion about them. However, we believe that an effort to move in the direction they indicate is urgently needed.

The economic challenge of today has many parallels with the political challenge that confronted the founders of our nation. In order to create a new form of political democracy they were compelled to develop ways of thinking and political institutions that had never existed before. Their efforts were arduous and their goals imperfectly realized, but they launched an experiment in the protection of civil and political rights that has prospered through the efforts of those who came after them. *We believe the time has come for a similar experiment in securing economic rights: the creation of an order that guarantees the minimum conditions of human dignity in the economic sphere for every person.* By drawing on the resources of the Catholic moral-religious tradition, we hope to make a contribution through this letter to such a new "American Experiment": a new venture to secure economic justice for all. . . .

OWNERS AND MANAGERS

The economy's success in fulfilling the demands of justice will depend on how its vast resources and wealth are managed. Property owners, managers, and investors of financial capital must all contribute to creating a more just society. Securing economic justice depends heavily on the leadership of men and women in business and on wise investment by private enterprises. Pope John Paul II has pointed out, "The degree of well-being which society today enjoys would be unthinkable without the dynamic figure of the business person, whose function consists of organizing human labor and the means of production so as to give rise to the goods and services necessary for the prosperity and progress of the

---

[r]Address on Christian Unity in a Technological Age (Toronto, September 14, 1984) in *Origins* 14:16 (October 4, 1984):248.

community."[s] The freedom of entrepreneurship, business, and finance should be protected, but the accountability of this freedom to the common good and the norms of justice must be assured.

Persons in management face many hard choices each day, choices on which the well-being of many others depends. Commitment to the public good and not simply the private good of their firms is at the heart of what it means to call their work a vocation and not simply a career or a job. We believe that the norms and priorities discussed in this letter can be of help as they pursue their important tasks. The duties of individuals in the business world, however, do not exhaust the ethical dimensions of business and finance. The size of a firm or bank is in many cases an indicator of relative power. Large corporations and large financial institutions have considerable power to help shape economic institutions within the United States and throughout the world. With this power goes responsibility and the need for those who manage it to be held to moral and institutional accountability.

Business and finance have the duty to be faithful trustees of the resources at their disposal. No one can ever own capital resources absolutely or control their use without regard for others and society as a whole.[t] This applies first of all to land and natural resources. Short-term profits reaped at the cost of depletion of natural resources or the pollution of the environment violate this trust.

Resources created by human industry are also held in trust. Owners and managers have not created this capital on their own. They have benefited from the work of many others and from the local communities that support their endeavors.[u] They are accountable to these workers and communities when making decisions. For example, reinvestment in technological innovation is often crucial for the long-term viability of a firm. The use of financial resources solely in pursuit of short-term profits can stunt the production of needed goods and services; a broader vision of managerial responsibility is needed.

The Catholic tradition has long defended the right to private ownership of productive property.[v] This right is an important element in a just economic policy. It enlarges our capacity for creativity and initiative.[w] Small and medium-sized farms, businesses, and entrepreneurial enterprises are among the most creative and efficient sectors of our economy. They should be highly valued by the people of the United States, as are land ownership and home ownership. Widespread distribution of property can help avoid excessive concentration of economic and

---

[s]Pope John Paul II, Address to Business Men and Economic Managers (Milan, May 22, 1983) in *L'Osservatore Romano,* weekly edition in English (June 20, 1983): 9:1.

[t]Thomas Aquinas, *Summa Theologiae,* IIa, IIae, q. 66.

[u]As Pope John Paul II has stated: "This gigantic and powerful instrument—the whole collection of the means of production that in a sense are considered synonymous with 'capital'—is the result of work and bears the signs of human labor" *On Human Work,* 12.

[v]*Rerum Novarum,* 10, 15, 36.

[w]*Mater et Magistra,* 109.

political power. For these reasons ownership should be made possible for a broad sector of our population.ˣ

The common good may sometimes demand that the right to own be limited by public involvement in the planning or ownership of certain sectors of the economy. Support of private ownership does not mean that anyone has the right to unlimited accumulation of wealth. "Private property does not constitute for anyone an absolute or unconditioned right. No one is justified in keeping for his exclusive use what he does not need, when others lack necessities."ʸ Pope John Paul II has referred to limits placed on ownership by the duty to serve the common good as a "social mortgage" on private property.ᶻ For example, these limits are the basis of society's exercise of eminent domain over privately owned land needed for roads or other essential public goods. The Church's teaching opposes collectivist and statist economic approaches. But it also rejects the notion that a free market automatically produces justice. Therefore, as Pope John Paul II has argued, "One cannot exclude the socialization, in suitable conditions, of certain means of production."ᴬ The determination of when such conditions exist must be made on a case by case basis in light of the demands of the common good.

CITIZENS AND GOVERNMENT

In addition to rights and duties related to specific roles in the economy, everyone has obligations based simply on membership in the social community. By fulfilling these duties, we create a true commonwealth. Volunteering time, talent, and money to work for greater justice is a fundamental expression of Christian love and social solidarity. All who have more than they need must come to the aid of the poor. People with professional or technical skills needed to enhance the lives of others have a duty to share them. And the poor have similar obligations: to work together as individuals and families to build up their communities by acts of social solidarity and justice. These voluntary efforts to overcome injustice are part of the Christian vocation. . . .

The traditional distinction between society and the state in Catholic social teaching provides the basic framework for such organized public efforts. The Church opposes all statist and totalitarian approaches to socioeconomic questions. Social life is richer than governmental power can encompass. All groups that compose society have responsibilities to respond to the demands of justice. We have just outlined some of the duties of labor unions and business and financial

---

ˣ*Rerum Novarum*, 65, 66; *Mater et Magistra*, 115.

ʸ*On the Development of Peoples*, 23.

ᶻPope John Paul II, Opening Address at the Puebla Conference (Puebla, Mexico, January 28, 1979) in John Eagleson and Philip Scharper, eds., *Puebla and Beyond*, 67.

ᴬ*On Human Work*, 14.

enterprises. These must be supplemented by initiatives by local community groups, professional associations, educational institutions, churches, and synagogues. All the groups that give life to this society have important roles to play in the pursuit of economic justice.

For this reason, it is all the more significant that the teachings of the Church insist that *government has a moral function: protecting human rights and securing basic justice for all members of the commonwealth.*[B] Society as a whole and in all its diversity is responsible for building up the common good. But it is government's role to guarantee the minimum conditions that make this rich social activity possible, namely, human rights and justice.[C] This obligation also falls on individual citizens as they choose their representatives and participate in shaping public opinion.

More specifically, it is the responsibility of all citizens, acting through their government, to assist and empower the poor, the disadvantaged, the handicapped, and the unemployed. Government should assume a positive role in generating employment and establishing fair labor practices, in guaranteeing the provision and maintenance of the economy's infrastructure, such as roads, bridges, harbors, public means of communication, and transport. It should regulate trade and commerce in the interest of fairness.[D] Government may levy the taxes necessary to meet these responsibilities, and citizens have a moral obligation to pay those taxes. The way society responds to the needs of the poor through its public policies is the litmus test of its justice or injustice. The political debate about these policies is the indispensable forum for dealing with the conflicts and tradeoffs that will always be present in the pursuit of a more just economy.

The primary norm for determining the scope and limits of governmental intervention is the "principle of subsidiarity" cited above. This principle states that, in order to protect basic justice, government should undertake only those initiatives which exceed the capacity of individuals or private groups acting indepen-

---

[B]*Peace on Earth*, 60–62.

[C]Vatican Council II, *Declaration on Religious Freedom (Dignitatis Humanae)*, 6. See John Courtney Murray, *The Problem of Religious Freedom*, Woodstock Papers, no. 7 (Westminster, Md.: Newman Press, 1965).

[D]*Peace on Earth*, 63–64. *Quadragesimo Anno*, 80. In *Rerum Novarum* Pope Leo XIII set down the basic norm that determines when government intervention is called for: "If, therefore, any injury has been done to or threatens either the common good or the interests of individual groups, which injury cannot in any other way be repaired or prevented, it is necessary for public authority to intervene" *Rerum Novarum*, 52. Pope John XXIII synthesized the Church's understanding of the function of governmental intervention this way: "The State, whose purpose is the realization of the common good in the temporal order, can by no means disregard the economic activity of its citizens. Indeed it should be present to promote in suitable manner the production of a sufficient supply of material goods, . . . contribute actively to the betterment of the living conditions of workers, . . . see to it that labor agreements are entered into according to the norms of justice and equity, and that in the environment of work the dignity of the human being is not violated either in body or spirit" *Mater et Magistra*, 20–21.

dently. Government should not replace or destroy smaller communities and individual initiative. Rather it should help them to contribute more effectively to social well-being and supplement their activity when the demands of justice exceed their capacities. This does not mean, however, that the government that governs least governs best. Rather it defines good government intervention as that which truly "helps" other social groups contribute to the common good by directing, urging, restraining, and regulating economic activity as "the occasion requires and necessity demands."[E] This calls for cooperation and consensus-building among the diverse agents in our economic life, including government. The precise form of government involvement in this process cannot be determined in the abstract. It will depend on an assessment of specific needs and the most effective ways to address them. . . .

ECONOMIC INEQUALITY

Important to our discussion of poverty in America is an understanding of the degree of economic inequality in our nation. Our economy is marked by a very uneven distribution of wealth and income. For example, it is estimated that 28 percent of the total net wealth is held by the richest 2 percent of families in the United States. The top ten percent holds 57 percent of the net wealth.[F] If homes and other real estate are excluded, the concentration of ownership of "financial wealth" is even more glaring. In 1983, 54 percent of the total net financial assets were held by 2 percent of all families, those whose annual income is over $125,000. Eighty-six percent of these assets were held by the top 10 percent of all families.[G]

Although disparities in the distribution of income are less extreme, they are still striking. In 1984 the bottom 20 percent of American families received only 4.7 percent of the total income in the nation and the bottom 40 percent received only 15.7 percent, the lowest share on record in U.S. history. In contrast, the top one-fifth received 42.9 percent of the total income, the highest share since 1948.[H] These figures are only partial and very imperfect measures of the inequality in our society.[I] However, they do suggest that the degree of inequality is quite large. In comparison with other industrialized nations, the United States is among the

---

[E] *Quadragesimo Anno,* 79.

[F]Federal Reserve Board, "Survey of Consumer Finances, 1983: A Second Report," reprint from the *Federal Reserve Bulletin* (Washington, D.C., December 1984), 857–868. This survey defines net worth as the difference between gross assets and gross liabilities. The survey's estimates include all financial assets, equity in homes and other real property, as well as all financial liabilities such as consumer credit and other debts.

[G]Ibid., 863–864.

[H]U.S. Bureau of the Census, series P-60, no. 149, 11.

[I]Income distribution figures give only a static picture of income shares. They do not reflect the significant movement of families in and out of different income categories over an extended period

more unequal in terms of income distribution.ᴶ Moreover, the gap between rich and poor in our nation has increased during the last decade.ᴷ These inequities are of particular concern because they reflect the uneven distribution of power in our society. They suggest that the level of participation in the political and social spheres is also very uneven.

Catholic social teaching does not require absolute equality in the distribution of income and wealth. Some degree of inequality not only is acceptable, but also may be considered desirable for economic and social reasons, such as the need for incentives and the provision of greater rewards for greater risks. However, unequal distribution should be evaluated in terms of several moral principles we have enunciated: the priority of meeting the basic needs of the poor and the importance of increasing the level of participation by all members of society in the economic life of the nation. These norms establish a strong presumption against *extreme* inequality of income and wealth as long as there are poor, hungry, and homeless people in our midst. They also suggest that *extreme* inequalities are detrimental to the development of social solidarity and community. In view of these norms we find the disparities of income and wealth in the United States to be unacceptable. Justice requires that all members of our society work for economic, political, and social reforms that will decrease these inequities.

GUIDELINES FOR ACTION

Our recommendations for dealing with poverty in the United States build upon several moral principles that were explored in chapter two of this letter. The themes of human dignity and the preferential option for the poor are at the heart of our approach; they compel us to confront the issue of poverty with a real sense of urgency.

The principle of social solidarity suggests that alleviating poverty will require fundamental changes in social and economic structures that perpetuate glaring inequalities and cut off millions of citizens from full participation in the economic and social life of the nation. The process of change should be one that draws together all citizens, whatever their economic status, into one community.

The principle of participation leads us to the conviction that the most appro-

---

of time. See *Years of Poverty, Years of Plenty,* 13. It should also be noted that these figures reflect pre-tax incomes. However, since the national tax structure is proportional for a large segment of the population, it does not have a significant impact on the distribution of income. See Joseph Pechman, *Who Paid Taxes, 1966–85?* (Washington, D.C.: The Brookings Institution, 1985), 51.

ᴶLars Osberg, *Economic Inequality in the United States* (New York: M. E. Sharpe, Inc., 1984), 24–28.

ᴷU.S. Bureau of the Census, series P-60, no. 149, 11.

priate and fundamental solutions to poverty will be those that enable people to take control of their own lives. For poverty is not merely the lack of adequate financial resources. It entails a more profound kind of deprivation, a denial of full participation in the economic, social, and political life of society and an inability to influence decisions that affect one's life. It means being powerless in a way that assaults not only one's pocketbook but also one's fundamental human dignity. Therefore, we should seek solutions that enable the poor to help themselves through such means as employment. Paternalistic programs which do too much *for* and too little *with* the poor are to be avoided.

The responsibility for alleviating the plight of the poor falls upon all members of society. As individuals, all citizens have a duty to assist the poor through acts of charity and personal commitment. But private charity and voluntary action are not sufficient. We also carry out our moral responsibility to assist and empower the poor by working collectively through government to establish just and effective public policies. . . .

We now wish to propose several elements which we believe are necessary for a national strategy to deal with poverty. We offer this not as a comprehensive list but as an invitation for others to join the discussion and take up the task of fighting poverty.

a. *The first line of attack against poverty must be to build and sustain a healthy economy that provides employment opportunities at just wages for all adults who are able to work.* Poverty is intimately linked to the issue of employment. Millions are poor because they have lost their jobs or because their wages are too low. The persistent high levels of unemployment during the last decade are a major reason why poverty has increased in recent years.[L] Expanded employment especially in the private sector would promote human dignity, increase social solidarity, and promote self-reliance of the poor. It should also reduce the need for welfare programs and generate the income necessary to support those who remain in need and cannot work: elderly, disabled, and chronically ill people, and single parents of young children. It should also be recognized that the persistence of poverty harms the larger society because the depressed purchasing power of the poor contributes to the periodic cycles of stagnation in the economy.

In recent years the minimum wage has not been adjusted to keep pace with inflation. Its real value has declined by 24 percent since 1981. We believe Congress should raise the minimum wage in order to restore some of the purchasing power it has lost due to inflation.

While job creation and just wages are major elements of a national strategy against poverty, they are clearly not enough. Other more specific policies are necessary to remedy the institutional causes of poverty and to provide for those who cannot work.

[L]"The Poverty of Losing Ground," 32–38.

b. *Vigorous action should be undertaken to remove barriers to full and equal employment for women and minorities.* Too many women and minorities are locked into jobs with low pay, poor working conditions, and little opportunity for career advancement. So long as we tolerate a situation in which people can work full-time and still be below the poverty line—a situation common among those earning the minimum wage—too many will continue to be counted among the "working poor." Concerted efforts must be made through job training, affirmative action, and other means to assist those now prevented from obtaining more lucrative jobs. Action should also be taken to upgrade poorer paying jobs and to correct wage differentials that discriminate unjustly against women.

c. *Self-help efforts among the poor should be fostered by programs and policies in both the private and public sectors.* We believe that an effective way to attack poverty is through programs that are small in scale, locally based, and oriented toward empowering the poor to become self-sufficient. Corporations, private organizations, and the public sector can provide seed money, training and technical assistance, and organizational support for self-help projects in a wide variety of areas such as low-income housing, credit unions, worker cooperatives, legal assistance, and neighborhood and community organizations. Efforts that enable the poor to participate in the ownership and control of economic resources are especially important.

Poor people must be empowered to take charge of their own futures and become responsible for their own economic advancement. Personal motivation and initiative, combined with social reform, are necessary elements to assist individuals in escaping poverty. By taking advantage of opportunities for education, employment, and training, and by working together for change, the poor can help themselves to be full participants in our economic, social, and political life.

d. *The tax system should be continually evaluated in terms of its impact on the poor.* This evaluation should be guided by three principles. First, the tax system should raise adequate revenues to pay for the public needs of society, especially to meet the basic needs of the poor. Secondly, the tax system should be structured according to the principle of progressivity, so that those with relatively greater financial resources pay a higher rate of taxation. The inclusion of such a principle in tax policies is an important means of reducing the severe inequalities of income and wealth in the nation. Action should be taken to reduce or offset the fact that most sales taxes and payroll taxes place a disproportionate burden on those with lower incomes. Thirdly, families below the official poverty line should not be required to pay income taxes. Such families are, by definition, without sufficient resources to purchase the basic necessities of life. They should not be forced to bear the additional burden of paying income taxes.[M]

[M]The tax reform legislation of 1986 did a great deal to achieve this goal. It removed from the federal income tax rules virtually all families below the official poverty line.

e. *All of society should make a much stronger commitment to education for the poor.* Any long-term solution to poverty in this country must pay serious attention to education, public and private, in school and out of school. Lack of adequate education, especially in the inner city setting, prevents many poor people from escaping poverty. In addition, illiteracy, a problem that affects tens of millions of Americans, condemns many to joblessness or chronically low wages. Moreover, it excludes them in many ways from sharing in the political and spiritual life of the community. [N] Since poverty is fundamentally a problem of powerlessness and marginalization, the importance of education as a means of overcoming it cannot be overemphasized. . . .

f. *Policies and programs at all levels should support the strength and stability of families, especially those adversely affected by the economy.* As a nation, we need to examine all aspects of economic life and assess their effects on families. Employment practices, health insurance policies, income security programs, tax policy, and service programs can either support or undermine the abilities of families to fulfill their roles in nurturing children and caring for infirm and dependent family members. . . .

g. *A thorough reform of the nation's welfare and income-support programs should be undertaken.* For millions of poor Americans the only economic safety net is the public welfare system. The programs that make up this system should serve the needs of the poor in a manner that respects their dignity and provides adequate support. In our judgment the present welfare system does not adequately meet these criteria.[O] We believe that several improvements can and should be made within the framework of existing welfare programs. However, in the long run, more far-reaching reforms that go beyond the present system will be necessary. Among the immediate improvements that could be made are the following:

(1) *Public assistance programs should be designed to assist recipients, wherever possible, to become self-sufficient through gainful employment.* Individuals should not be worse off economically when they get jobs than when they rely only on public assistance. Under current rules, people who give up welfare benefits to work in low-paying jobs soon lose their Medicaid benefits. To help recipients become self-sufficient and reduce dependency on welfare, public assistance programs should work in tandem with job creation programs that include provisions for training, counseling, placement, and child care. Jobs for recipients of public assistance should be fairly compensated so that workers receive the full benefits and status associated with gainful employment.

(2) *Welfare programs should provide recipients with adequate levels of support.*

[N]Jonathan Kozol, *Illiterate America* (New York: Anchor Press/Doubleday, 1985).

[O]H.R. Rodgers, Jr., *The Cost of Human Neglect: America's Welfare* (Armonk, N.Y.: W.E. Sharpe, Inc., 1982); C.T. Waxman, *The Stigma of Poverty*, second edition (New York: Pergamon Press, 1983), especially ch. 5; and S. A. Levitan and C. M. Johnson, *Beyond the Safety Net: Reviving the Promise of Opportunity in America* (Cambridge, Mass.: Ballinger, 1984).

This support should cover basic needs in food, clothing, shelter, health care, and other essentials. At present only 4 percent of poor families with children receive enough cash welfare benefits to lift them out of poverty.[P] The combined benefits of AFDC and food stamps typically come to less than three-fourths of the official poverty level.[Q] Those receiving public assistance should not face the prospect of hunger at the end of the month, homelessness, sending children to school in ragged clothing, or inadequate medical care.

(3) *National eligibility standards and a national minimum benefit level for public assistance programs should be established.* Currently welfare eligibility and benefits vary greatly among states. In 1985 a family of three with no earnings had a maximum AFDC benefit of $96 a month in Mississippi and $558 a month in Vermont.[R] To remedy these great disparities, which are far larger than the regional differences in the cost of living, and to assure a floor of benefits for all needy people, our nation should establish and fund national minimum benefit levels and eligibility standards in cash assistance programs.[S] The benefits should also be indexed to reflect changes in the cost of living. These changes reflect standards that our nation has already put in place for aged and disabled people and veterans. Is it not possible to do the same for the children and their mothers who receive public assistance?

(4) *Welfare programs should be available to two-parent as well as single-parent families.* Most states now limit participation in AFDC to families headed by single parents, usually women.[T] The coverage of this program should be extended to two-parent families so that fathers who are unemployed or poorly paid do not have to leave home in order for their children to receive help. Such a change would be a significant step toward strengthening two-parent families who are poor.

[P]*Children in Poverty.*

[Q]U.S. House of Representative Committee on Ways and Means, *Background Materials and Data on Programs Within the Jurisdiction of the Committee on Ways and Means* (Washington, D. C., February 22, 1985). 345–346

[R]Ibid., 347–348.

[S]In 1982, similar recommendations were made by eight former Secretaries of Health, Education, and Welfare (now Health and Human Services). In a report called "Welfare Policy in the United States," they suggested a number of ways in which national minimal standards might be set and strongly urged the establishment of a floor for all states and territories.

[T]Committee on Ways and Means, *Background Materials and Data on Programs.*

CHAPTER *15*

Socialist Thought—New Trends: "Perestroika"

Established Marxist countries of the East appear to be rapidly moving away from what has hitherto been perceived as Marxist orthodoxy. In recent years both China and the U.S.S.R. have taken major steps away from past practice. If, after all the change underway now, socialism still remains, it will be at the very least a new variant for those countries.

In the eighties and nineties, Soviet leader Mikhail Gorbachev fascinated both his own people and those of the predominantly capitalist West with his program of "perestroika." The word means "restructuring," and truly it is an ambitious program of change that Gorbachev is pushing upon the Soviet system.

Gorbachev's more or less articulated major premise is that Marxist socialism has failed to achieve the gains in economic efficiency and human happiness promised in revolutionary ideology. Sensing that if trends are not reversed, major social, economic, and political upheavals loom on the horizon, Gorbachev calls for restructuring now. More decentralized economic production management, more democracy, more "openness" (*glasnost*), more *economic justice*—these are major planks in Gorbachev's perestroika platform.

For all the radicalness of his proposals, however, Gorbachev denies that he advocates the abandonment of Marxist socialism for something resembling Western capitalist forms. "Just think," he asks, "how can we agree that 1917 was a mistake and all the seventy years of our life, work, and battles were also a complete mistake, that we were going in the 'wrong direction'?"

Does Gorbachev perhaps protest too much? Even if he favored capitalism for Russia, he could not admit it. But whatever we may think of Gorbachev's real intentions, it is striking how he has redefined *socialism*, equating the word with *democracy*. And it is difficult not to be impressed with the boldness of this daring man whose dynamic speeches and deeds have ignited the Marxist East with new and great expectations.

Perestroika

Mikhail Gorbachev

I think one thing should be borne in mind when studying the origins and essence of perestroika in the USSR. Perestroika is no whim on the part of some ambitious individuals or a group of leaders. If it were, no exhortations, plenary meetings or even a party congress could have rallied the people to the work which we are now doing and which involves more and more Soviet people each day.

Perestroika is an urgent necessity arising from the profound processes of development in our socialist society. This society is ripe for change. It has long been yearning for it. Any delay in beginning perestroika could have led to an exacerbated internal situation in the near future, which, to put it bluntly, would have been fraught with serious social, economic and political crises.

We have drawn these conclusions from a broad and frank analysis of the situation that has developed in our society by the middle of the eighties. This situation and the problems arising from it presently confront the country's leadership, in which new people have gradually appeared in the last few years. I would like to discuss here the main results of this analysis, in the course of which we had to reassess many things and look back at our history, both recent and not so recent. . . .

At some stage—this became particularly clear in the latter half of the seventies—something happened that was at first sight inexplicable. The country began to lose momentum. Economic failures became more frequent. Difficulties began to accumulate and deteriorate, and unresolved problems to multiply. Elements of what we call stagnation and other phenomena alien to socialism began to appear in the life of society. A kind of "braking mechanism" affecting social and economic development formed. And all this happened at a time when scientific and technological revolution opened up new prospects for economic and social progress.

Something strange was taking place: the huge fly-wheel of a powerful machine was revolving, while either transmission from it to work places was skidding or drive belts were too loose.

Analyzing the situation, we first discovered a slowing economic growth. In the last fifteen years the national income growth rates had declined by more than a half and by the beginning of the eighties had fallen to a level close to economic stagnation. A country that was once quickly closing on the world's advanced nations began to lose one position after another. Moreover, the gap in the efficiency of production, quality of products, scientific and technological development, the production of advanced technology and the use of advanced techniques began to widen, and not to our advantage.

The gross output drive, particularly in heavy industry, turned out to be a "top-priority" task, just an end in itself. The same happened in capital construction, where a sizable portion of the national wealth became idle capital. There were costly projects that never lived up to the highest scientific and technological standards. The worker or the enterprise that had expended the greatest amount of labor, material and money was considered the best. It is natural for the producer to "please" the consumer, if I may put it that way. With us, however, the consumer found himself totally at the mercy of the producer and had to make do with what the latter chose to give him. This was again a result of the gross output drive.

It became typical of many of our economic executives to think not of how to build up the national asset, but of how to put more material, labor and working time into an item to sell it at a higher price. Consequently, for all "gross output," there was a shortage of goods. We spent, in fact we are still spending, far more on raw materials, energy and other resources per unit of output than other developed nations. Our country's wealth in terms of natural and manpower resources has spoilt, one may even say corrupted, us. That, in fact, is chiefly the reason why it was possible for our economy to develop extensively for decades.

Accustomed to giving priority to quantitative growth in production, we tried to check the falling rates of growth, but did so mainly by continually increasing expenditures: we built up the fuel and energy industries and increased the use of natural resources in production.

As time went on, material resources became harder to get and more expensive. On the other hand, the extensive methods of fixed capital expansion resulted in an artificial shortage of manpower. In an attempt to rectify the situation somehow, large, unjustified, i.e., in fact unearned, bonuses began to be paid and all kinds of undeserved incentives introduced under the pressure of this shortage, and that led, at a later stage, to the practice of padding reports merely for gain. Parasitical attitudes were on the rise, the prestige of conscientious and high-quality labor began to diminish and a "wage-leveling" mentality was becoming widespread. The imbalance between the measure of work and the measure of consumption, which had become something like the linchpin of the braking mechanism, not only obstructed the growth of labor productivity, but led to the distortion of the principle of social justice.

So the inertia of extensive economic development was leading to an economic deadlock and stagnation. . . .

This, unfortunately, is not all. A gradual erosion of the ideological and moral values of our people began.

It was obvious to everyone that the growth rates were sharply dropping and that the entire mechanism of quality control was not working properly; there was a lack of receptivity to the advances in science and technology; the improvement in living standards was slowing down and there were difficulties in the supply of foodstuffs, housing, consumer goods and services.

On the ideological plane as well, the braking mechanism brought about ever greater resistance to the attempts to constructively scrutinize the problems that were emerging and to the new ideas. Propaganda of success—real or imagined—was gaining the upper hand. Eulogizing and servility were encouraged; the needs and opinions of ordinary working people, of the public at large, were ignored. In the social sciences scholastic theorization was encouraged and developed, but creative thinking was driven out from the social sciences, and superfluous and voluntarist assessments and judgments were declared indisputable truths. Scientific, theoretical and other discussions, which are indispensable for the development of thought and for creative endeavor, were emasculated. Similar negative tendencies also affected culture, the arts and journalism, as well as the teaching process and medicine, where mediocrity, formalism and loud eulogizing surfaced, too.

The presentation of a "problem-free" reality backfired: a breach had formed between word and deed, which bred public passivity and disbelief in the slogans being proclaimed. It was only natural that this situation resulted in a credibility gap: everything that was proclaimed from the rostrums and printed in newspapers and textbooks was put in question. Decay began in public morals; the great feeling of solidarity with each other that was forged during the heroic times of the Revolution, the first five-year plans, the Great Patriotic War and postwar rehabilitation was weakening; alcoholism, drug addiction and crime were growing; and the penetration of the stereotypes of mass culture alien to us, which bred vulgarity and low tastes and brought about ideological barrenness, increased.

Party guidance was relaxed, and initiative lost in some of the vital social processes. Everybody started noticing the stagnation among the leadership and the violation of the natural process of change there. At a certain stage this made for a poorer performance by the Politburo and the Secretariat of the CPSU Central Committee, by the government and throughout the entire Central Committee and the Party apparatus, for that matter.

Political flirtation and mass distribution of awards, titles and bonuses often replaced genuine concern for the people, for their living and working conditions, for a favorable social atmosphere. An atmosphere emerged of "everything goes," and fewer and fewer demands were made on discipline and responsibility. Attempts were made to cover it all up with pompous campaigns and undertakings and celebrations of numerous anniversaries centrally and locally. The world of day-to-day realities and the world of feigned prosperity were diverging more and more.

Many Party organizations in the regions were unable to uphold principles or to attack with determination bad tendencies, slack attitudes, the practice of covering up for one another and lax discipline. More often than not, the principles of equality among Party members were violated. Many Party members in leading posts stood beyond control and criticism, which led to failures in work and to serious malpractices.

At some administrative levels there emerged a disrespect for the law and encouragement of eyewash and bribery, servility and glorification. Working people were justly indignant at the behavior of people who, enjoying trust and responsibility, abused power, suppressed criticism, made fortunes and, in some cases, even became accomplices in—if not organizers of—criminal acts.

In fairness, it must be said that over those years many vitally important issues were also resolved, one way or another. But, first, those were just a few of the problems which had long demanded attention, and, second, even where decisions were taken, they were only partially enacted, or not at all. And, most significantly, none of those measures were comprehensive; they affected only some aspects of the life of society, while leaving the existing braking mechanism intact. . . .

The need for change was brewing not only in the material sphere of life but also in public consciousness. People who had practical experience, a sense of justice and commitment to the ideals of Bolshevism criticized the established practice of doing things and noted with anxiety the symptoms of moral degradation and erosion of revolutionary ideals and socialist values.

Workers, farmers and intellectuals, Party functionaries centrally and locally, came to ponder the situation in the country. There was a growing awareness that things could not go on like this much longer. Perplexity and indignation welled up that the great values born of the October Revolution and the heroic struggle for socialism were being trampled underfoot.

All honest people saw with bitterness that people were losing interest in social affairs, that labor no longer had its respectable status, that people, especially the young, were after profit at all cost. Our people have always had an intrinsic ability to discern the gap between word and deed. No wonder Russian folk tales are full of mockery aimed against people who like pomp and trappings; and literature, which has always played a great role in our country's spiritual life, is merciless to every manifestation of injustice and abuse of power. In their best works writers, film-makers, theater producers and actors tried to boost people's belief in the ideological achievements of socialism and hope for a spiritual revival of society and, despite bureaucratic bans and even persecution, prepared people morally for perestroika.

By saying all this I want to make the reader understand that the energy for revolutionary change has been accumulating amid our people and in the Party for some time. And the ideas of perestroika have been prompted not just by pragmatic interests and considerations but also by our troubled conscience, by the indomitable commitment to ideals which we inherited from the Revolution and as a result of a theoretical quest which gave us a better knowledge of society and reinforced our determination to go ahead. . . .

The first question to arise was one of improving the economic situation, stopping and reversing the unfavorable trends in that sphere.

The most immediate priority, which we naturally first looked to, was to put the economy into some kind of order, to tighten up discipline, to raise the level of organization and responsibility, and to catch up in areas where we were behind. A great deal of hard work was done and, for that matter, is continuing. As expected, it has produced its first results. The rates of economic growth have stopped declining and are even showing some signs of improvement.

To be sure, we saw that these means alone would not impart a great dynamism to the economy. The principal priorities are known to lie elsewhere—in a profound structural reorganization of the economy, in reconstruction of its material base, in new technologies, in investment policy changes, and in high standards in management. All that adds up to one thing—acceleration of scientific and technological progress. . . .

The economy has, of course, been and remains our main concern. But at the same time we have set about changing the moral and psychological situation in society. Back in the 1970s many people realized that we could not do without drastic changes in thinking and psychology, in the organization, style and methods of work everywhere—in the Party, the state machinery, and upper echelons. And this has happened, in the Party's Central Committee, in the government, as well as elsewhere. Certain personnel changes at all levels were needed. New people took over leadership positions, people who understood the situation well and had ideas as to what should be done and how.

An uncompromising struggle was launched against violations of the principles of socialist justice with no account being taken of who committed these violations. A policy of openness was proclaimed. Those who spoke in favor of Party, government and economic bodies and public organizations conducting their activities openly were allowed to have their say and unwarranted restrictions and bans were removed.

We have come to the conclusion that unless we activate the human factor, that is, unless we take into consideration the diverse interests of people, work collectives, public bodies, and various social groups, unless we rely on them, and draw them into active, constructive endeavor, it will be impossible for us to accomplish any of the tasks set, or to change the situation in the country.

I have long appreciated a remarkable formula advanced by Lenin: socialism is the living creativity of the masses. Socialism is not an *a priori* theoretical scheme, in keeping with which society is divided into two groups: those who give instructions and those who follow them. I am very much against such a simplified and mechanical understanding of socialism.

People, human beings with all their creative diversity, are the makers of history. So the initial task of restructuring—an indispensable condition, necessary if it is to be successful—is to "wake up" those people who have "fallen asleep" and make them truly active and concerned, to ensure that everyone feels as if he is the master of the country, of his enterprise, office, or institute. This is the main thing.

To get the individual involved in all processes is the most important aspect of what we are doing. Perestroika is to provide a "melting-pot" for society and, above all, the individual himself. It will be a renovated society. This is how serious the job is that we have begun to tackle, and it is a very difficult task. But the goal is worth the effort. . . .

To do something better, you must work an extra bit harder. I like this phrase: working an *extra bit harder*. For me it is not just a slogan, but a habitual state of mind, a disposition. Any job one takes on must be grasped and felt with one's soul, mind and heart; only then will one work an extra bit harder.

A weak-spirited person won't work an extra bit harder. On the contrary, he gives in before difficulties, they overwhelm him. But if a person is strong in his convictions and knowledge, is morally strong, he can't be broken, he can weather any storms. We know this from our history.

Today our main job is to lift the individual spiritually, respecting his inner world and giving him moral strength. We are seeking to make the whole intellectual potential of society and all the potentialities of culture work to mold a socially active person, spiritually rich, just and conscientious. An individual must know and feel that his contribution is needed, that his dignity is not being infringed upon, that he is being treated with trust and respect. When an individual sees all this, he is capable of accomplishing much.

Of course, perestroika somehow affects everybody; it jolts many out of their customary state of calm and satisfaction at the existing way of life. Here I think it is appropriate to draw your attention to one specific feature of socialism. I have in mind the high degree of social protection in our society. On the one hand, it is, doubtless, a benefit and a major achievement of ours. On the other, it makes some people spongers.

There is virtually no unemployment. The state has assumed concern for ensuring employment. Even a person dismissed for laziness or a breach of labor discipline must be given another job. Also, wage-leveling has become a regular feature of our everyday life: even if a person is a bad worker, he gets enough to live fairly comfortably. The children of an outright parasite will not be left to the mercy of fate. We have enormous sums of money concentrated in the social funds from which people receive financial assistance. The same funds provide subsidies for the upkeep of kindergartens, orphanages, Young Pioneer houses and other institutions related to children's creativity and sport. Health care is free, and so is education. People are protected from the vicissitudes of life, and we are proud of this.

But we also see that dishonest people try to exploit these advantages of socialism; they know only their rights, but they do not want to know their duties: they work poorly, shirk and drink hard. There are quite a few people who have adapted the existing laws and practices to their own selfish interests. They give little to society, but nevertheless managed to get from it all that is possible and what even seems impossible; they have lived on unearned incomes.

The policy of restructuring puts everything in its place. We are fully restoring the principle of socialism: "From each according to his ability, to each according to his work," and we seek to affirm social justice for all, equal rights for all, one law for all, one kind of discipline for all, and high responsibilities for each. Perestroika raises the level of social responsibility and expectation. The only people to resent the changes are those who believe that they already have what they need, so why should they readjust? But if a person has conscience, if he does not forget about the good of his people, he cannot—and must not—reason in such a way. And then glasnost, or openness, reveals that someone enjoys illegal privileges. We can no longer tolerate stagnation. . . .

It is essential to look ahead. We must have enough political experience, theoretical scope and civic courage to achieve success, to make sure that perestroika meets the high moral standards of socialism.

We need wholesome, full-blooded functioning by all public organizations, all production teams and creative unions, new forms of activity by citizens and the revival of those which have been forgotten. In short, *we need broad democratization of all aspects of society.* That democratization is also the main guarantee that the current processes are irreversible.

We know today that we would have been able to avoid many of these difficulties if the democratic process had developed normally in our country.

We have learned this lesson of our history well and will never forget it. We will now firmly stick to the line that only through the consistent development of the democratic forms inherent in socialism and through the expansion of self-government can we make progress in production, science and technology, culture and art, and in all social spheres. This is the only way we can ensure conscious discipline. Perestroika itself can only come through democracy. Since we see our task as unfolding and utilizing the potential of socialism through the intensification of the human factor, there can be no other way but democratization, including reform of the economic mechanism and management, a reform whose main element is promotion of the role of work collectives.

It is exactly because we place emphasis on the development of socialist democracy that we pay so much attention to the intellectual sphere, public consciousness and an active social policy. Thereby we want to invigorate the human factor.

In the West, Lenin is often portrayed as an advocate of authoritarian methods of administration. This is a sign of total ignorance of Lenin's ideas and, not infrequently, of their deliberate distortion. In effect, according to Lenin, socialism and democracy are indivisible. By gaining democratic freedoms the working masses come to power. It is also only in conditions of expanding democracy that they can consolidate and realize that power. There is another remarkably true idea of Lenin's: the broader the scope of the work and the deeper the reform, the greater the need to increase the interest in it and convince millions and millions of people of its necessity. This means that if we have set out for a radical and all-round restructuring, we must also unfold the entire potential of democracy.

The democratic process has promoted the entire perestroika, elevated its goals and has made our society understand its problems better. This process allowed us to take a wider view of economic issues, and put forward a program for radical economic reforms. The economic mechanism now well fits the overall system of social management which is based on renewed democratic principles.

We did this work at the June 1987 Plenary Meeting of the CPSU Central Committee, which adopted "Fundamentals of Radical Restructuring of Economic Management." Perhaps this is the most important and most radical program for economic reform our country has had since Lenin introduced his New Economic Policy in 1921. The present economic reform envisages that the emphasis will be shifted from primarily administrative to primarily economic management methods at every level, and calls for extensive democratization of management, and the overall activization of the human factor.

The reform is based on dramatically increased independence of enterprises and associations, their transition to full self-accounting and self-financing, and granting all appropriate rights to work collectives. They will now be fully responsible for efficient management and end results. A collective's profits will be directly proportionate to its efficiency.

In this connection, a radical reorganization of centralized economic management is envisaged in the interests of enterprises. We will free the central management of operational functions in the running of enterprises and this will enable it to concentrate on key processes determining the strategy of economic growth. To make this a reality we launched a serious radical reform in planning, price formation, the financial and crediting mechanism, the network of material and technological production supplies, and management of scientific and technological progress, labor and the social sphere. The aim of this reform is to ensure—within the next two or three years—the transition from an excessively centralized management system relying on orders, to a democratic one, based on the combination of democratic centralism and self-management.

The adoption of fundamental principles for a radical change in economic management was a big step forward in the program of perestroika. Now perestroika concerns virtually every main aspect of public life. Of course, our notions about the contents, methods and forms of perestroika will be developed, clarified and corrected later on. This is inevitable and natural. This is a living process. No doubt, changes will pose new major problems which will require unorthodox solutions. But the overall concept, and the overall plan of perestroika, not only from the point of view of substance, but also of its component parts, are clear to us.

Perestroika means overcoming the stagnation process, breaking down the braking mechanism, creating a dependable and effective mechanism for the acceleration of social and economic progress and giving it greater dynamism.

Perestroika means mass initiative. It is the comprehensive development of democracy, socialist self-government, encouragement of initiative and creative endeavor, improved order and discipline, more glasnost, criticism and self-criticism in all spheres of our society. It is utmost respect for the individual and consideration for personal dignity.

Perestroika is the all-round intensification of the Soviet economy, the revival and development of the principles of democratic centralism in running the national economy, the universal introduction of economic methods, the renunciation of management by injunction and by administrative methods, and the overall encouragement of innovation and socialist enterprise.

Perestroika means a resolute shift to scientific methods, an ability to provide a solid scientific basis for every new initiative. It means the combination of the achievements of the scientific and technological revolution with a planned economy.

Perestroika means priority development of the social sphere aimed at ever better satisfaction of the Soviet people's requirements for good living and working conditions, for good rest and recreation, education and health care. It means unceasing concern for cultural and spiritual wealth, for the culture of every individual and society as a whole.

Perestroika means the elimination from society of the distortions of socialist ethics, the consistent implementation of the principles of social justice. It means the unity of words and deeds, rights and duties. It is the elevation of honest, highly-qualified labor, the overcoming of leveling tendencies in pay and consumerism.

This is how we see perestroika today. This is how we see our tasks, and the substance and content of our work for the forthcoming period. It is difficult now to say how long that period will take. Of course, it will be much more than two or three years. We are ready for serious, strenuous and tedious work to ensure that our country reaches new heights by the end of the twentieth century. . . .

I stress once again: perestroika is not some kind of illumination or revelation. To restructure our life means to understand the objective necessity for renovation and acceleration. And that necessity emerged in the heart of our society. The essence of perestroika lies in the fact that *it unites socialism with democracy* and revives the Leninist concept of socialist construction both in theory and in practice. Such is the essence of perestroika, which accounts for its genuine revolutionary spirit and its all-embracing scope.

The goal is worth the effort. And we are sure that our effort will be a worthy contribution to humanity's social progress. Perestroika is closely connected with socialism as a system. That side of the matter is being widely discussed, especially abroad, and our talk about perestroika won't be entirely clear if we don't touch upon that aspect.

Does perestroika mean that we are giving up socialism or at least some of its foundations? Some ask this question with hope, others with misgiving.

There are people in the West who would like to tell us that socialism is in a deep crisis and has brought our society to a dead end. That's how they interpret our critical analysis of the situation at the end of the seventies and beginning of the eighties. We have only one way out, they say: to adopt capitalist methods of economic management and social patterns, to drift toward capitalism.

They tell us that nothing will come of perestroika within the framework of our system. They say we should change this system and borrow from the experience of another socio-political system. To this they add that, if the Soviet Union takes this path and gives up its socialist choice, close links with the West will supposedly become possible. They go so far as to claim that the October 1917 Revolution was a mistake which almost completely cut off our country from world social progress.

To put an end to all the rumors and speculations that abound in the West about this, I would like to point out once again that we are conducting all our reforms in accordance with the socialist choice. We are looking within socialism, rather than outside it, for the answers to all the questions that arise. We assess our successes and errors alike by socialist standards. Those who hope that we shall move away from the socialist path will be greatly disappointed. Every part of our program of perestroika—and the program as a whole, for that matter—is fully based on the principle of more socialism and more democracy.

More socialism means a more dynamic pace and creative endeavor, more organization, law and order, more scientific methods and initiative in economic management, efficiency in administration, and a better and materially richer life for the people.

More socialism means more democracy, openness and collectivism in everyday life, more culture and humanism in production, social and personal relations among people, more dignity and self-respect for the individual.

More socialism means more patriotism and aspiration to noble ideals, more active civic concern about the country's internal affairs and about their positive influence on international affairs.

In other words, more of all those things which are inherent in socialism and in the theoretical precepts which characterize it as a distinct socio-economic formation.

We will proceed toward better socialism rather than away from it. We are saying this honestly, without trying to fool our own people or the world. Any hopes that we will begin to build a different, non-socialist society and go over to the other camp are unrealistic and futile. Those in the West who expect us to give up socialism will be disappointed. It is high time they understood this, and, even more importantly, proceeded from that understanding in practical relations with the Soviet Union. . . .

We want more socialism and, therefore, more democracy.

As we understand it, the difficulties and problems of the seventies and eighties did not signify some kind of crisis for socialism as a social and political system, but rather were the result of insufficient consistency in applying the principles of socialism, of departures from them and even distortions of them, and of continued adherence to the methods and forms of social management that arose under specific historical conditions in the early stages of socialist development.

On the contrary, socialism as a young social system, as a way of living, possesses vast possibilities for self-development and self-perfection that have yet to be revealed, and for the solution of the fundamental problems of contemporary society's scientific, technological, economic, cultural and intellectual progress, and of the development of the human individual. This is indicated by the path our country has taken since October 1917, a path that has been full of innumerable difficulties, drama and strenuous work, and at the same time full of great triumphs and accomplishments.

. . . . In order to save the revolutionary gains, we had to build—and quickly—a national industrial base with our internal resources, holding down consumption and reducing it to a minimum. The material burden of that new construction fell on the people, of whom the peasants formed the bulk.

In effect, we had to build up industry, especially heavy industry and the power and machine-building industries, from scratch. And we set out boldly to accomplish this task. The viability of the Party's plans, which the masses understood and accepted, and of the slogans and projects permeated with the ideological energy of our revolution manifested itself in the enthusiasm with which millions of Soviet people joined in the efforts to build up national industry. And that enthusiasm astounded the world. Under incredibly trying conditions, often far away from their homes, usually without any machinery, and half-fed, they worked wonders, so to say, out of nothing, from scratch. They drew inspiration from the fact that theirs was a great and historic cause. Although not very literate, they realized what a grand and unique job they were doing. That was truly a great feat in the name of their motherland's future and a demonstration of the people's loyalty to the free choice which they had made in 1917.

And we cannot but mention one more aspect of the matter which is frequently ignored or hushed up in the West, but without which it is simply impossible to understand us, Soviet people; along with the economic and social achievements, there was also a new life, there was the enthusiasm of the builders of a new world, an inspiration from things new and unusual, a keen feeling of pride that we alone, unassisted and not for the first time, were raising the country on our shoulders. People thirsted for knowledge and culture and mastered them. They rejoiced at life, reared their children, and did their day-to-day chores. All this we did in an entirely new atmosphere which differed greatly from what had been before the Revolution, in an atmosphere of ease, equality and immense opportunities for the working people. We know very well what we received from socialism. In short, people lived and worked creatively at all stages of the peaceful development of our country. Letters which I receive from my compatriots say proudly: sure, we were poorer than others, but our life was more full-blooded and interesting.

Fourteen out of fifteen citizens living in the USSR today were born after the Revolution. And we are still being urged to give up socialism. Why should the Soviet people, who have grown and gained in strength under socialism, abandon that system? We will spare no effort to develop and strengthen socialism. I think that a minimum of the new system's potential has been tapped so far.

This is why we find strange those proposals—some even sincere—to alter our social system and turn to methods and forms typical of a different social set-up. People who make such suggestions do not realize that this is just impossible even if there were someone wishing to turn the Soviet Union to capitalism. Just think: how can we agree that 1917 was a mistake and all the seventy years of our life, work, effort and battles were also a complete mistake, that we were going in the "wrong direction"? No, a strict and impartial view of the facts of history suggests only one conclusion: it is the socialist option that has brought formerly backward Russia to the "right place"—the place the Soviet Union now occupies in human progress.

We have no reason to speak about the October Revolution and socialism in a low voice, as though ashamed of them. Our successes are immense and indisputable. But we see the past in its entirety and complexity. Our most tremendous achievements do not prevent us from seeing contradictions in the development of our society, our errors and omissions. And our ideology itself is critical and revolutionary by nature. . . .

What conclusions have we drawn from the lessons of history?

First, socialism as a social system has proved that it has immense potentialities for resolving the most complex problems of social progress. We are convinced of its capacity for self-perfection, for still greater revelation of its possibilities, and for dealing with the present major problems of social progress which arise as we approach the twenty-first century.

At the same time, we realize that improving socialism is not a spontaneous process, but a job requiring tremendous attention, a truthful and unbiased analysis of problems, and a resolute rejection of anything outdated. We have come to see that half-hearted measures will not work here. We must act on a wide front, consistently and energetically, without failing to take the boldest steps.

One more conclusion—the most important one I would say—is that we should rely on the initiative and creativity of the masses; on the active participation of the widest sections of the population in the implementation of the reforms planned; that is, on democratization and again democratization.

CHAPTER 16

Critique of Socialism: Von Mises' Thoughts on Socialism

Those who favor socialism as a form of economic organization argue that the ideals of justice and equality are best served under socialism rather than under capitalism. By abolishing private property, economic democracy can be achieved, giving workers a larger voice rather than permitting capitalists to make decisions affecting workers and consumers. Moralists and theologians, claiming that the teachings of Christ and the behavior of His disciples seemingly point toward communism, use the Bible to argue the moral superiority of socialism over capitalism. Socialism stands on the moral high ground, while defenders of capitalism typically base their case on acceptance of people's greed, selfishness, and sinful nature.

In *Socialism*, Ludwig von Mises offers an apologetic work to defend capitalism and show the shortcomings of socialism. Democracy can best be achieved by capitalism, not socialism. Those interpreting the Christian scriptures as advocating socialism twist passages and teachings out of context. Von Miss argues that socialism does not require a person of greater moral purity than does capitalism; the failures of socialism have nothing to do with the morality of man, or the work attributes of socialist man and bourgeois capitalist man. Rather, the failure of socialism is due to the impossibility of economic calculation—the calculation of value—in a socialist economy.

In the first part of the excerpt below, von Mises discusses economic calculation and how attempts to modify socialism so as to allow price setting in a capitalistic-like market are doomed to failure. In a capitalistic market, prices are determined by a free, fair, unforced exchange. Thus, without a free market, one cannot determine price, and there can be no economic calculation of value. By eliminating the profit motive, the market mechanism cannot work, and so prices cannot be successfully determined under socialism.

Using a labor theory of value to determine the value of output will not work, as labor differs in quality from person to person; labor skills are not homogenous. Also, the labor theory of value cannot value naturally occurring inputs to production, such as plants, dirt, trees, rocks, and so on.

Setting up an artificial market under socialism and letting socialist managers pretend to maximize "profit" will not be successful either. Price determination involves a joint effort between entrepreneurs seeking profit, capitalists seeking interest, landlords seeking rent, and workers seeking wages, as firms try to maximize profit by meeting consumers' needs. Without profit prospects, the price-setting market mechanism cannot work correctly. Managers cannot pretend to maximize profit as it is the capitalist, by investing and withdrawing capital from various industries and enterprises, who "creates the data" the managers need to direct business and make appropriate investment decisions.

Letting the state play the role of capitalist is doomed to failure also. The state will direct capital to those state-appointed managers who are more aggressive and optimistic in their business projections. In capitalism, investors and the impersonal financial markets objectively balance risk and expected return prospects. A socialist state cannot do that successfully and consistently.

Due to this inability to calculate value and determine resource allocation, socialism is doomed to fail. It is not because of immoral man that socialism cannot successfully work as an economic system. Rather, it is man's lack of intellectual capacity to solve the problem of value calculation that dooms socialism. Due to the impossibility of value calculation, socialists must develop and elevate a socialist utopia where man is unlike man as hitherto seen on this earth. This ideal human socialist type is not due so much to the desire to develop an alternative to the alleged immorality of capitalism as it is to the socialists' grasping for ideas in the face of the impossible task of calculating value.

Socialism

Ludwig von Mises

ECONOMIC CALCULATION IN THE SOCIALIST COMMUNITY

The theory of economic calculation shows that in the socialistic community economic calculation would be impossible.

In any large undertaking the individual works or departments are partly independent in their accounts. They can reckon the cost of materials and labour, and it is possible at any time for an individual group to strike a separate balance and to sum up the results of its activity in figures. In this way it is possible to ascertain with what success each separate branch has been operated and thereby to make decisions concerning the reorganization, limitations or extension of existing branches or the establishment of new ones. Some mistakes are of course unavoidable in these calculations. They arise partly from the difficulty of allocating overhead costs. Other mistakes again arise from the necessity of calculating from insufficiently determined data, as, e.g. when in calculating the profitability of a certain process, depreciation of the machinery employed is determined by assuming a certain working life for the machine. But all such errors can be confined within certain narrow limits which do not upset the total result of the calculation. Whatever uncertainty remains is attributed to the uncertainty of future conditions inevitable in any imaginable state of affairs.

It seems natural then to ask why individual branches of production in a socialistic community should not make separate accounts in the same manner. But this is impossible. Separate accounts for a single branch of one and the same undertaking are possible only when prices for all kinds of goods and services are established in the market and furnish a basis of reckoning. Where there is no market there is no price system, and where there is no price system there can be no economic calculation.

Some may think that it is possible to permit exchange between the different groups of undertakings so as to establish a system of exchange relations (prices) and in this way create a basis for economic calculation in the socialistic community. Thus within a framework of a unitary economic system which does not recognize private property in the means of production, individual branches of industry with separate administration could be set up, subject of course, to the supreme economic authority, but able to transfer to each other goods and services for a consideration reckoned in a common medium of exchange. This roughly, is how people conceive the productive organization of socialistic industry when they speak nowadays of complete socialization and the like. But here again the decisive point is evaded. Exchange relations in productive goods can only be established on the basis of private property in the means of production. If the Coal Syndicate delivers coal to the Iron Syndicate a price can be fixed only if both syndicates own the means of production in the industry. But that would not be Socialism but Syndicalism.

For those socialist writers who accept the labour theory of value the problem is, of course, quite simple. . . .

At first sight it would appear that calculations based on labour take into account the natural conditions of production, as well as conditions arising from the human element. The Marxian concept of the socially necessary labour time takes the law of diminishing returns into consideration in so far as it results from different natural conditions of production. If the demand for a commodity increases and less favourable natural conditions have to be exploited, then the average socially necessary time for the production of a unit also increases. If more favourable conditions of production are discovered then the necessary quantum of social labour declines. But this is not enough. Computation of changes in marginal labour costs only take account of natural conditions in so far as they influence labour costs. Beyond that, the 'labour' calculation breaks down. It leaves, for instance, the consumption of material factors of production entirely out of account. Suppose the socially necessary labour time for producing two commodities P and Q is ten hours, and that the production of a unit both of P and of Q requires material A, one unit of which is produced by one hour of socially necessary labour, and that the production of P involves two units of A and eight hours of labour, and of Q one unit of A and nine hours of labour. In a calculation based on labour time P and Q are equivalent, but in a calculation based on value P must be worth more than Q. The former calculation is false. Only the latter corresponds to the essence and object of economic calculation. It is true that this surplus by which the value of P exceeds that of Q, this material substratum, 'is furnished by nature without the help of man', but provided it is present only in such quantities that it becomes an economic factor it must also in some form enter into economic calculation.

The second deficiency of the labour calculation theory is that it disregards differences in the quality of labour. For Marx all human labour is economically homogeneous, because it is always the 'productive expenditure of human brain, muscles, nerves, hands, etc.' 'Skilled labour is only intensified, or rather multiplied simple labour, so that a small quantity of skilled labour equals a larger quantity of simple labour. Experience shows that this resolution of skilled into simple constantly happens. A commodity may be the product of highly skilled labour, but its value equates it to the product of simple labour and represents only a certain quantity of simple labour.' Böhm-Bawerk was justified in describing this argument as a master-piece of astounding naivety. In criticizing it one may conveniently leave undecided whether one can discover a unitary physiological measure of all human labour, physical as well as 'mental'. For it is certain that between men themselves there are differences of capability and skill which result in differing qualities of the goods and services produced. What is ultimately decisive for the solution of the problem of the feasibility of using labour as a basis of economic calculation is the question whether one can assimilate different kinds of work to a common denominator without a valuation of the products by the consumer. It is clear that the argument which Marx brings to bear on this point has failed. Experience does indeed show that commodities enter into exchange regardless of the question whether they are the products of skilled or simple labour. But this would only prove that a definite quantity of simple labour is equal to a definite quantity of skilled labour if it were proved that labour is the source of exchange value. But not only is this unproven; it is exactly what Marx originally set out to prove. The fact that in exchange a substitute relation between simple and skilled labour has arisen in the form of wage rates—a point to which Marx does not here allude—is not in the least a proof of this homogeneity. This process of equating is a result of the working of the market, not its presupposition. Calculations based on labour cost rather than on monetary values would have to establish a purely arbitrary relation by which to resolve skilled into simple labour, and this would make them useless as an instrument for the economic organization of resources.

It was long thought that the labour theory of value provided a necessary ethical basis for the demand to socialize the means of production. We know now that this was an error. Although the majority of socialists have adopted this view and although even Marx with his professedly non-ethical standpoint could not shake it off, it is clear that, on the one hand, the political demands for the introduction of the socialistic method of production neither need nor receive support from the labour theory of value, and, on the other hand, that those who hold different views on the nature and causes of value can also have socialistic tendencies. But from another point of view, the labour theory of value is still an essential dogma for the advocates of the socialistic method of production. For socialistic production in a society based on division of labour seems practicable only if there is an objective recognizable unit of value which would enable economic calculations to be made in an exchangeless and moneyless community and labour seems the only thing to serve this purpose. . . .

THE ARTIFICIAL MARKET AS THE SOLUTION OF THE PROBLEM OF ECONOMIC CALCULATION

Some of the younger socialists believe that the socialist community could solve the problem of economic calculation by the creation of an artificial market for the means of production. They admit that it was an error on the part of the older socialists to have sought to realize Socialism through the suspension of the market and the abolition of pricing for goods of higher orders; they hold that it was an error to have seen in the suppression of the market and of the price system the essence of the socialistic ideal. And they contend that if it is not to degenerate into a meaningless chaos in which the whole of our civilization would disappear, the socialist community equally with the capitalistic community, must create a market in which all goods and services may be priced. On the basis of such arrangements, they think, the socialist community will be able to make its calculations as easily as the capitalist entrepreneurs.

Unfortunately the supporters of such proposals do not see (or perhaps *will* not see) that it is not possible to divorce the market and its functions in regard to the formation of prices from the working of a society which is based on private property in the means of production and in which, subject to the rules of such a society, the landlords, capitalists and entrepreneurs can dispose of their property as they think fit. For the motive force of the whole process which gives rise to market prices for the factors of production is the ceaseless search on the part of the capitalists and the entrepreneurs to maximize their profits by serving the consumers' wishes. Without the striving of the entrepreneurs (including the shareholders) for profit, of the landlords for rent, of the capitalists for interest and the labourers for wages, the successful functioning of the whole mechanism is not to be thought of. It is only the prospect of profit which directs production into those channels in which the demands of the consumer are best satisfied at least cost. If the prospect of profit disappears the mechanism of the market loses its mainspring, for it is only this prospect which sets it in motion and maintains it in operation. The market is thus the focal point of the capitalist order of society; it is the essence of Capitalism. Only under Capitalism, therefore, it is possible; it cannot be 'artificially' imitated under Socialism.

The advocates of the artificial market, however, are of the opinion that an artificial market can be created by instructing the controllers of the different industrial units to act *as if* they were entrepreneurs in a capitalistic state. They argue that even under Capitalism the managers of joint stock companies work not for themselves but for the companies, that is to say, for the shareholders. Under Socialism, therefore, it would be possible for them to act in exactly the same way as before, with the same circumspection and devotion to duty. The only difference would be that under Socialism the product of the manager's labours would go to the community rather than to the shareholders. In such a way, in contrast to all socialists who have written on the subject hitherto, especially the Marxians, they think it would be possible to construct a decentralized, as opposed to a centralized, Socialism.

In order to judge properly such proposals, it is necessary in the first place to realize that these controllers of individual industrial units would have to be appointed. Under Capitalism the managers of the joint stock companies are appointed either directly or indirectly by the shareholders. In so far as the shareholders give to the managers power to produce by the means of the company's (i.e. the shareholders') stock they are risking their own property or a part of their own property. The speculation (for it is necessarily a speculation) may succeed and bring profit; it may, however, misfire and bring about the loss of the whole or a part of the capital concerned. This committing of one's own capital to a business whose outcome is uncertain and to men whose future ability is still a matter of conjecture whatever one may know of their past, is the essence of joint stock company enterprise.

Now it is a complete fallacy to suppose that the problem of economic calculation in a socialist community relates solely to matters which fall into the sphere of the daily business routine of managers of joint stock companies. It is clear that such a belief can only arise from exclusive concentration on the idea of a stationary economic system—a conception which no doubt is useful for the solution of many theoretical problems but which has no counterpart in fact and which, if exclusively regarded, can even be positively misleading. It is clear that under stationary conditions the problem of economic calculation does not really arise. When we think of the stationary society, we think of an economy in which all the factors of production are already used in such a way as, under the given conditions, to provide the maximum of the things which are demanded by consumers. That is to say, under stationary conditions there no longer exists a problem for economic calculation to solve. The essential function of economic calculation has *by hypothesis* already been performed. There is no need for an apparatus of calculation. To use a popular but not altogether satisfactory terminology we can say that the problem of economic calculation is of economic dynamics: it is no problem of economic statics.

The problem of economic calculation is a problem which arises in an economy which is perpetually subject to change, an economy which every day is confronted with new problems which have to be solved. Now in order to solve such problems it is above all necessary that capital should be withdrawn from particular lines of production, from particular undertakings and concerns and should be applied in other lines of production, in other undertakings and concerns. This is not a matter for the managers of joint stock companies, it is essentially a matter for the capitalists—the capitalists who buy and sell stocks and shares, who make loans and recover them, who make deposits in the banks and draw them out of the banks again, who speculate in all kinds of commodities. It is these operations of speculative capitalists which create those conditions of the money market, the stock exchanges and the wholesale markets which have to be taken for granted by the manager of the joint stock company, who, according to the socialist writers we are considering, is to be conceived as nothing but the reliable and conscientious servant of the company. It is the speculative capitalists who create the data to which he has to adjust his business and which therefore gives direction to his trading operations.

It follows therefore that it is a fundamental deficiency of all these socialistic constructions which invoke the 'artificial market' and artificial competition as a way out of the problem of economic calculation, that they rest on the belief that the market for factors of production is affected only by producers buying and selling commodities. It is not possible to eliminate from such markets the influence of the supply of capital from the capitalists and the demand for capital by the entrepreneurs, without destroying the mechanism itself.

Faced with this difficulty, the socialist is likely to propose that the socialist state as owner of all capital and all means of production should simply direct capital to those undertakings which promise the highest return. The available capital, he will contend, should go to those undertakings which offer the highest rate of profit. But such a state of affairs would simply mean that those managers who were less cautious and more optimistic would receive capital to enlarge their undertakings while more cautious and more sceptical managers would go away empty-handed. Under Capitalism, the capitalist decides to whom he will entrust *his own* capital. The beliefs of the managers of joint stock companies regarding the future prospects of their undertakings and the hopes of project-makers regarding the profitability of their plans are not in any way decisive. The mechanism of the money market and the capital market decides. This indeed is its main task: to serve the economic system as a whole, to judge the profitability of alternative openings and not blindly to follow what the managers of particular concerns, limited by the narrow horizon of their own undertakings, are tempted to propose.

To understand this completely, it is essential to realise that the capitalist does not just invest his capital in those undertakings which offer high interest or high profit; he attempts rather to strike a balance between his desire for profit and his estimate of the risk of loss. He must exercise foresight. If he does not do so then he suffers losses—losses that bring it about that his disposition over the factors of production is transferred to the hands of others who know better how to weigh the risks and the prospects of business speculation.

Now if it is to remain socialistic, the socialist State cannot leave to other hands that disposition over capital which permits the enlargement of existing undertakings, the contraction of others and the bringing into being of undertakings that are completely new. And it is scarcely to be assumed that socialists of whatever persuasion would seriously propose that this function should be made over to some group of people who would 'simply' have the business of doing what capitalists and speculators do under capitalistic conditions, the only difference being that the product of their foresight should not belong to them but to the community. Proposals of this sort may well be made concerning the managers of joint stock companies. They can never be extended to capitalists and speculators, for no socialist would dispute that the function which capitalists and speculators perform under Capitalism, namely directing the use of capital goods into that direction in which they best serve the demands of the consumer, is only performed because they are under the incentive to preserve their property and to make profits which increase it or at least allow them to live without diminishing their capital.

It follows therefore that the socialist community can do nothing but place the disposition over capital in the hands of the State or to be exact in the hands of the men who, as the governing authority, carry out the business of the State. And that signifies elimination of the market, which indeed is the fundamental aim of

Socialism, for the guidance of economic activity by the market implies organization of production and a distribution of the product according to that disposition of the spending power of individual members of society which makes itself felt on the market; that is to say, it implies precisely that which it is the goal of Socialism to eliminate.

If the socialists attempt to belittle the significance of the problem of economic calculation in the Socialist community, on the ground that the forces of the market do not lead to ethically justifiable arrangements, they simply show that they do not understand the real nature of the problem. It is not a question of whether there shall be produced cannons or clothes, dwelling houses or churches, luxuries or subsistence. In any social order, even under Socialism, it can very easily be decided which kind and what number of consumption goods should be produced. No one has ever denied that. But once this decision has been made, there still remains the problem of ascertaining how the existing means of production can be used most effectively to produce these goods in question. In order to solve this problem it is necessary that there should be economic calculation. And economic calculation can only take place by means of money prices established in the market for production goods in a society resting on private property in the means of production. That is to say, there must exist money prices of land, raw materials, semi-manufactures; that is to say, there must be money wages and interest rates.

Thus the alternative is still *either* Socialism or a market economy.

PRIMITIVE CHRISTIANITY AND SOCIETY

Primitive Christianity was not ascetic. With a joyful acceptance of life it deliberately pushed into the background the ascetic ideals which permeated many contemporary sects. (Even John the Baptist lived as an ascetic.) Only in the third and fourth centuries was asceticism introduced into Christianity, from this time dates the ascetic re-interpretation and reformation of gospel teachings. The Christ of the Gospels enjoys life among his disciples, refreshes himself with food and drink and shares the feasts of the people. He is as far removed from asceticism and a desire to flee the world as he is from intemperance and debauchery. Alone his attitude to the relations of the sexes strikes us as ascetic, but we can explain this, as we can explain all practical Gospel Teachings—and they offer no rules of life except practical ones—by the basic conception which gives us our whole idea of Jesus, the conception of the Messiah.

'The Time is fulfilled, and the Kingdom of God is at hand: repent ye, and believe the gospel.' These are the words with which, in the Gospel of Mark, the Redeemer makes his entry. Jesus regards himself as the prophet of the approaching Kingdom of God, the Kingdom which according to ancient prophecy shall bring redemption from all earthly insufficiency, and with it from all economic cares. His followers have nothing to do but to prepare themselves for this Day. The time for worrying about earthly matters is past, for now, in expectation of the Kingdom, men must attend to more important things. Jesus offers no rules for earthly action and struggle; his Kingdom is not of this world. Such rules of conduct as he gives his followers are valid only for the short interval of time which has still to be lived while waiting for the great things to come. In the Kingdom of God there will be no economic cares. There the believers will eat and drink at the Lord's table. For this Kingdom therefore, all economic and political counsel would be superfluous. Any preparations made by Jesus must be regarded as merely transitional expedients.

It is only in this way that we can understand why, in the Sermon on the Mount, Jesus recommends his own people to take no thought for food, drink, and clothing; why he exhorts them not to sow or reap or gather in barns, not to labour or spin. It is the only explanation, too, of his and his disciples' 'communism'. This 'communism' is not Socialism; it is not production with means of production belonging to the community. It is nothing more than a distribution of consumption goods among the members of the community—'unto each, according as any one had need'. It is a communism of consumption goods, not of the means of production, a community of consumers, not of producers. The primitive Christians do not produce, labour, or gather anything at all. The newly converted realize their possessions and divide the proceeds with the brethren and sisters. Such a way of living is untenable in the long run. It can be looked upon only as a temporary order which is what it was in fact intended to be. Christ's disciples lived in daily expectation of Salvation.

The primitive Christian's idea of imminent fulfillment transforms itself gradually into that conception of the Last Judgment which lies at the root of all ecclesiastical movements that have had any prolonged existence. Hand in hand with this transformation went the entire reconstruction of the Christian rules of life. Expectation of the coming of the Kingdom of God could no longer serve as a basis. When the congregations sought to organize themselves for a prolonged life on earth they had to cease demanding that their members should abstain from work and dedicate themselves to the contemplative life in preparation for the Divine Kingdom. Not only did they have to tolerate their brethren's participation in the world's work, they had to insist upon it, as otherwise they would have destroyed the conditions necessary to the existence of their religion. And thus, Christianity, which began with complete indifference to all social conditions, practically canonized the social order of the declining Roman Empire once the process of adapting the Church to that order had begun.

It is an error to speak of the social teachings of primitive Christianity. The historical Christ and his teachings, as the oldest part of the New Testament represents them, are quite indifferent to all social considerations. Not that Christ did not sharply criticize the existing state of affairs, but he did not think it worth while to consider how matters could be improved or even to think about them at all. That was God's affair. He would set up his own glorious and faultless Kingdom, and its coming would be soon. Nobody knew what this Kingdom would look like, but one thing was certain: in it one would live carefree. Jesus omits all minuter details, and they were not needed; for the Jews of his time did not doubt the splendour of life in the Kingdom of God. The Prophets had announced this Kingdom and their words continued to live in the minds of the people, forming indeed the essential content of their religious thought.

The expectation of God's own reorganization when the time came and the exclusive transfer of all action and thought to the future Kingdom of God, made Jesus's teaching utterly negative. He rejects everything that exists without offering anything to replace it. He arrives at dissolving all existing social ties. The disciple shall not merely be indifferent to supporting himself, shall not merely refrain from work and dispossess himself of all goods, but he shall hate 'father and mother and wife and children and brethren and sisters, yea, and his own life'. Jesus is able to tolerate the worldly laws of the Roman Empire and the prescriptions of the Jewish Law because he is indifferent to them, despising them as things important only within the narrow limits of time and not because he acknowledges their value. His zeal in destroying social ties knows no limits. The motive force behind the purity and power of this complete negation is ecstatic inspiration and enthusiastic hope of a new world. Hence his passionate attack upon everything that exists. Everything may be destroyed because God in His omnipotence will rebuild the future order. No need to scrutinize whether anything can be carried over from the old to the new order, because this new order will arise without human aid. It demands therefore from its adherents no system of ethics, no particular conduct in any positive direction. Faith and faith alone, hope, expectation—that is all he needs. He need contribute nothing to the reconstruction of the future, this God Himself has provided for. The clearest modern parallel to the attitude of complete negation of primitive Christianity is Bolshevism. The Bolshevists, too, wish to destroy everything that exists because they regard it as hopelessly bad. But they have in mind ideas, indefinite and contradictory though they may be, of the future social order. They demand not only that their followers shall destroy all that is, but also that they pursue a definite line of conduct leading towards the future Kingdom of which they have dreamt. Jesus's teaching in this respect, on the other hand, is merely negation.

Jesus was no social reformer. His teachings had no moral application to life on earth, and his instructions to the disciples only have a meaning in the light of their immediate aim—to await the Lord with girded loins and burning lamps, 'that when he cometh and knocketh, they may straightaway open unto him'. It is just this that has enabled Christianity to make its triumphant progress through the world. Being neutral to any social system, it was able to traverse the centuries without being destroyed by the tremendous social revolutions which took place. Only for this reason could it become the religion of Roman Emperors and Anglo-Saxon entrepreneurs, of African negroes and European Teutons, medieval feudal lords and modern industrial labourers. Each epoch and every party has been able to take from it what they wanted, because it contains nothing which binds it to a definite social order.

THE SLOGAN 'ECONOMIC DEMOCRACY'

One of the more important arguments in favour of Socialism is that contained in the slogan 'self-government in industry'. As in the political sphere the King's absolutism was broken by the peoples' right to share decisions and later by its sole right to decide, so the absolutism of owners of the means of production and of entrepreneurs is to be abolished by consumers and workers. Democracy is incomplete as long as everyone is obliged to submit to the dictatorship of the owners. The worst part of Capitalism is by no means inequality of income; more unbearable still is the power which it gives the capitalists over their fellow citizens. As long as this state of affairs continues there can be no personal freedom. The People must take the administration of economic matters into its own hands, just as it has taken over the government of the state.

There is a double error in this argument. It misconceives on the one hand, the nature and function of political democracy, and on the other, the nature of the social order based on private ownership in the means of production.

We have already shown that the essence of democracy is to be found neither in the electoral system, nor in the discussions and resolutions of national councils, nor in any sort of committee appointed by these councils. These are merely the technical tools of political democracy. Its real function is to make peace. Democratic institutions make the will of the people effective in political matters, seem arbitrary and capricious. Seen from too close up the shape of things lose their true significance. If the entrepreneur's disposal of production injures the worker's momentary interest, it is sure to seem to him unfounded and arbitrary. He will not realize that the entrepreneur works under the rule of a strict law. True, the entrepreneur is free to give full rein to his whims, to dismiss workers off hand, to cling stubbornly to antiquated processes, deliberately to choose unsuitable methods of production and to allow himself to be guided by motives which conflict with the demands of consumers. But when and in so far as he does this he must pay for it, and if he does not restrain himself in time he will be driven, by the loss of his property, into a position where he can inflict no further damage. Special means of controlling his behaviour are unnecessary. The market controls him more strictly and exactingly than could any government or other organ of society. . . .

THE CONSUMER AS THE DECIDING FACTOR IN PRODUCTION

People sometimes maintain that in guarding their own interests, entrepreneurs force production in a direction opposed to the interests of consumers. The entrepreneurs have no scruples about 'creating or intensifying the public's need for things which provide for merely sensual gratification but inflict harm on health or spiritual welfare'. For instance the fight against alcoholism, the dread menace to national health and welfare, is said to be made more difficult because of the opposition 'of the vested interests of alcohol capitalism to all attempts to combat it'. The habit of smoking would not be 'so widespread and so greatly on the increase among the young if economic interests played no role in promoting it'. 'Luxury articles, baubles and tinsel of all kinds, trashy and obscene publications' are to-day 'forced upon the public because the producers profit by them or hope to do so'. It is common knowledge that the large-scale arming of the Powers and therefore, indirectly, war itself are ascribed to the machinations of 'armament-capital'.

Entrepreneurs and capitalists in search of investments turn towards those branches of production from which they hope to obtain the greatest profit. They try to fathom the future wants of consumers so as to gain a general survey of demand. As Capitalism is constantly creating new wealth for all and extending the satisfaction of wants, consumers are frequently in the position of being able to satisfy wants which formerly remained unsatisfied. Thus it becomes a special task of the capitalist entrepreneur to find out what formerly unsatisfied wants can now be provided for. This is what people have in mind when they say that Capitalism creates wants in order to satisfy them.

The nature of the things demanded by the consumer does not concern the entrepreneur and the capitalist. They are merely the obedient servants of the consumer and it is not their business to prescribe what the consumer shall enjoy. They give him poison and murderous weapons if he wants them. But nothing could be more erroneous than to suppose that products which serve a bad or harmful purpose bring in more than those which serve a good one. The highest profit is obtained from articles for which there is the most urgent demand. The profit-seeker therefore sets about producing those commodities in which there is the greatest disproportion between supply and demand. Of course, once he has invested his capital, it is to his interest to see that the demand for his product increases. He tries to expand sales. But in the long run he cannot prevail against a change of demand. Neither can he obtain much advantage from growth in the demand for his products, for new enterprises turn their attention to his branch of industry and thereby tend to reduce his profits to the average.

Mankind does not drink alcohol because there are breweries, distilleries, and vineyards; men brew beer, distil spirits, and grow grapes because of the demand for alcoholic drinks. 'Alcohol-capital' has not created drinking habits any more than it has created drinking songs. The capitalists who own shares in breweries and distilleries would have preferred shares in publishing firms for devotional books, had the demand been for spiritual and not spirituous sustenance. 'Armament capital' did not create wars; wars created 'armament capital'. It was not Krupp and Schneider who incited the nations to war, but imperialist writers and politicians.

If a man thinks alcohol and nicotine harmful, let him abstain from them. Let him try, if he will, to convert his fellows to his own views on abstinence. What is certain is that he cannot, in a capitalist society, whose basic principle is the self-determination and self-responsibility of each individual, force them against their will to renounce alcohol and nicotine. If this inability to impose his will on others causes him regret, then at least he can console himself with the thought that neither is he at the mercy of the commands of others.

Some socialists reproach the capitalist social order primarily for the rich variety of its goods. Instead of producing uniform products, which could be brought out on the largest scale, people manufacture hundreds and thousands of types of each commodity, and production is made much more expensive thereby. Socialism would put at the comrades' disposal only uniform goods; it would unify production and thereby raise national productivity. Simultaneously Socialism would dissolve separate family households, and in their place provide communal kitchens and hotel-like dwellings; this, too, would increase social wealth by eliminating the waste of labour power in tiny kitchens which serve only a few consumers. . . .

Under Capitalism each buyer has to decide whether he prefers the cheaper uniformity of mass production or the greater expense of articles specially manufactured to suit the taste of the individual or the small group. There is unmistakably a tendency towards progressive uniformity of production and consumption through standardization. Commodities used in the productive process itself are daily becoming more standardized. The shrewd entrepreneur soon discovers the advantage of using the standard type—with its lower purchasing cost, its replaceability and adaptability to other productive processes rather than articles produced by a special process. The movement to standardize the implements of production is impeded to-day by the fact that numerous enterprises are indirectly or directly socialized. As they are not rationally controlled, no stress is laid on the advantage of using standard types. Army administrations, municipal building departments, State railways, and similar authorities resist, with bureaucratic obstinacy, the adoption of types in universal use. The unification of the production of machines, factory equipment, and semi-finished products does not require a change to Socialism. On the contrary, Capitalism does this more quickly of its own accord. . . .

If the socialist community does not supply the comrades with the goods which they themselves want to enjoy, but with those which the rulers think they ought to enjoy, the sum of satisfactions is not increased, but diminished. One certainly could not call this violation of the individual will 'economic democracy'.

For it is an essential difference between capitalist and socialist production that in the first men provide for themselves, while in the second they are provided for. The socialist wants to feed and house humanity and cover its nakedness. But men prefer to eat, dwell, dress and generally to seek happiness after their own fashion. . . .

CHAPTER 17

Philosophical Dialogue on Justice: John Rawls on Distributive Justice

By the middle of the twentieth century, American philosophy had largely retreated from any attempt to deal directly with the substantive questions of economic justice—or indeed any substantive questions at all. Under the influence first of logical positivism and later of linguistic analysis, philosophers often took the position that they had to confine inquiry to questions about logic and language. The grand old questions of metaphysics, ethics, and other branches of philosophy that had aimed at an understanding of nature, man, and morals were either considered "meaningless" or food for linguistic and logical analysis. "Analytical philosophy," as it came to be called, seemed content to assign to the metaphysical dustbin such questions as what is the most just economic system and what is the ideal human type.

It was in this context that John Rawls's book, A *Theory of Justice*, appeared in 1971. While writing within the analytic tradition, Rawls boldly went where his philosophical contemporaries feared to go. Synthesizing his own speculations, which span more than a decade (a representative example of which is excerpted here), Rawls raised anew the old questions of justice: "What are the fundamental principles by which we should judge whether any proposed scheme of economic arrangements is morally justified or not?"[1]

---

[1]John Rawls, A *Theory of Justice* (Cambridge, Mass.: Harvard University Press, 1971).

Virginia Held has succinctly and brilliantly summarized Rawls's rather complicated argument as follows:

> John Rawls has presented one of the most powerful and widely discussed formulations of such principles in many years. In his view, the fundamental principles of justice are those principles for the regulation of society to which we could all, unanimously, agree, if we chose them impartially from a standpoint outside any actual society, without knowing in which positions—rich or poor, male or female, white, tan, or black, untalented or talented, and so on—we would actually find ourselves. A society's basic social institutions, and their arrangement into a structure, should accord with such principles of justice. The principles would, Rawls holds, require first of all as extensive a scheme of equal basic liberties for each of us as would be compatible with the similar liberties of others. Once such liberties are assured, we should apply what Rawls calls "the difference principle" to the basic structure of society. The difference principle would require that *all* inequalities of social primary goods—rights, opportunities, income, wealth, and so on—could only be justified if such inequalities would contribute to raising the position in these respects of the least advantaged groups in the society. Thus, high rewards for entrepreneurs could only be justified if their effect was to improve the lot of the least advantaged members of the society, who might benefit from new economic activity that otherwise would not take place.
>
> Government should, in Rawls's view, continually adjust the rewards allowed to various groups by its scheme of property rights and economic policies so that the results will accord with this principle. Government should tax those whose economic benefits would exceed those allowed by this principle, and government should redistribute these funds, in some form, to those least advantaged in the society, such as those who cannot work because of illness (within a normal range), those unable to find work, or those working for the most meager wages.
>
> In Rawls's view, we would certainly choose, from his equivalent of the "state of nature" of traditional social contract theory, to insure ourselves against the worst outcome that could befall us in organized society: being among the "least advantaged." If we did not know where we ourselves would wind up, we would choose principles of economic justice that would raise us from the bottom, and we would want those at the top to be taxed up to the point at which it would decrease their contribution to our well-being to be taxed further.[2]

It would be difficult to overestimate the impact that Rawls's theory has had in the philosophical community and beyond. Whatever one may finally think of Rawls's views, it cannot be denied that A *Theory of Justice* is one of the most influential books of the day. Its novel approach to justifying the kind of activist, redistributionist state often accompanying late twentieth-century capitalism has struck responsive chords in many.

---

[2]Virginia Held, *Property, Profits, and Economic Justice* (Belmont, Calif.: Wadsworth, 1980), p. 14.

A Theory of Justice

John Rawls

THE MAIN IDEA OF THE THEORY OF JUSTICE

My aim is to present a conception of justice which generalizes and carries to a higher level of abstraction the familiar theory of the social contract as found, say, in Locke, Rousseau, and Kant.[a] In order to do this we are not to think of the original contract as one to enter a particular society or to set up a particular form of government. Rather, the guiding idea is that the principles of justice for the basic structure of society are the object of the original agreement. They are the principles that free and rational persons concerned to further their own interests would accept in an initial position of equality as defining the fundamental terms of their association. These principles are to regulate all further agreements; they specify the kinds of social cooperation that can be entered into and the forms of government that can be established. This way of regarding the principles of justice I shall call justice as fairness.

Thus we are to imagine that those who engage in social cooperation choose together, in one joint act, the principles which are to assign basic rights and duties and to determine the division of social benefits. Men are to decide in advance how they are to regulate their claims against one another and what is to be the foundation charter of their society. Just as each person must decide by rational reflection what constitutes his good, that is, the system of ends which it is rational for him to pursue, so a group of persons must decide once and for all what is to count among them as just and unjust. The choice which rational men would make in this hypothetical situation of equal liberty, assuming for the present that this choice problem has a solution, determines the principles of justice.

---

[a]As the text suggests, I shall regard Locke's *Second Treatise of Government*, Rousseau's *The Social Contract*, and Kant's ethical works beginning with *The Foundations of the Metaphysics of Morals* as definitive of the contract tradition. For all of its greatness, Hobbes's *Leviathan* raises special problems. A general historical survey is provided by J. W. Gough, *The Social Contract*, 2nd ed. (Oxford, The Clarendon Press, 1957), and Otto Gierke, *Natural Law and the Theory of Society*, trans. with an introduction by Ernest Barker (Cambridge, The University Press, 1934). A presentation of the contract view as primarily an ethical theory is to be found in G. R. Grice, *The Grounds of Moral Judgment* (Cambridge, The University Press, 1967). See also §19, note 30.

In justice as fairness the original position of equality corresponds to the state of nature in the traditional theory of the social contract. This original position is not, of course, thought of as an actual historical state of affairs, much less as a primitive condition of culture. It is understood as a purely hypothetical situation characterized so as to lead to a certain conception of justice.[b] Among the essential features of this situation is that no one knows his place in society, his class position or social status, nor does any one know his fortune in the distribution of natural assets and abilities, his intelligence, strength, and the like. I shall even assume that the parties do not know their conceptions of the good or their special psychological propensities. The principles of justice are chosen behind a veil of ignorance. This ensures that no one is advantaged or disadvantaged in the choice of principles by the outcome of natural chance or the contingency of social circumstances. Since all are similarly situated and no one is able to design principles to favor his particular condition, the principles of justice are the result of a fair agreement or bargain. For given the circumstances of the original position, the symmetry of everyone's relations to each other, this initial situation is fair between individuals as moral persons, that is, as rational beings with their own ends and capable, I shall assume, of a sense of justice. The original position is, one might say, the appropriate initial status quo, and thus the fundamental agreements reached in it are fair. This explains the propriety of the name "justice as fairness": it conveys the idea that the principles of justice are agreed to in an initial situation that is fair. The name does not mean that the concepts of justice and fairness are the same, any more than the phrase "poetry as metaphor" means that the concepts of poetry and metaphor are the same.

Justice as fairness begins, as I have said, with one of the most general of all choices which persons might make together, namely, with the choice of the first principles of a conception of justice which is to regulate all subsequent criticism and reform of institutions. Then, having chosen a conception of justice, we can suppose that they are to choose a constitution and a legislature to enact laws, and so on, all in accordance with the principles of justice initially agreed upon. Our social situation is just if it is such that by this sequence of hypothetical agreements we would have contracted into the general system of rules which defines it. Moreover, assuming that the original position does determine a set of principles (that

---

[b]Kant is clear that the original agreement is hypothetical. See *The Metaphysics of Morals*, pt. I (*Rechtslehre*), especially §§47,52; and pt. II of the essay "Concerning the Common Saying: This May Be True in Theory but It Does Not Apply in Practice," in *Kant's Political Writings*, ed. Hans Reiss and trans. by H. B. Nisbet (Cambridge, The University Press, 1970), pp. 73-87. See Georges Vlachos, *La Pensée politique de Kant* (Paris, Presses Universitaires de France, 1962), pp. 326-335; and J. G. Murphy, *Kant: The Philosophy of Right* (London, Macmillan, 1970), pp. 109-112, 133-136, for a further discussion.

is, that a particular conception of justice would be chosen), it will then be true that whenever social institutions satisfy these principles those engaged in them can say to one another that they are cooperating on terms to which they would agree if they were free and equal persons whose relations with respect to one another were fair. They could all view their arrangements as meeting the stipulations which they would acknowledge in an initial situation that embodies widely accepted and reasonable constraints on the choice of principles. The general recognition of this fact would provide the basis for a public acceptance of the corresponding principles of justice. No society can, of course, be a scheme of cooperation which men enter voluntarily in a literal sense; each person finds himself placed at birth in some particular position in some particular society, and the nature of this position materially affects his life prospects. Yet a society satisfying the principles of justice as fairness comes as close as a society can to being a voluntary scheme, for it meets the principles which free and equal persons would assent to under circumstances that are fair. In this sense its members are autonomous and the obligations they recognize self-imposed.

One feature of justice as fairness is to think of the parties in the initial situation as rational and mutually disinterested. This does not mean that the parties are egoists, that is, individuals with only certain kinds of interests, say in wealth, prestige, and domination. But they are conceived as not taking an interest in one another's interests. They are to presume that even their spiritual aims may be opposed, in the way that the aims of those of different religions may be opposed. Moreover, the concept of rationality must be interpreted as far as possible in the narrow sense, standard in economic theory, of taking the most effective means to given ends. I shall modify this concept to some extent, as explained later, but one must try to avoid introducing into it any controversial ethical elements. The initial situation must be characterized by stipulations that are widely accepted.

In working out the conception of justice as fairness one main task clearly is to determine which principles of justice would be chosen in the original position. To do this we must describe this situation in some detail and formulate with care the problem of choice which it presents. These matters I shall take up in the immediately succeeding chapters. It may be observed, however, that once the principles of justice are thought of as arising from an original agreement in a situation of equality, it is an open question whether the principle of utility would be acknowledged. Offhand it hardly seems likely that persons who view themselves as equals, entitled to press their claims upon one another, would agree to a principle which may require lesser life prospects for some simply for the sake of a greater sum of advantages enjoyed by others. Since each desires to protect his interests, his capacity to advance his conception of the good, no one has a reason to acquiesce in an enduring loss for himself in order to bring about a greater net balance of satisfaction. In the absence of strong and lasting benevolent impulses, a rational man would not accept a basic structure merely because it maximized the algebraic sum of advantages irrespective of its permanent effects on his own basic rights and interests. Thus it seems that the principle of utility is incompatible with the conception of social cooperation among equals for mutual advantage. It appears to be inconsistent with the idea of reciprocity implicit in the notion of a well-ordered society. Or, at any rate, so I shall argue.

I shall maintain instead that the persons in the initial situation would choose two rather different principles: the first requires equality in the assignment of basic rights and duties, while the second holds that social and economic inequalities, for example inequalities of wealth and authority, are just only if they result in compensating benefits for everyone, and in particular for the least advantaged members of society. These principles rule out justifying institutions on the grounds that the hardships of some are offset by a greater good in the aggregate. It may be expedient but it is not just that some should have less in order that others may prosper. But there is no injustice in the greater benefits earned by a few provided that the situation of persons not so fortunate is thereby improved. The intuitive idea is that since everyone's well-being depends upon a scheme of cooperation without which no one could have a satisfactory life, the division of advantages should be such as to draw forth the willing cooperation of everyone taking part in it, including those less well situated. Yet this can be expected only if reasonable terms are proposed. The two principles mentioned seem to be a fair agreement on the basis of which those better endowed, or more fortunate in their social position, neither of which we can be said to deserve, could expect the willing cooperation of others when some workable scheme is a necessary condition of the welfare of all.ᶜ Once we decide to look for a conception of justice that nullifies the accidents of natural endowment and the contingencies of social circumstance as counters in quest for political and economic advantage, we are led to these principles. They express the result of leaving aside those aspects of the social world that seem arbitrary from a moral point of view.

The problem of the choice of principles, however, is extremely difficult. I do not expect the answer I shall suggest to be convincing to everyone. It is, therefore, worth noting from the outset that justice as fairness, like other contract views, consists of two parts: (1) an interpretation of the initial situation and of the problem of choice posed there, and (2) a set of principles which, it is argued, would be agreed to. One may accept the first part of the theory (or some variant thereof), but not the other, and conversely. The concept of the initial contractual situation may seem reasonable although the particular principles proposed are rejected. To be sure, I want to maintain that the most appropriate conception of this situation does lead to principles of justice contrary to utilitarianism and perfectionism, and therefore that the contract doctrine provides an alternative to these views. Still, one may dispute this contention even though one grants that the contractarian

---

ᶜFor the formulation of this intuitive idea I am indebted to Allan Gibbard.

method is a useful way of studying ethical theories and of setting forth their underlying assumptions.

Justice as fairness is an example of what I have called a contract theory. Now there may be an objection to the term "contract" and related expressions, but I think it will serve reasonably well. Many words have misleading connotations which at first are likely to confuse. The terms "utility" and "utilitarianism" are surely no exception. They too have unfortunate suggestions which hostile critics have been willing to exploit; yet they are clear enough for those prepared to study utilitarian doctrine. The same should be true of the term "contract" applied to moral theories. As I have mentioned, to understand it one has to keep in mind that it implies a certain level of abstraction. In particular, the content of the relevant agreement is not to enter a given society or to adopt a given form of government, but to accept certain moral principles. Moreover, the undertakings referred to are purely hypothetical: a contract view holds that certain principles would be accepted in a well-defined initial situation.

The merit of the contract terminology is that it conveys the idea that principles of justice may be conceived as principles that would be chosen by rational persons, and that in this way conceptions of justice may be explained and justified. The theory of justice is a part, perhaps the most significant part, of the theory of rational choice. Furthermore, principles of justice deal with conflicting claims upon the advantages won by social cooperation; they apply to the relations among several persons or groups. The word "contract" suggests this plurality as well as the condition that the appropriate division of advantages must be in accordance with principles acceptable to all parties. The condition of publicity for principles of justice is also connoted by the contract phraseology. Thus, if these principles are the outcome of an agreement, citizens have a knowledge of the principles that others follow. It is characteristic of contract theories to stress the public nature of political principles. Finally there is the long tradition of the contract doctrine. Expressing the tie with this line of thought helps to define ideas and accords with natural piety. There are then several advantages in the use of the term "contract." With due precautions taken, it should not be misleading.

A final remark. Justice as fairness is not a complete contract theory. For it is clear that the contractarian idea can be extended to the choice of more or less an entire ethical system, that is, to a system including principles for all the virtues and not only for justice. Now for the most part I shall consider only principles of justice and others closely related to them; I make no attempt to discuss the virtues in a systematic way. Obviously if justice as fairness succeeds reasonably well, a next step would be to study the more general view suggested by the name "rightness as fairness." But even this wider theory fails to embrace all moral relationships, since it would seem to include only our relations with other persons and to leave out of account how we are to conduct ourselves toward animals and the rest of nature. I do not contend that the contract notion offers a way to approach these questions which are certainly of the first importance; and I shall have to put them aside. We must recognize the limited scope of justice as fairness and of the general type of view that it exemplifies. How far its conclusions must be revised once these other matters are understood cannot be decided in advance.

THE ORIGINAL POSITION AND JUSTIFICATION

I have said that the original position is the appropriate initial status quo which insures that the fundamental agreements reached in it are fair. This fact yields the name "justice as fairness." It is clear, then, that I want to say that one conception of justice is more reasonable than another, or justifiable with respect to it, if rational persons in the initial situation would choose its principles over those of the other for the role of justice. Conceptions of justice are to be ranked by their acceptability to persons so circumstanced. Understood in this way the question of justification is settled by working out a problem of deliberation: we have to ascertain which principles it would be rational to adopt given the contractual situation. This connects the theory of justice with the theory of rational choice.

If this view of the problem of justification is to succeed, we must, of course, describe in some detail the nature of this choice problem. A problem of rational decision has a definite answer only if we know the beliefs and interests of the parties, their relations with respect to one another, the alternatives between which they are to choose, the procedure whereby they make up their minds, and so on. As the circumstances are presented in different ways, correspondingly different principles are accepted. The concept of the original position, as I shall refer to it, is that of the most philosophically favored interpretation of this initial choice situation for the purposes of a theory of justice.

But how are we to decide what is the most favored interpretation? I assume, for one thing, that there is a broad measure of agreement that principles of justice should be chosen under certain conditions. To justify a particular description of the initial situation one shows that it incorporates these commonly shared presumptions. One argues from widely accepted but weak premises to more specific conclusions. Each of the presumptions should by itself be natural and plausible; some of them may seem innocuous or even trivial. The aim of the contract approach is to establish that taken together they impose significant bounds on acceptable principles of justice. The ideal outcome would be that these conditions determine a unique set of principles; but I shall be satisfied if they suffice to rank the main traditional conceptions of social justice.

One should not be misled, then, by the somewhat unusual conditions which characterize the original position. The idea here is simply to make vivid to ourselves the restrictions that it seems reasonable to impose on arguments for principles of justice, and therefore on these principles themselves. Thus it seems reasonable and generally acceptable that no one should be advantaged or disadvantaged by natural fortune or social circumstances in the choice of principles. It also seems widely agreed that it should be impossible to tailor principles to the circumstances of one's own case. We should insure further that particular inclinations and aspirations, and persons' conceptions of their good do not affect the principles adopted. The aim is to rule out those principles that it would be rational to propose for acceptance, however little the chance of success, only if one knew certain things that are irrelevant from the standpoint of justice. For example, if a man knew that he was wealthy, he might find it rational to advance the principle that various taxes for welfare measures be counted unjust; if he knew that he was poor, he would most likely propose the contrary principle. To represent the desired restrictions one imagines a situation in which everyone is deprived of this sort of information. One excludes the knowledge of those contingencies which sets men at odds and allows them to be guided by their prejudices. In this manner the veil of ignorance is arrived at in a natural way. This concept should cause no difficulty if we keep in mind the constraints on arguments that it is meant to express. At any time we can enter the original position, so to speak, simply by following a certain procedure, namely, by arguing for principles of justice in accordance with these restrictions.

It seems reasonable to suppose that the parties in the original position are equal. That is, all have the same rights in the procedure for choosing principles; each can make proposals, submit reasons for their acceptance, and so on. Obviously the purpose of these conditions is to represent equality between human beings as moral persons, as creatures having a conception of their good and capable of a sense of justice. The basis of equality is taken to be similarity in these two respects. Systems of ends are not ranked in value; and each man is presumed to have the requisite ability to understand and to act upon whatever principles are adopted. Together with the veil of ignorance, these conditions define the principles of justice as those which rational persons concerned to advance their interests would consent to as equals when none are known to be advantaged or disadvantaged by social and natural contingencies. . . .

TWO PRINCIPLES OF JUSTICE

I shall now state in a provisional form the two principles of justice that I believe would be chosen in the original position. In this section I wish to make only the most general comments, and therefore the first formulation of these principles is tentative. As we go on I shall run through several formulations and approximate step by step the final statement to be given much later. I believe that doing this allows the exposition to proceed in a natural way.

The first statement of the two principles reads as follows.

First: each person is to have an equal right to the most extensive basic liberty compatible with a similar liberty for others.

Second: social and economic inequalities are to be arranged so that they are both (a) reasonably expected to be to everyone's advantage, and (b) attached to positions and offices open to all. . . .

There are two ambiguous phrases in the second principle, namely "everyone's advantage" and "open to all."

By way of general comment, these principles primarily apply, as I have said, to the basic structure of society. They are to govern the assignment of rights and duties and to regulate the distribution of social and economic advantages. As their formulation suggests, these principles presuppose that the social structure can be divided into two more or less distinct parts, the first principle applying to the one, the second to the other. They distinguish between those aspects of the social system that define and secure the equal liberties of citizenship and those that specify and establish social and economic inequalities. The basic liberties of citizens are, roughly speaking, political liberty (the right to vote and to be eligible for public office) together with freedom of speech and assembly; liberty of conscience and freedom of thought; freedom of the person along with the right to hold (personal) property; and freedom from arbitrary arrest and seizure as defined by the concept of the rule of law. These liberties are all required to be equal by the first principle, since citizens of a just society are to have the same basic rights.

The second principle applies, in the first approximation, to the distribution of income and wealth and to the design of organizations that make use of differences in authority and responsibility, or chains of command. While the distribution of wealth and income need not be equal, it must be to everyone's advantage, and at the same time, positions of authority and offices of command must be accessible to all. One applies the second principle by holding positions open, and then, subject to this constraint, arranges social and economic inequalities so that everyone benefits.

These principles are to be arranged in a serial order with the first principle prior to the second. This ordering means that a departure from the institutions of equal liberty required by the first principle cannot be justified by, or compensated for, by greater social and economic advantages. The distribution of wealth and income, and the hierarchies of authority, must be consistent with both the liberties of equal citizenship and equality of opportunity.

It is clear that these principles are rather specific in their content, and their acceptance rests on certain assumptions that I must eventually try to explain and justify. A theory of justice depends upon a theory of society in ways that will become evident as we proceed. For the present, it should be observed that the two principles (and this holds for all formulations) are a special case of a more general conception of justice that can be expressed as follows.

All social values—liberty and opportunity, income and wealth, and the bases of self-respect—are to be distributed equally unless an unequal distribution of any, or all, of these values is to everyone's advantage. Injustice, then, is simply inequalities that are not to the benefit of all. Of course, this conception is extremely vague and requires interpretation.

As a first step, suppose that the basic structure of society distributes certain primary goods, that is, things that every rational man is presumed to want. These goods normally have a use whatever a person's rational plan of life. For simplicity, assume that the chief primary goods at the disposition of society are rights and liberties, powers and opportunities, income and wealth. (Later on in Part Three the primary good of self-respect has a central place.) These are the social primary goods. Other primary goods such as health and vigor, intelligence and imagination, are natural goods; although their possession is influenced by the basic structure, they are not so directly under its control. Imagine, then, a hypothetical initial arrangement in which all the social primary goods are equally distributed: everyone has similar rights and duties, and income and wealth are evenly shared. This state of affairs provides a benchmark for judging improvements. If certain inequalities of wealth and organizational powers would make everyone better off than in this hypothetical starting situation, then they accord with the general conception.

Now it is possible, at least theoretically, that by giving up some of their fundamental liberties men are sufficiently compensated by the resulting social and economic gains. The general conception of justice imposes no restrictions on what sort of inequalities are permissible; it only requires that everyone's position be improved. We need not suppose anything so drastic as consenting to a condition of slavery. Imagine instead that men forego certain political rights when the economic returns are significant and their capacity to influence the course of policy by the exercise of these rights would be marginal in any case. It is this kind of exchange which the two principles as stated rule out; being arranged in serial order they do not permit exchanges between basic liberties and economic and social gains. The serial ordering of principles expresses an underlying preference among primary social goods. When this preference is rational so likewise is the choice of these principles in this order.

In developing justice as fairness I shall, for the most part, leave aside the general conception of justice and examine instead the special case of the two principles in serial order. The advantage of this procedure is that from the first the matter of priorities is recognized and an effort made to find principles to deal with it. One is led to attend throughout to the conditions under which the acknowledgment of the absolute weight of liberty with respect to social and economic advantages, as defined by the lexical order of the two principles, would be reasonable. Offhand, this ranking appears extreme and too special a case to be of much interest; but there is more justification for it than would appear at first sight. Or at any rate, so I shall maintain (§82). Furthermore, the distinction between fundamental rights and liberties and economic and social benefits marks a difference among primary social goods that one should try to exploit. It suggests an important division in the social system. Of course, the distinctions drawn and the ordering proposed are bound to be at best only approximations. There are surely circumstances in which they fail. But it is essential to depict clearly the main lines of a reasonable conception of justice; and under many conditions anyway, the two principles in serial order may serve well enough. When necessary we can fall back on the more general conception.

The fact that the two principles apply to institutions has certain consequences. Several points illustrate this. First of all, the rights and liberties referred to by these principles are those which are defined by the public rules of the basic structure. Whether men are free is determined by the rights and duties established by the major institutions of society. Liberty is a certain pattern of social forms. The first principle simply requires that certain sorts of rules, those defining basic liberties, apply to everyone equally and that they allow the most extensive liberty compatible with a like liberty for all. The only reason for circumscribing the rights defining liberty and making men's freedom less extensive than it might otherwise be is that these equal rights as institutionally defined would interfere with one another.

Another thing to bear in mind is that when principles mention persons, or require that everyone gain from an inequality, the reference is to representative persons holding the various social positions, or offices, or whatever, established by the basic structure. Thus in applying the second principle I assume that it is possible to assign an expectation of well-being to representative individuals holding these positions. This expectation indicates their life prospects as viewed from their social station. In general, the expectations of representative persons depend upon the distribution of rights and duties throughout the basic structure. When this changes, expectations change. I assume, then, that expectations are connected: by raising the prospects of the representative man in one position we presumably increase or decrease the prospects of representative men in other positions. Since it applies to institutional forms, the second principle (or rather the first part of it) refers to the expectations of representative individuals. As I shall discuss below, neither principle applies to distributions of particular goods to particular individuals who may be identified by their proper names. The situation where someone is considering how to allocate certain commodities to needy persons who are known to him is not within the scope of the principles. They are meant to regulate basic institutional arrangements. We must not assume that there is much similarity from the standpoint of justice between an administrative allotment of goods to specific persons and the appropriate design of society. Our common sense intuitions for the former may be a poor guide to the latter.

Now the second principle insists that each person benefit from permissible inequalities in the basic structure. This means that it must be reasonable for each relevant representative man defined by this structure, when he views it as a going concern, to prefer his prospects with the inequality to his prospects without it. One is not allowed to justify differences in income or organizational powers on the ground that the disadvantages of those in one position are out-weighed by the greater advantages of those in another. Much less can infringements of liberty be counterbalanced in this way. Applied to the basic structure, the principle of utility would have us maximize the sum of expectations of representative men (weighted by the number of persons they represent, on the classical view); and this would permit us to compensate for the losses of some by the gains of others. Instead, the two principles require that everyone benefit from economic and social inequalities. It is obvious, however, that there are indefinitely many ways in which all may be advantaged when the initial arrangement of equality is taken as a benchmark. How then are we to choose among these possibilities? The principles must be specified so that they yield a determinate conclusion. I now turn to this problem. . . .

THE VEIL OF IGNORANCE

The idea of the original position is to set up a fair procedure so that any principles agreed to will be just. The aim is to use the notion of pure procedural justice as a basis of theory. Somehow we must nullify the effects of specific contingencies which put men at odds and tempt them to exploit social and natural circumstances to their own advantage. Now in order to do this I assume that the parties are situated behind a veil of ignorance. They do not know how the various alternatives will affect their own particular case and they are obliged to evaluate principles solely on the basis of general considerations.[d]

It is assumed, then, that the parties do not know certain kinds of particular facts. First of all, no one knows his place in society, his class position or social status; nor does he know his fortune in the distribution of natural assets and abilities, his intelligence and strength, and the like. Nor, again, does anyone know his conception of the good, the particulars of his rational plan of life, or even the special features of his psychology such as his aversion to risk or liability to optimism or pessimism. More than this, I assume that the parties do not know the particular circumstances of their own society. That is, they do not know its economic or political situation, or the level of civilization and culture it has been able to achieve. The persons in the original position have no information as to which generation they belong. These broader restrictions on knowledge are appropriate in part because questions of social justice arise between generations as well as within them, for example, the question of the appropriate rate of capital saving and of the conservation of natural resources and the environment of nature. There is also, theoretically anyway, the question of a reasonable genetic policy. In these cases too, in order to carry through the idea of the original position, the parties must not know the contingencies that set them in opposition. They must choose principles the consequences of which they are prepared to live with whatever generation they turn out to belong to.

As far as possible, then, the only particular facts which the parties know is that their society is subject to the circumstances of justice and whatever this implies.

---

[d]The veil of ignorance is so natural a condition that something like it must have occurred to many. The closest explicit statement of it known to me is found in J. C. Harsanyi, "Cardinal Utility in Welfare Economics and in the Theory of Risk-Taking," *Journal of Political Economy*, vol. 61 (1953). Harsanyi uses it to develop a utilitarian theory.

It is taken for granted, however, that they know the general facts about human society. They understand political affairs and the principles of economic theory; they know the basis of social organization and the laws of human psychology. Indeed, the parties are presumed to know whatever general facts affect the choice of the principles of justice. There are no limitations on general information, that is, on general laws and theories, since conceptions of justice must be adjusted to the characteristics of the systems of social cooperation which they are to regulate, and there is no reason to rule out these facts. It is, for example, a consideration against a conception of justice that, in view of the laws of moral psychology, men would not acquire a desire to act upon it even when the institutions of their society satisfied it. For in this case there would be difficulty in securing the stability of social cooperation. It is an important feature of a conception of justice that it should generate its own support. That is, its principles should be such that when they are embodied in the basic structure of society men tend to acquire the corresponding sense of justice. Given the principles of moral learning, men develop a desire to act in accordance with its principles. In this case a conception of justice is stable. This kind of general information is admissible in the original position.

The notion of the veil of ignorance raises several difficulties. Some may object that the exclusion of nearly all particular information makes it difficult to grasp what is meant by the original position. Thus it may be helpful to observe that one or more persons can at any time enter this position, or perhaps, better, simulate the deliberations of this hypothetical situation, simply by reasoning in accordance with the appropriate restrictions. In arguing for a conception of justice we must be sure that it is among the permitted alternatives and satisfies the stipulated formal constraints. No considerations can be advanced in its favor unless they would be rational ones for us to urge were we to lack the kind of knowledge that is excluded. The evaluation of principles must proceed in terms of the general consequences of their public recognition and universal application, it being assumed that they will be complied with by everyone. To say that a certain conception of justice would be chosen in the original position is equivalent to saying that rational deliberation satisfying certain conditions and restrictions would reach a certain conclusion. If necessary, the argument to this result could be set out more formally. I shall, however, speak throughout in terms of the notion of the original position. It is more economical and suggestive, and brings out certain essential features that otherwise one might easily overlook.

These remarks show that the original position is not to be thought of as a general assembly which includes at one moment everyone who will live at some time; or, much less, as an assembly of everyone who could live at some time. It is not a gathering of all actual or possible persons. To conceive of the original position in either of these ways is to stretch fantasy too far; the conception would cease to be a natural guide to intuition. In any case, it is important that the original position be interpreted so that one can at any time adopt its perspective. It must make no difference when one takes up this viewpoint, or who does so:

the restrictions must be such that the same principles are always chosen. The veil of ignorance is a key condition in meeting this requirement. It insures not only that the information available is relevant, but that it is at all times the same.

It may be protested that the condition of the veil of ignorance is irrational. Surely, some may object, principles should be chosen in the light of all the knowledge available. There are various replies to this contention. Here I shall sketch those which emphasize the simplifications that need to be made if one is to have any theory at all. . . . To begin with, it is clear that since the differences among the parties are unknown to them, and everyone is equally rational and similarly situated, each is convinced by the same arguments. Therefore, we can view the choice in the original position from the standpoint of one person selected at random. If anyone after due reflection prefers a conception of justice to another, then they all do, and a unanimous agreement can be reached. We can, to make the circumstances more vivid, imagine that the parties are required to communicate with each other through a referee as intermediary, and that he is to announce which alternatives have been suggested and the reasons offered in their support. He forbids the attempt to form coalitions, and he informs the parties when they have come to an understanding. But such a referee is actually superfluous, assuming that the deliberations of the parties must be similar.

Thus there follows the very important consequence that the parties have no basis for bargaining in the usual sense. No one knows his situation in society nor his natural assets, and therefore no one is in a position to tailor principles to his advantage. We might imagine that one of the contractees threatens to hold out unless the others agree to principles favorable to him. But how does he know which principles are especially in his interests? The same holds for the formation of coalitions: if a group were to decide to band together to the disadvantage of the others, they would not know how to favor themselves in the choice of principles. Even if they could get everyone to agree to their proposal, they would have no assurance that it was to their advantage, since they cannot identify themselves either by name or description. The one case where this conclusion fails is that of saving. Since the persons in the original position know that they are contemporaries (taking the present time of entry interpretation), they can favor their generation by refusing to make any sacrifices at all for their successors; they simply acknowledge the principle that no one has a duty to save for posterity. Previous generations have saved or they have not; there is nothing the parties can now do to affect that. So in this instance the veil of ignorance fails to secure the desired result. Therefore I resolve the question of justice between generations in a different way by altering the motivation assumption. But with this adjustment no one is able to formulate principles especially designed to advance his own cause. Whatever his temporal position, each is forced to choose for everyone.[c]

---

[c]Rousseau, *The Social Contract*, bk. II, ch. IV, par. 5.

The restrictions on particular information in the original position are, then, of fundamental importance. Without them we would not be able to work out any definite theory of justice at all. We would have to be content with a vague formula stating that justice is what would be agreed to without being able to say much, if anything, about the substance of the agreement itself. The formal constraints of the concept of right, those applying to principles directly, are not sufficient for our purpose. The veil of ignorance makes possible a unanimous choice of a particular conception of justice. Without these limitations on knowledge the bargaining problem of the original position would be hopelessly complicated. Even if theoretically a solution were to exist, we would not, at present anyway, be able to determine it.

The notion of the veil of ignorance is implicit, I think, in Kant's ethics (§40). Nevertheless the problem of defining the knowledge of the parties and of characterizing the alternatives open to them has often been passed over, even by contract theories. Sometimes the situation definitive of moral deliberation is presented in such an indeterminate way that one cannot ascertain how it will turn out. Thus Perry's doctrine is essentially contractarian: he holds that social and personal integration must proceed by entirely different principles, the latter by rational prudence, the former by the concurrence of persons of good will. He would appear to reject utilitarianism on much the same grounds suggested earlier: namely, that it improperly extends the principle of choice for one person to choices facing society. The right course of action is characterized as that which best advances social aims as these would be formulated by reflective agreement given that the parties have full knowledge of the circumstances and are moved by a benevolent concern for one another's interests. No effort is made, however, to specify in any precise way the possible outcomes of this sort of agreement. Indeed, without a far more elaborate account, no conclusions can be drawn.[f] I do not wish here to criticize others; rather, I want to explain the necessity for what may seem at times like so many irrelevant details.

Now the reasons for the veil of ignorance go beyond mere simplicity. We want to define the original position so that we get the desired solution. If a knowledge of particulars is allowed, then the outcome is biased by arbitrary contingencies. As already observed, to each according to his threat advantage is not a principle of justice. If the original position is to yield agreements that are just, the parties must be fairly situated and treated equally as moral persons. The arbitrariness of the world must be corrected for by adjusting the circumstances of the initial contractual situation. Moreover, if in choosing principles we required unanimity even when there is full information, only a few rather obvious cases could be decided. A conception of justice based on unanimity in these circumstances would

---

[f] See R. B. Perry, *The General Theory of Value* (New York, Longmans, Green and Company, 1926), pp. 674–682.

indeed be weak and trivial. But once knowledge is excluded, the requirement of unanimity is not out of place and the fact that it can be satisfied is of great importance. It enables us to say of the preferred conception of justice that it represents a genuine reconciliation of interests.

A final comment. For the most part I shall suppose that the parties possess all general information. No general facts are closed to them. I do this mainly to avoid complications. Nevertheless a conception of justice is to be the public basis of the terms of social cooperation. Since common understanding necessitates certain bounds on the complexity of principles, there may likewise be limits on the use of theoretical knowledge in the original position. Now clearly it would be very difficult to classify and to grade for complexity the various sorts of general facts. I shall make no attempt to do this. We do however recognize an intricate theoretical construction when we meet one. Thus it seems reasonable to say that other things equal one conception of justice is to be preferred to another when it is founded upon markedly simpler general facts, and its choice does not depend upon elaborate calculations in the light of a vast array of theoretically defined possibilities. It is desirable that the grounds for a public conception of justice should be evident to everyone when circumstances permit. This consideration favors, I believe, the two principles of justice over the criterion of utility.

CHAPTER 18

Philosophical Dialogue on Justice: Robert Nozick on Distributive Justice

Many consider Robert Nozick's *Anarchy, State, and Utopia,* published in 1974, to be the most important work of ethical philosophy in the analytical tradition since the appearance of Rawls's book in 1971.

Also from Harvard, Nozick writes in a style similar to that of Rawls. As Nozick describes what he calls his "flashy tools": "I write in the mode of much contemporary philosophical work. . . . There are elaborate arguments, claims rebutted by unlikely counterexamples, surprising theses, puzzles, abstract structural conditions, challenges to find another theory which fits a specified range of cases, startling conclusions, and so on."[1]

Unlike Rawls's redistributionist, activist state conclusions, however, Nozick's positions are best described as "libertarian." Nozick argues for what he calls the "minimal state," which *only* has the right or obligation to enforce voluntary contracts between individuals and to protect citizens from violence, theft, and other violations of individual rights. He contends that any more "extensive state" is not justified.

Claims that a more "extensive state" is morally required typically rest, as in Rawls, on the view that it is necessary to achieve true distributive justice. Against

[1]Robert Nozick, *Anarchy, State, and Utopia* (New York: Basic Books, 1974), p. x.

such claims Nozick develops his own "entitlement theory" of justice, according to which individuals have a right or "entitlement" to economic benefits that derive either from their own production or from voluntary transfers of property between individuals.

The latter notion of "transfers" plays an important role in Nozick's theory. He holds that property transfers are just if they result from voluntary agreements among individuals. Thus, if in a society people have acquired what they own justly, the subsequent distribution of wealth that results from voluntary transfers of property is also just. There is no need for an "extensive" state to redistribute wealth in order to achieve "distributive justice."

On the other hand, *nonvoluntary* transfers of property—as, for example, would occur under the redistributionist programs of Rawls's more "extensive" state—are unjust. Thus, Nozick condemns any taxation for purposes other than the narrow ones of the "minimal" state to be "forced labor."

Anarchy, State, and Utopia

Robert Nozick

DISTRIBUTIVE JUSTICE

The minimal state is the most extensive state that can be justified. Any state more extensive violates people's rights. Yet many persons have put forth reasons purporting to justify a more extensive state. It is impossible within the compass of this book to examine all the reasons that have been put forth. Therefore, I shall focus upon those generally acknowledged to be most weighty and influential, to see precisely wherein they fail. In this chapter we consider the claim that a more extensive state is justified, because necessary (or the best instrument) to achieve distributive justice; in the next chapter we shall take up diverse other claims.

The term "distributive justice" is not a neutral one. Hearing the term "distribution," most people presume that some thing or mechanism uses some principle or criterion to give out a supply of things. Into this process of distributing shares some error may have crept. So it is an open question, at least, whether *re*distribution should take place; whether we should do again what has already been done once, though poorly. However, we are not in the position of children who have been given portions of pie by someone who now makes last minute adjustments to rectify careless cutting. There is no *central* distribution, no person or group entitled to control all the resources, jointly deciding how they are to be doled out. What each person gets, he gets from others who give to him in exchange for something, or as a gift. In a free society, diverse persons control different resources, and new holdings arise out of the voluntary exchanges and actions of persons. There is no more a distributing or distribution of shares than there is a distributing of mates in a society in which persons choose whom they shall marry. The total result is the product of many individual decisions which the different individuals involved are entitled to make. Some uses of the term "distribution," it is true, do not imply a previous distributing appropriately judged by some criterion (for example, "probability distribution"); nevertheless, despite the title of this chapter, it would be best to use a terminology that clearly is neutral. We shall speak of people's holdings; a principle of justice in holdings describes (part of) what justice tells us (requires) about holdings. I shall state first what I take to be the correct view about justice in holdings, and then turn to the discussion of alternate views.

THE ENTITLEMENT THEORY

The subject of justice in holdings consists of three major topics. The first is the original acquisition of holdings, the appropriation of unheld things. This includes the issues of how unheld things may come to be held, the process, or processes, by which unheld things may come to be held, the things that may come to be held by these processes, the extent of what comes to be held by a particular process, and so on. We shall refer to the complicated truth about this topic, which we shall not formulate here, as the principle of justice in acquisition. The second topic concerns the transfer of holdings from one person to another. By what processes may a person transfer holdings to another? How may a person acquire a holding from another who holds it? Under this topic come general descriptions of voluntary exchange, and gift and (on the other hand) fraud, as well as reference to particular conventional details fixed upon in a given society. The complicated truth about this subject (with placeholders for conventional details) we shall call the principle of justice in transfer. (And we shall suppose it also includes principles governing how a person may divest himself of a holding, passing it into an unheld state.)

If the world were wholly just, the following inductive definition would exhaustively cover the subject of justice in holdings.

1. A person who acquires a holding in accordance with the principle of justice in acquisition is entitled to that holding.
2. A person who acquires a holding in accordance with the principle of justice in transfer, from someone else entitled to the holding, is entitled to the holding.
3. No one is entitled to a holding except by (repeated) applications of 1 and 2.

The complete principle of distributive justice would say simply that a distribution is just if everyone is entitled to the holdings they possess under the distribution.

A distribution is just if it arises from another just distribution by legitimate means. The legitimate means of moving from one distribution to another are specified by the principle of justice in transfer. The legitimate first "moves" are specified by the principle of justice in acquisition.[a] Whatever arises from a just situation by just steps is itself just. The means of change specified by the principle of justice in transfer preserve justice. As correct rules of inference are truth-

---

[a]Applications of the principle of justice in acquisition may also occur as part of the move from one distribution to another. You may find an unheld thing now and appropriate it. Acquisitions also are to be understood as included when, to simplify, I speak only of transitions by transfers.

preserving, and any conclusion deduced via repeated application of such rules from only true premises is itself true, so the means of transition from one situation to another specified by the principle of justice in transfer are justice-preserving, and any situation actually arising from repeated transitions in accordance with the principle from a just situation is itself just. The parallel between justice-preserving transformations and truth-preserving transformations illuminates where it fails as well as where it holds. That a conclusion could have been deduced by truth-preserving means from premises that are true suffices to show its truth. That from a just situation a situation *could* have arisen via justice-preserving means does *not* suffice to show its justice. The fact that a thief's victims voluntarily *could* have presented him with gifts does not entitle the thief to his ill-gotten gains. Justice in holdings is historical: it depends upon what actually has happened. We shall return to this point later.

Not all actual situations are generated in accordance with the two principles of justice in holdings: the principle of justice in acquisition and the principle of justice in transfer. Some people steal from others, or defraud them, or enslave them, seizing their product and preventing them from living as they choose, or forcibly exclude others from competing in exchanges. None of these are permissible modes of transition from one situation to another. And some persons acquire holdings by means not sanctioned by the principle of justice in acquisition. The existence of past injustice (previous violations of the first two principles of justice in holdings) raises the third major topic under justice in holdings: the rectification of injustice in holdings. If past injustice has shaped present holdings in various ways, some identifiable and some not, what now, if anything, ought to be done to rectify these injustices? What obligations do the performers of injustice have toward those whose position is worse than it would have been had the injustice not been done? Or, than it would have been had compensation been paid promptly? How, if at all, do things change if the beneficiaries and those made worse off are not the direct parties in the act of injustice, but, for example, their descendants? Is an injustice done to someone whose holding was itself based upon an unrectified injustice? How far back must one go in wiping clean the historical slate of injustices? What may victims of injustice permissibly do in order to rectify the injustices being done to them, including the many injustices done by persons acting through their government? I do not know of a thorough or theoretically sophisticated treatment of such issues. Idealizing greatly, let us suppose theoretical investigation will produce a principle of rectification. This principle uses historical information about previous situations and injustices done in them (as defined by the first two principles of justice and rights against interference), and information about the actual course of events that flowed from these injustices, until the present, and it yields a description (or descriptions) of holdings in the society. The principle of rectification presumably will make use of its best estimate of subjunctive information about what would have occurred (or a probability distribution over what might have occurred, using the expected value) if the injustice had not taken place. If the actual description of holdings turns out not to be one of the descriptions yielded by the principle, then one of the descriptions yielded must be realized.[b]

The general outlines of the theory of justice in holdings are that the holdings of a person are just if he is entitled to them by the principles of justice in acquisition and transfer, or by the principle of rectification of injustice (as specified by the first two principles). If each person's holdings are just, then the total set (distribution) of holdings is just. To turn these general outlines into a specific theory we would have to specify the details of each of the three principles of justice in holdings: the principle of acquisition of holdings, the principle of transfer of holdings, and the principle of rectification of violations of the first two principles. I shall not attempt that task here. (Locke's principle of justice in acquisition is discussed below.)

HISTORICAL PRINCIPLES AND END-RESULT PRINCIPLES

The general outlines of the entitlement theory illuminate the nature and defects of other conceptions of distributive justice. The entitlement theory of justice in distribution is historical; whether a distribution is just depends upon how it came about. In contrast, current time-slice principles of justice hold that the justice of a distribution is determined by how things are distributed (who has what) as judged by some *structural* principle(s) of just distribution. A utilitarian who judges between any two distributions by seeing which has the greater sum of utility and, if the sums tie, applies some fixed equality criterion to choose the more equal distribution, would hold a current time-slice principle of justice. As would someone who had a fixed schedule of trade-offs between the sum of happiness and equality. According to a current time-slice principle, all that needs to be looked at, in judging the justice of a distribution, is who ends up with what; in comparing any two distributions one need look only at the matrix presenting the distributions. No further information need be fed into a principle of justice. It is a consequence of such principles of justice that any two structurally identical distributions are equally just. (Two distributions are structurally identical if they present the same profile, but perhaps have different persons occupying the particular slots. My having ten and your having five, and my having five and your having ten are structurally identical distributions.) Welfare economics is the theory of current time-slice principles of justice. The subject is conceived as operating on matrices

---

[b]If the principle of rectification of violations of the first two principles yields more than one description of holdings, then some choice must be made as to which of these is to be realized. Perhaps the sort of considerations about distributive justice and equality that I argue against play a legitimate role in *this* subsidiary choice. Similarly, there may be room for such considerations in deciding which otherwise arbitrary features a statute will embody, when such features are unavoidable because other considerations do not specify a precise line; yet a line must be drawn.

representing only current information about distribution. This, as well as some of the usual conditions (for example, the choice of distribution is invariant under relabeling of columns), guarantees that welfare economics will be a current time-slice theory, with all of its inadequacies.

Most persons do not accept current time-slice principles as constituting the whole story about distributive shares. They think it relevant in assessing the justice of a situation to consider not only the distribution it embodies, but also how that distribution came about. If some persons are in prison for murder or war crimes, we do not say that to assess the justice of the distribution in the society we must look only at what this person has, and that person has, and that person has, . . . at the current time. We think it relevant to ask whether someone did something so that he deserved to be punished, deserved to have a lower share. Most will agree to the relevance of further information with regard to punishments and penalties. Consider also desired things. One traditional socialist view is that workers are entitled to the product and full fruits of their labor; they have earned it; a distribution is unjust if it does not give the workers what they are entitled to. Such entitlements are based upon some past history. No socialist holding this view would find it comforting to be told that because the actual distribution A happens to coincide structurally with the one he desires D, A therefore is no less just than D; it differs only in that the "parasitic" owners of capital receive under A what the workers are entitled to under D, and the workers receive under A what the owners are entitled to under D, namely very little. This socialist rightly, in my view, holds onto the notions of earning, producing, entitlement, desert, and so forth, and he rejects current time-slice principles that look only to the structure of the resulting set of holdings. (The set of holdings resulting from what? Isn't it implausible that how holdings are produced and come to exist has no effect at all on who should hold what?) His mistake lies in his view of what entitlements arise out of what sorts of productive processes.

We construe the position we discuss too narrowly by speaking of *current* time-slice principles. Nothing is changed if structural principles operate upon a time sequence of current time-slice profiles and, for example, give someone more now to counterbalance the less he has had earlier. A utilitarian or an egalitarian or any mixture of the two over time will inherit the difficulties of his more myopic comrades. He is not helped by the fact that *some* of the information others consider relevant in assessing a distribution is reflected, unrecoverably, in past matrices. Henceforth, we shall refer to such unhistorical principles of distributive justice, including the current time-slice principles, as end-result principles or end-state principles.

In contrast to end-result principles of justice, historical principles of justice hold that past circumstances or actions of people can create differential entitlements or differential deserts to things. An injustice can be worked by moving from one distribution to another structurally identical one, for the second, in profile the same, may violate people's entitlements or deserts; it may not fit the actual history.

PATTERNING

The entitlement principles of justice in holdings that we have sketched are historical principles of justice. To better understand their precise character, we shall distinguish them from another subclass of the historical principles. Consider, as an example, the principle of distribution according to moral merit. This principle requires that total distributive shares vary directly with moral merit; no person should have a greater share than anyone whose moral merit is greater. (If moral merit could be not merely ordered but measured on an interval or ratio scale, stronger principles could be formulated.) Or consider the principle that results by substituting "usefulness to society" for "moral merit" in the previous principle. Or instead of "distribute according to moral merit," or "distribute according to usefulness to society," we might consider "distribute according to the weighted sum of moral merit, usefulness to society, and need," with the weights of the different dimensions equal. Let us call a principle of distribution patterned if it specifies that a distribution is to vary along with some natural dimension, weighted sum of natural dimensions, or lexicographic ordering of natural dimensions. And let us say a distribution is patterned if it accords with some patterned principle. (I speak of natural dimensions, admittedly without a general criterion for them, because for any set of holdings some artificial dimensions can be gimmicked up to vary along with the distribution of the set.) The principle of distribution in accordance with moral merit is a patterned historical principle, which specifies a patterned distribution. "Distribute according to I.Q." is a patterned principle that looks to information not contained in distributional matrices. It is not historical, however, in that it does not look to any past actions creating differential entitlements to evaluate a distribution; it requires only distributional matrices whose columns are labeled by I.Q. scores. The distribution in a society, however, may be composed of such simple patterned distributions, without itself being simply patterned. Different sectors may operate different patterns, or some combination of patterns may operate in different proportions across a society. A distribution composed in this manner, from a small number of patterned distributions, we also shall term "patterned." And we extend the use of "pattern" to include the overall designs put forth by combinations of end-state principles.

Almost every suggested principle of distributive justice is patterned: to each according to his moral merit, or needs, or marginal product, or how hard he tries, or the weighted sum of the foregoing, and so on. The principle of entitlement we have sketched is not patterned.[c] There is no one natural dimension or weighted

---

[c] One might try to squeeze a patterned conception of distributive justice into the framework of the entitlement conception, by formulating a gimmicky obligatory "principle of transfer" that would lead to the pattern. For example, the principle that if one has more than the mean income one must transfer everything one holds above the mean to persons below the mean so as to bring them up to (but not over) the mean. We can formulate a criterion for a "principle of transfer" to rule out such

sum or combination of a small number of natural dimensions that yields the distributions generated in accordance with the principle of entitlement. The set of holdings that results when some persons receive their marginal products, others win at gambling, others receive a share of their mate's income, others receive gifts from foundations, others receive interest on loans, others receive gifts from admirers, others receive returns on investment, others make for themselves much of what they have, others find things, and so on, will not be patterned. Heavy strands of patterns will run through it; significant portions of the variance in holdings will be accounted for by pattern-variables. If most people most of the time choose to transfer some of their entitlements to others only in exchange for something from them, then a large part of what many people hold will vary with what they held that others wanted. More details are provided by the theory of marginal productivity. But gifts to relatives, charitable donations, bequests to children, and the like, are not best conceived, in the first instance, in this manner. Ignoring the strands of pattern, let us suppose for the moment that a distribution actually arrived at by the operation of the principle of entitlement is random with respect to any pattern. Though the resulting set of holdings will be unpatterned, it will not be incomprehensible, for it can be seen as arising from the operation of a small number of principles. These principles specify how an initial distribution may arise (the principle of acquisition of holdings) and how distributions may be transformed into others (the principle of transfer of holdings). The process whereby the set of holdings is generated will be intelligible, though the set of holdings itself that results from this process will be unpatterned.

The writings of F. A. Hayek focus less than is usually done upon what patterning distributive justice requires. Hayek argues that we cannot know enough about each person's situation to distribute to each according to his moral merit (but would justice demand we do so if we did have this knowledge?); and he goes on to say, "our objection is against all attempts to impress upon society a deliberately chosen pattern of distribution, whether it be an order of equality or of inequality." However, Hayek concludes that in a free society there will be distribution in accordance with value rather than moral merit; that is, in accordance with the perceived value of a person's actions and services to others. Despite his rejection of a patterned conception of distributive justice, Hayek himself suggests a pattern he thinks justifiable: distribution in accordance with the perceived benefits given to others, leaving room for the complaint that a free society does not realize exactly this pattern. Stating this patterned strand of a free capitalist society more precisely, we get "To each according to how much he benefits others who have

---

obligatory transfers, or we can say that no correct principle of transfer, no principle of transfer in a free society will be like this. The former is probably the better course, though the latter also is true.

Alternatively, one might think to make the entitlement conception instantiate a pattern, by using matrix entries that express the relative strength of a person's entitlements as measured by some real-valued function. But even if the limitation to natural dimensions failed to exclude this function, the resulting edifice would *not* capture our system of entitlements to *particular* things.

the resources for benefiting those who benefit them." This will seem arbitrary unless some acceptable initial set of holdings is specified, or unless it is held that the operation of the system over time washes out any significant effects from the initial set of holdings. As an example of the latter, if almost anyone would have bought a car from Henry Ford, the supposition that it was an arbitrary matter who held the money then (and so bought) would not place Henry Ford's earnings under a cloud. In any event, *his* coming to hold it is not arbitrary. Distribution according to benefits to others is a major patterned strand in a free capitalist society, as Hayek correctly points out, but it is only a strand and does not constitute the whole pattern of a system of entitlements (namely, inheritance, gifts for arbitrary reasons, charity, and so on) or a standard that one should insist a society fit. Will people tolerate for long a system yielding distributions that they believe are unpatterned? No doubt people will not long accept a distribution they believe is *unjust*. People want their society to be and to look just. But must the look of justice reside in a resulting pattern rather than in the underlying generating principles? We are in no position to conclude that the inhabitants of a society embodying an entitlement conception of justice in holdings will find it unacceptable. Still, it must be granted that were people's reasons for transferring some of their holdings to others always irrational or arbitrary, we would find this disturbing. (Suppose people always determined what holdings they would transfer, and to whom, by using a random device.) We feel more comfortable upholding the justice of an entitlement system if most of the transfers under it are done for reasons. This does not mean necessarily that all deserve what holdings they receive. It means only that there is a purpose or point to someone's transferring a holding to one person rather than to another; that usually we can see what the transferrer thinks he's gaining, what cause he thinks he's serving, what goals he thinks he's helping to achieve, and so forth. Since in a capitalist society people often transfer holdings to others in accordance with how much they perceive these others benefiting them, the fabric constituted by the individual transactions and transfers is largely reasonable and intelligible.[d] (Gifts to loved ones, bequests to children, charity to the needy also are nonarbitrary components of the fabric.) In stressing the large strand of distribution in accordance with benefit to others, Hayek shows the point of many transfers, and so shows that the system of transfer of entitlements is not just spinning its gears aimlessly. The system of entitlements is defensible when

---

[d]We certainly benefit because great economic incentives operate to get others to spend much time and energy to figure out how to serve us by providing things we will want to pay for. It is not mere paradox mongering to wonder whether capitalism should be criticized for most rewarding and hence encouraging, not individualists like Thoreau who go about their own lives, but people who are occupied with serving others and winning them as customers. But to defend capitalism one need not think businessmen are the finest human types. (I do not mean to join here the general maligning of businessmen, either.) Those who think the finest should acquire the most can try to convince their fellows to transfer resources in accordance with *that* principle.

constituted by the individual aims of individual transactions. No overarching aim is needed, no distributional pattern is required.

To think that the task of a theory of distributive justice is to fill in the blank in "to each according to his———" is to be predisposed to search for a pattern; and the separate treatment of "from each according to his———" treats production and distribution as two separate and independent issues. On an entitlement view these are not two separate questions. Whoever makes something, having bought or contracted for all other held resources used in the process (transferring some of his holdings for these cooperating factors), is entitled to it. The situation is *not* one of something's getting made, and there being an open question of who is to get it. Things come into the world already attached to people having entitlements over them. From the point of view of the historical entitlement conception of justice in holdings, those who start afresh to complete "to each according to his———" treat objects as if they appeared from nowhere, out of nothing. A complete theory of justice might cover this limit case as well; perhaps here is a use for the usual conceptions of distributive justice.

So entrenched are maxims of the usual form that perhaps we should present the entitlement conception as a competitor. Ignoring acquisition and rectification, we might say:

> From each according to what he chooses to do, to each according to what he makes for himself (perhaps with the contracted aid of others) and what others choose to do for him and choose to give him of what they've been given previously (under this maxim) and haven't yet expended or transferred.

This, the discerning reader will have noticed, has its defects as a slogan. So as a summary and great simplification (and not as a maxim with any independent meaning) we have:

> From each as they choose, to each as they are chosen.

HOW LIBERTY UPSETS PATTERNS

It is not clear how those holding alternative conceptions of distributive justice can reject the entitlement conception of justice in holdings. For suppose a distribution favored by one of these nonentitlement conceptions is realized. Let us suppose it is your favorite one and let us call this distribution D_1; perhaps everyone has an equal share, perhaps shares vary in accordance with some dimension you treasure. Now suppose that Wilt Chamberlain is greatly in demand by basketball teams, being a great gate attraction. (Also suppose contracts run only for a year, with players being free agents.) He signs the following sort of contract with a team: In each home game, twenty-five cents from the price of each ticket of admission goes to him. (We ignore the question of whether he is "gouging" the owners, letting them look out for themselves.) The season starts, and people cheerfully attend his team's games; they buy their tickets, each time dropping a separate twenty-five cents of their admission price into a special box with Chamberlain's name on it. They are excited about seeing him play; it is worth the total admission price to them. Let us suppose that in one season one million persons attend his home games, and Wilt Chamberlain winds up with $250,000, a much larger sum than the average income and larger even than anyone else has. Is he entitled to this income? Is this new distribution D_2, unjust? If so, why? There is *no* question about whether each of the people was entitled to the control over the resources they held in D_1; because that was the distribution (your favorite) that (for the purposes of argument) we assumed was acceptable. Each of these persons *chose* to give twenty-five cents of their money to Chamberlain. They could have spent it on going to the movies, or on candy bars, or on copies of *Dissent* magazine, or of *Monthly Review*. But they all, at least one million of them, converged on giving it to Wilt Chamberlain in exchange for watching him play basketball. If D_1 was a just distribution, and people voluntarily moved from it to D_2, transferring parts of their shares they were given under D_1 (what was it for if not to do something with?), isn't D_2 also just? If the people were entitled to dispose of the resources to which they were entitled (under D_1), didn't this include their being entitled to give it to, or exchange it with, Wilt Chamberlain? Can anyone else complain on grounds of justice? Each other person already has his legitimate share under D_1. Under D_1, there is nothing that anyone has that anyone else has a claim of justice against. After someone transfers something to Wilt Chamberlain, third parties *still* have their legitimate shares; *their* shares are not changed. By what process could such a transfer among two persons give rise to a legitimate claim of distributive justice on a portion of what was transferred, by a third party who had no claim of justice on any holding of the others *before* the transfer?[e] To cut off objections irrelevant here, we might imagine the exchanges occurring in a socialist society, after hours. After playing whatever basketball he does in his daily work, or doing whatever other daily work he does, Wilt Chamberlain decides to put in *overtime*

---

[e]Might not a transfer have instrumental effects on a third party, changing his feasible options? (But what if the two parties to the transfer independently had used their holdings in this fashion?) I discuss this question below, but note here that this question concedes the point for distributions of ultimate intrinsic noninstrumental goods (pure utility experiences, so to speak) that are transferable. It also might be objected that the transfer might make a third party more envious because it worsens his position relative to someone else. I find it incomprehensible how this can be thought to involve a claim of justice. On envy, see Chapter 8.

Here and elsewhere in this chapter, a theory which incorporates elements of pure procedural justice might find what I say acceptable, *if* kept in its proper place; that is, if background institutions exist to ensure the satisfaction of certain conditions on distributive shares. But if these institutions are not themselves the sum or invisible-hand result of people's voluntary (nonaggressive) actions, the constraints they impose require justification. At no point does *our* argument assume any background institutions more extensive than those of the minimal night-watchman state, a state limited to protecting persons against murder, assault, theft, fraud, and so forth.

to earn additional money. (First his work quota is set; he works time over that.) Or imagine it is a skilled juggler people like to see, who puts on shows after hours.

Why might someone work overtime in a society in which it is assumed their needs are satisfied? Perhaps because they care about things other than needs. I like to write in books that I read, and to have easy access to books for browsing at odd hours. It would be very pleasant and convenient to have the resources of Widener Library in my back yard. No society, I assume, will provide such resources close to each person who would like them as part of his regular allotment (under D_1). Thus, persons either must do without some extra things that they want, or be allowed to do something extra to get some of these things. On what basis could the inequalities that would eventuate be forbidden? Notice also that small factories would spring up in a socialist society, unless forbidden. I melt down some of my personal possessions (under D_1) and build a machine out of the material. I offer you, and others, a philosophy lecture once a week in exchange for your cranking the handle on my machine, whose products I exchange for yet other things, and so on. (The raw materials used by the machine are given to me by others who possess them under D_1, in exchange for hearing lectures.) Each person might participate to gain things over and above their allotment under D_1. Some persons even might want to leave their job in socialist industry and work full time in this private sector. I shall say something more about these issues in the next chapter. Here I wish merely to note how private property even in means of production would occur in a socialist society that did not forbid people to use as they wished some of the resources they are given under the socialist distribution. D_1 The socialist society would have to forbid capitalist acts between consenting adults.

The general point illustrated by the Wilt Chamberlain example and the example of the entrepreneur in a socialist society is that no end-state principle or distributional patterned principle of justice can be continuously realized without continuous interference with people's lives. Any favored pattern would be transformed into one unfavored by the principle, by people choosing to act in various ways; for example, by people exchanging goods and services with other people, or giving things to other people, things the transferrers are entitled to under the favored distributional pattern. To maintain a pattern one must either continually interfere to stop people from transferring resources as they wish to, or continually (or periodically) interfere to take from some persons resources that others for some reason chose to transfer to them. (But if some time limit is to be set on how long people may keep resources others voluntarily transfer to them, why let them keep these resources for *any* period of time? Why not have immediate confiscation?) It might be objected that all persons voluntarily will choose to refrain from actions which would upset the pattern. This presupposes unrealistically (I) that all will most want to maintain the pattern (are those who don't, to be "reeducated" or forced to undergo "self-criticism"?), (2) that each can gather enough information about his own actions and the ongoing activities of others to discover which of his actions will upset the pattern, and (3) that diverse and far-flung persons can coordinate their actions to dove-tail into the pattern. Compare the manner in which the market is neutral among persons' desires, as it reflects and transmits widely scattered information via prices, and coordinates persons' activities.

It puts things perhaps a bit too strongly to say that every patterned (or end-state) principle is liable to be thwarted by the voluntary actions of the individual parties transferring some of their shares they receive under the principle. For perhaps some *very* weak patterns are not so thwarted.[f] Any distributional pattern with any egalitarian component is overturnable by the voluntary actions of individual persons over time; as is every patterned condition with sufficient content so as actually to have been proposed as presenting the central core of distributive justice. Still, given the possibility that some weak conditions or patterns may not be unstable in this way, it would be better to formulate an explicit description of the kind of interesting and contentful patterns under discussion, and to prove a theorem about their instability. Since the weaker the patterning, the more likely it is that the entitlement system itself satisfies it, a plausible conjecture is that any patterning either is unstable or is satisfied by the entitlement system.

SEN'S ARGUMENT

Our conclusions are reinforced by considering a recent general argument of Amartya K. Sen. Suppose individual rights are interpreted as the right to choose which of two alternatives is to be more highly ranked in a social ordering of the alternatives. Add the weak condition that if one alternative unanimously is preferred to another then it is ranked higher by the social ordering. If there are two different individuals each with individual rights, interpreted as above, over different pairs of alternatives (having no members in common), then for some possible preference rankings of the alternatives by the individuals, there is no linear social ordering. For suppose that person A has the right to decide among (X, Y) and person B has the right to decide among (Z, W); and suppose their individual preferences are as follows (and that there are no other individuals). Person A prefers W to X to Y to Z, and person B prefers Y to Z to W to X. By the unanimity condition, in the social ordering W is preferred to X (since each individual prefers it to X), and Y is preferred to Z (since each individual prefers it to Z). Also in the social ordering, X is preferred to Y, by person A's right of choice among these two alternatives. Combining these three binary rankings, we get W preferred to X preferred to Y preferred to Z, in the social ordering. However, by person B's right of choice, Z must be preferred to W in the social ordering. There is no transitive social ordering satisfying all these conditions, and the social ordering, therefore, is nonlinear. Thus far, Sen.

---

[f] Is the patterned principle stable that requires merely that a distribution be Pareto-optimal? One person might give another a gift or bequest that the second could exchange with a third to their mutual benefit. Before the second makes this exchange, there is not Pareto-optimality. Is a stable pattern presented by a principle choosing that among the Pareto-optimal positions that satisfies some

The trouble stems from treating an individual's right to choose among alternatives as the right to determine the relative ordering of these alternatives within a social ordering. The alternative which has individuals rank *pairs* of alternatives, and separately rank the individual alternatives is no better; their ranking of pairs feeds into some method of amalgamating preferences to yield a social ordering of pairs; and the choice among the alternatives in the highest ranked pair in the social ordering is made by the individual with the right to decide between this pair. This system also has the result that an alternative may be selected although *everyone* prefers some other alternative; for example, A selects X over Y, where (X, Y) somehow is the highest ranked *pair* in the social ordering of pairs, although everyone, including A, prefers W to X. (But the choice person A was given, however, was only between X and Y.)

A more appropriate view of individual rights is as follows. Individual rights are co-possible; each person may exercise his rights as he chooses. The exercise of these rights fixes some features of the world. Within the constraints of these fixed features, a choice may be made by a social choice mechanism based upon a social ordering; if there are any choices left to make! Rights do not determine a social ordering but instead set the constraints within which a social choice is to be made, by excluding certain alternatives, fixing others, and so on. (If I have a right to choose to live in New York or in Massachusetts, and I choose Massachusetts, then alternatives involving my living in New York are not appropriate objects to be entered in a social ordering.) Even if all possible alternatives are ordered first, apart from anyone's rights, the situation is not changed: for then the highest ranked alternative *that is not excluded by anyone's exercise of his rights* is instituted. Rights do not determine the position of an alternative or the relative position of two alternatives in a social ordering; they *operate upon* a social ordering to constrain the choice it can yield.

If entitlements to holdings are rights to dispose of them, then social choice must take place *within* the constraints of how people choose to exercise these rights. If any patterning is legitimate, it falls within the domain of social choice, and hence is constrained by people's rights. *How else can one cope with Sen's result?* The alternative of first having a social ranking with rights exercised within *its* constraints is no alternative at all. Why not just select the top-ranked alternative and forget about rights? If that top-ranked alternative itself leaves some room for

---

further condition C? It may seem that there cannot be a counterexample, for won't any voluntary exchange made away from a situation show that the first situation wasn't Pareto-optimal? (Ignore the implausibility of this last claim for the case of bequests.) But principles are to be satisfied over time, during which new possibilities arise. A distribution that at one time satisfies the criterion of Pareto-optimality might not do so when some new possibilities arise (Wilt Chamberlain grows up and starts playing basketball); and though people's activities will tend to move then to a new Pareto-optimal position, *this* new one need not satisfy the contentful condition C. Continual interference will be needed to insure the continual satisfaction of C. (The theoretical possibility of a pattern's being maintained by some invisible-hand process that brings it back to an equilibrium that fits the pattern when deviations occur should be investigated.)

individual choice (and here is where "rights" of choice is supposed to enter in) there must be something to stop these choices from transforming it into another alternative. Thus Sen's argument leads us again to the result that patterning requires continuous interference with individuals' actions and choices.

REDISTRIBUTION AND PROPERTY RIGHTS

Apparently, patterned principles allow people to choose to expend upon themselves, but not upon others, those resources they are entitled to (or rather, receive) under some favored distributional pattern D_1. For if each of several persons chooses to expend some of his D_1 resources upon one other person, then that other person will receive more than his D_1 share, disturbing the favored distributional pattern. Maintaining a distributional pattern is individualism with a vengeance! Patterned distributional principles do not give people what entitlement principles do, only better distributed. For they do not give the right to choose what to do with what one has; they do not give the right to choose to pursue an end involving (intrinsically, or as a means) the enhancement of another's position. To such views, families are disturbing; for within a family occur transfers that upset the favored distributional pattern. Either families themselves become units to which distribution takes place, the column occupiers (on what rationale?), or loving behavior is forbidden. We should note in passing the ambivalent position of radicals toward the family. Its loving relationships are seen as a model to be emulated and extended across the whole society, at the same time that it is denounced as a suffocating institution to be broken and condemned as a focus of parochial concerns that interfere with achieving radical goals. Need we say that it is not appropriate to enforce across the wider society the relationships of love and care appropriate within a family, relationships which are voluntarily undertaken?[g] Incidentally, love is an interesting instance of another relationship that is historical, in that (like justice) it depends upon what actually occurred. An adult may come to love another because of the other's characteristics; but it is the other person, and not the characteristics, that is loved. The love is not transferrable to someone else with the same characteristics, even to one who "scores" higher for these characteristics. And the love endures through changes of the characteristics that gave rise to it. One loves the particular person one actually encountered.

---

[g]One indication of the stringency of Rawls' difference principle, which we attend to in the second part of this chapter, is its inappropriateness as a governing principle even within a family of individuals who love one another. Should a family devote its resources to maximizing the position of its least well off and least talented child, holding back the other children or using resources for their education and development only if they will follow a policy through their life-times of maximizing the position of their least fortunate sibling? Surely not. How then can this even be considered as the appropriate policy for enforcement in the wider society? (I discuss below what I think would be Rawls' reply: that some principles apply at the macro level which do not apply to micro-situations.)

Why love is historical, attaching to persons in this way and not to characteristics, is an interesting and puzzling question.

Proponents of patterned principles of distributive justice focus upon criteria for determining who is to receive holdings; they consider the reasons for which someone should have something, and also the total picture of holdings. Whether or not it is better to give than to receive, proponents of patterned principles ignore giving altogether. In considering the distribution of goods, income, and so forth, their theories are theories of recipient justice; they completely ignore any right a person might have to give something to someone. Even in exchanges where each party is simultaneously giver and recipient, patterned principles of justice focus only upon the recipient role and its supposed rights. Thus discussions tend to focus on whether people (should) have a right to inherit, rather than on whether people (should) have a right to bequeath or on whether persons who have a right to hold also have a right to choose that others hold in their place. I lack a good explanation of why the usual theories of distributive justice are so recipient oriented; ignoring givers and transferrers and their rights is of a piece with ignoring producers and their entitlements. But why is it *all* ignored?

Patterned principles of distributive justice necessitate redistributive activities. The likelihood is small that any actual freely-arrived-at set of holdings fits a given pattern; and the likelihood is nil that it will continue to fit the pattern as people exchange and give. From the point of view of an entitlement theory, redistribution is a serious matter indeed, involving, as it does, the violation of people's rights. (An exception is those takings that fall under the principle of the rectification of injustices.) From other points of view, also, it is serious.

Taxation of earnings from labor is on a par with forced labor.[h] Some persons find this claim obviously true: taking the earnings of n hours labor is like taking n hours from the person; it is like forcing the person to work n hours for another's purpose. Others find the claim absurd. But even these, *if* they object to forced labor, would oppose forcing unemployed hippies to work for the benefit of the needy.[i] And they would also object to forcing each person to work five extra hours each week for the benefit of the needy. But a system that takes five hours' wages in taxes does not seem to them like one that forces someone to work five hours, since it offers the person forced a wider range of choice in activities than does taxation in kind with the particular labor specified. (But we can imagine a grada-

---

[h]I am unsure as to whether the arguments I present below show that such taxation merely *is* forced labor; so that "is on a par with" means "is one kind of." Or alternatively, whether the arguments emphasize the great similarities between such taxation and forced labor, to show it is plausible and illuminating to view such taxation in the light of forced labor. This latter approach would remind one of how John Wisdom conceives of the claims of metaphysicians.

[i]Nothing hangs on the fact that here and elsewhere I speak loosely of *needs*, since I go on, each time, to reject the criterion of justice which includes it. If, however, something did depend upon the notion, one would want to examine it more carefully. For a skeptical view, see Kenneth Minogue, *The Liberal Mind*, (New York: Random House, 1963), pp. 103–112.

tion of systems of forced labor, from one that specifies a particular activity, to one that gives a choice among two activities, to . . . ; and so on up.) Furthermore, people envisage a system with something like a proportional tax on everything above the amount necessary for basic needs. Some think this does not force someone to work extra hours, since there is no fixed number of extra hours he is forced to work, and since he can avoid the tax entirely by earning only enough to cover his basic needs. This is a very uncharacteristic view of forcing for those who *also* think people are forced to do something *whenever* the alternatives they face are considerably worse. However, *neither* view is correct. The fact that others intentionally intervene, in violation of a side constraint against aggression, to threaten force to limit the alternatives, in this case to paying taxes or (presumably the worse alternative) bare subsistence, makes the taxation system one of forced labor and distinguishes it from other cases of limited choices which are not forcings.

The man who chooses to work longer to gain an income more than sufficient for his basic needs prefers some extra goods or services to the leisure and activities he could perform during the possible nonworking hours; whereas the man who chooses not to work the extra time prefers the leisure activities to the extra goods or services he could acquire by working more. Given this, if it would be illegitimate for a tax system to seize some of a man's leisure (forced labor) for the purpose of serving the needy, how can it be legitimate for a tax system to seize some of a man's goods for that purpose? Why should we treat the man whose happiness requires certain material goods or services differently from the man whose preferences and desires make such goods unnecessary for his happiness? Why should the man who prefers seeing a movie (and who has to earn money for a ticket) be open to the required call to aid the needy, while the person who prefers looking at a sunset (and hence need earn no extra money) is not? Indeed, isn't it surprising that redistributionists choose to ignore the man whose pleasures are so easily attainable without extra labor, while adding yet another burden to the poor unfortunate who must work for his pleasures? If anything, one would have expected the reverse. Why is the person with the nonmaterial or nonconsumption desire allowed to proceed unimpeded to his most favored feasible alternative, whereas the man whose pleasures or desires involve material things and who must work for extra money (thereby serving whomever considers his activities valuable enough to pay him) is constrained in what he can realize? Perhaps there is no difference in principle. And perhaps some think the answer concerns merely administrative convenience. (These questions and issues will not disturb those who think that forced labor to serve the needy or to realize some favored end-state pattern is acceptable.) In a fuller discussion we would have (and want) to extend our argument to include interest, entrepreneurial profits, and so on. Those who doubt that this extension can be carried through, and who draw the line here at taxation of income from labor, will have to state rather complicated patterned *historical* principles of distributive justice, since end-state principles would not distinguish *sources* of income in any way. It is enough for now to get away from end-state principles and to make clear how various patterned principles are dependent upon particular views about the sources or the illegitimacy or the lesser legitimacy of profits, interest, and so on; which particular views may well be mistaken.

What sort of right over others does a legally institutionalized end-state pattern give one? The central core of the notion of a property right in X, relative to which other parts of the notion are to be explained, is the right to determine what shall be done with X; the right to choose which of the constrained set of options concerning X shall be realized or attempted. The constraints are set by other principles or laws operating in the society; in our theory, by the Lockean rights people possess (under the minimal state). My property rights in my knife allow me to leave it where I will, but not in your chest. I may choose which of the acceptable options involving the knife is to be realized. This notion of property helps us to understand why earlier theorists spoke of people as having property in themselves and their labor. They viewed each person as having a right to decide what would become of himself and what he would do, and as having a right to reap the benefits of what he did.

This right of selecting the alternative to be realized from the constrained set of alternatives may be held by an *individual* or by a *group* with some procedure for reaching a joint decision; or the right may be passed back and forth, so that one year I decide what's to become of X, and the next year you do (with the alternative of destruction, perhaps, being excluded). Or, during the same time period, some types of decisions about X may be made by me, and others by you. And so on. We lack an adequate, fruitful, analytical apparatus for classifying the *types* of constraints on the set of options among which choices are to be made, and the *types* of ways decision powers can be held, divided, and amalgamated. A *theory* of property would, among other things, contain such a classification of constraints and decision modes, and from a small number of principles would follow a host of interesting statements about the *consequences* and effects of certain combinations of constraints and modes of decision.

When end-result principles of distributive justice are built into the legal structure of a society, they (as do most patterned principles) give each citizen an enforceable claim to some portion of the total social product; that is, to some portion of the sum total of the individually and jointly made products. This total product is produced by individuals laboring, using means of production others have saved to bring into existence, by people organizing production or creating means to produce new things or things in a new way. It is on this batch of individual activities that patterned distributional principles give each individual an enforceable claim. Each person has a claim to the activities and the products of other persons, independently of whether the other persons enter into particular relationships that give rise to these claims, and independently of whether they voluntarily take these claims upon themselves, in charity or in exchange for something.

Whether it is done through taxation on wages or on wages over a certain amount, or through seizure of profits, or through there being a big *social pot* so that it's not clear what's coming from where and what's going where, patterned principles of distributive justice involve appropriating the actions of other persons. Seizing the results of someone's labor is equivalent to seizing hours from him and directing him to carry on various activities. If people force you to do certain work, or unrewarded work, for a certain period of time, they decide what you are to do and what purposes your work is to serve apart from your decisions. This process whereby they take this decision from you makes them a *part-owner* of you; it gives them a property right in you. Just as having such partial control and power of decision, by right, over an animal or inanimate object would be to have a property right in it.

End-state and most patterned principles of distributive justice institute (partial) ownership by others of people and their actions and labor. These principles involve a shift from the classical liberals' notion of self-ownership to a notion of (partial) property rights in *other* people.

Considerations such as these confront end-state and other patterned conceptions of justice with the question of whether the actions necessary to achieve the selected pattern don't themselves violate moral side constraints. Any view holding that there are moral side constraints on actions, that not all moral considerations can be built into end states that are to be achieved must face the possibility that some of its goals are not achievable by any morally permissible available means. An entitlement theorist will face such conflicts in a society that deviates from the principles of justice for the generation of holdings, if and only if the only actions available to realize the principles themselves violate some moral constraints. Since deviation from the first two principles of justice (in acquisition and transfer) will involve other persons' direct and aggressive intervention to violate rights, and since moral constraints will not exclude defensive or retributive action in such cases, the entitlement theorist's problem rarely will be pressing. And whatever difficulties he has in applying the principle of rectification to persons who did not themselves violate the first two principles are difficulties in balancing the conflicting considerations so as correctly to formulate the complex principle of rectification itself; he will not violate moral side constraints by applying the principle. Proponents of patterned conceptions of justice, however, often will face head-on clashes (and poignant ones if they cherish each party to the clash) between moral side constraints on how individuals may be treated and their patterned conception of justice that presents an end state or other pattern that must be realized.

May a person emigrate from a nation that has institutionalized some end-state or patterned distributional principle? For some principles (for example, Hayek's) emigration presents no theoretical problem. But for others it is a tricky matter. Consider a nation having a compulsory scheme of minimal social provision to aid the neediest (or one organized so as to maximize the position of the worst-off group); no one may opt out of participating in it. (None may say, "Don't compel me to contribute to others and don't provide for me via this compulsory mechanism if I am in need.") Everyone above a certain level is forced to contribute to aid the needy. But if emigration from the country were allowed, anyone could choose to move to another country that did not have compulsory social provision but otherwise was (as much as possible) identical. In such a case, the person's *only* motive for leaving would be to avoid participating in the compulsory scheme of social provision. And if he does leave, the needy in his initial country will receive no (compelled) help from him. What rationale yields the result that the person be permitted to emigrate, yet forbidden to stay and opt out of the compulsory scheme of social provision? If providing for the needy is of overriding importance, this does militate against allowing internal opting out; but it also speaks against allowing external emigration. (Would it also support, to some extent, the kidnapping of persons living in a place without compulsory social provision, who could be forced to make a contribution to the needy in your community?) Perhaps the crucial component of the position that allows emigration solely to avoid certain arrangements, while not allowing anyone internally to opt out of them, is a concern for fraternal feelings within the country. "We don't want anyone here who doesn't contribute, who doesn't care enough about the others to contribute." That concern, in this case, would have to be tied to the view that forced aiding tends to produce fraternal feelings between the aided and the aider (or perhaps merely to the view that the knowledge that someone or other voluntarily is not aiding produces unfraternal feelings).

LOCKE'S THEORY OF ACQUISITION

Before we turn to consider other theories of justice in detail, we must introduce an additional bit of complexity into the structure of the entitlement theory. This is best approached by considering Locke's attempt to specify a principle of justice in acquisition. Locke views property rights in an unowned object as originating through someone's mixing his labor with it. This gives rise to many questions. What are the boundaries of what labor is mixed with? If a private astronaut clears a place on Mars, has he mixed his labor with (so that he comes to own) the whole planet, the whole uninhabited universe, or just a particular plot? Which plot does an act bring under ownership? The minimal (possibly disconnected) area such that an act decreases entropy in that area, and not elsewhere? Can virgin land (for the purposes of ecological investigation by high-flying airplane) come under ownership by a Lockean process? Building a fence around a territory presumably would make one the owner of only the fence (and the land immediately underneath it).

Why does mixing one's labor with something make one the owner of it? Perhaps because one owns one's labor, and so one comes to own a previously unowned thing that becomes permeated with what one owns. Ownership seeps over into the rest. But why isn't mixing what I own with what I don't own a way of losing what I own rather than a way of gaining what I don't? If I own a can of tomato juice and spill it in the sea so that its molecules (made radioactive, so I can check this) mingle evenly throughout the sea, do I thereby come to own the sea, or have I foolishly dissipated my tomato juice? Perhaps the idea, instead, is that laboring on something improves it and makes it more valuable; and anyone is entitled to own a thing whose value he has created. (Reinforcing this, perhaps, is the view that laboring is unpleasant. If some people made things effortlessly, as the cartoon characters in *The Yellow Submarine* trail flowers in their wake, would they have lesser claim to their own products whose making didn't cost them anything?) Ignore the fact that laboring on something may make it less valuable (spraying pink enamel paint on a piece of driftwood that you have found). Why should one's entitlement extend to the whole object rather than just to the *added value* one's labor has produced? (Such reference to value might also serve to delimit the extent of ownership; for example, substitute "increases the value of" for "decreases entropy in" in the above entropy criterion.) No workable or coherent value-added property scheme has yet been devised, and any such scheme presumably would fall to objections (similar to those) that fell the theory of Henry George.

It will be implausible to view improving an object as giving full ownership to it, if the stock of unowned objects that might be improved is limited. For an object's coming under one person's ownership changes the situation of all others. Whereas previously they were at liberty (in Hohfeld's sense) to use the object, they now no longer are. This change in the situation of others (by removing their liberty to act on a previously unowned object) need not worsen their situation. If I appropriate a grain of sand from Coney Island, no one else may now do as they will with *that* grain of sand. But there are plenty of other grains of sand left for them to do the same with. Or if not grains of sand, then other things. Alternatively, the things I do with the grain of sand I appropriate might improve the position of others, counterbalancing their loss of the liberty to use that grain. The crucial point is whether appropriation of an unowned object worsens the situation of others.

Locke's proviso that there be "enough and as good left in common for others" (sect. 27) is meant to ensure that the situation of others is not worsened. (If this proviso is met is there any motivation for his further condition of nonwaste?) It is often said that this proviso once held but now no longer does. But there appears to be an argument for the conclusion that if the proviso no longer holds, then it cannot ever have held so as to yield permanent and inheritable property rights. Consider the first person Z for whom there is not enough and as good left to appropriate. The last person Y to appropriate left Z without his previous liberty to act on an object, and so worsened Z's situation. So Y's appropriation is not allowed under Locke's proviso. Therefore the next to last person X to appropriate left Y in a worse position, for X's act ended permissible appropriation. Therefore X's appropriation wasn't permissible. But then the appropriator two from last, W, ended permissible appropriation and so, since it worsened X's position, W's appropriation wasn't permissible. And so on back to the first person A to appropriate a permanent property right.

This argument, however, proceeds too quickly. Someone may be made worse off by another's appropriation in two ways: first, by losing the opportunity to improve his situation by a particular appropriation or any one; and second, by no longer being able to use freely (without appropriation) what he previously could. A stringent requirement that another not be made worse off by an appropriation would exclude the first way if nothing else counterbalances the diminution in opportunity, as well as the second. A weaker requirement would exclude the second way, though not the first. With the weaker requirement, we cannot zip back so quickly from Z to A, as in the above argument; for though person Z can no longer *appropriate,* there may remain some for him to *use* as before. In this case Y's appropriation would not violate the weaker Lockean condition. (With less remaining that people are at liberty to use, users might face more inconvenience, crowding, and so on; in that way the situation of others might be worsened, unless appropriation stopped far short of such a point.) It is arguable that no one legitimately can complain if the weaker provision is satisfied. However, since this is less clear than in the case of the more stringent proviso, Locke may have intended this stringent proviso by "enough and as good" remaining, and perhaps he meant the nonwaste condition to delay the end point from which the argument zips back.

Is the situation of persons who are unable to appropriate (there being no more accessible and useful unowned objects) worsened by a system allowing appropriation and permanent property? Here enter the various familiar social considerations favoring private property: it increases the social product by putting means of production in the hands of those who can use them most efficiently (profitably); experimentation is encouraged, because with separate persons controlling resources, there is no one person or small group whom someone with a new idea must convince to try it out; private property enables people to decide on the pattern and types of risks they wish to bear, leading to specialized types of risk bearing; private property protects future persons by leading some to hold back resources from current consumption for future markets; it provides alternate sources of employment for unpopular persons who don't have to convince any one person or small group to hire them, and so on. These considerations enter a Lockean theory to support the claim that appropriation of private property satisfies the intent behind the "enough and as good left over" proviso, *not* as a utilitarian justification of property. They enter to rebut the claim that because the proviso is violated no natural right to private property can arise by a Lockean process. The difficulty in working such an argument to show that the proviso is satisfied is in fixing the appropriate base line for comparison. Lockean appropriation makes people no worse off than they would be *how?* This question of fixing the baseline needs more detailed investigation than we are able to give it here. It would be desirable to have an estimate of the general economic importance of original appropriation in order to see how much leeway there is for differing theories of appropriation and of the location of the baseline. Perhaps this importance can be measured by the percentage of all income that is based upon untransformed raw materials and given resources (rather than upon human actions), mainly rental income representing the unimproved value of land, and the price of raw material *in situ,* and by the percentage of current wealth which represents such income in the past.[j]

We should note that it is not only persons favoring *private* property who need a theory of how property rights legitimately originate. Those believing in collective property, for example those believing that a group of persons living in an area jointly own the territory, or its mineral resources, also must provide a theory of how such property rights arise; they must show why the persons living there have rights to determine what is done with the land and resources there that persons living elsewhere don't have (with regard to the same land and resources).

THE PROVISO

Whether or not Locke's particular theory of appropriation can be spelled out so as to handle various difficulties, I assume that any adequate theory of justice in acquisition will contain a proviso similar to the weaker of the ones we have attributed to Locke. A process normally giving rise to a permanent bequeathable property right in a previously unowned thing will not do so if the position of others no longer at liberty to use the thing is thereby worsened. It is important to specify *this* particular mode of worsening the situation of others, for the proviso does not encompass other modes. It does not include the worsening due to more limited opportunities to appropriate (the first way above, corresponding to the more stringent condition), and it does not include how I "worsen" a seller's position if I appropriate materials to make some of what he is selling, and then enter into competition with him. Someone whose appropriation otherwise would violate the proviso still may appropriate provided he compensates the others so that their situation is not thereby worsened; unless he does compensate these others, his appropriation will violate the proviso of the principle of justice in acquisition and will be an illegitimate one.[k] A theory of appropriation incorporating this Lockean

---

[j] I have not seen a precise estimate. David Friedman, *The Machinery of Freedom* (N.Y.: Harper & Row, 1973), pp. xiv, xv, discusses this issue and suggests 5 percent of U.S. national income as an upper limit for the first two factors mentioned. However he does not attempt to estimate the percentage of current wealth which is based upon such income in the past. (The vague notion of "based upon" merely indicates a topic needing investigation.)

[k] Fourier held that since the process of civilization had deprived the members of society of certain liberties (to gather, pasture, engage in the chase), a socially guaranteed minimum provision for persons was justified as compensation for the loss (Alexander Gray, *The Socialist Tradition* (New York: Harper & Row, 1968), p. 188). But this puts the point too strongly. This compensation would be due those persons, if any, for whom the process of civilization was a *net loss,* for whom the benefits of civilization did not counterbalance being deprived of these particular liberties.

proviso will handle correctly the cases (objections to the theory lacking the proviso) where someone appropriates the total supply of something necessary for life.[1]

A theory which includes this proviso in its principle of justice in acquisition must also contain a more complex principle of justice in transfer. Some reflection of the proviso about appropriation constrains later actions. If my appropriating all of a certain substance violates the Lockean proviso, then so does my appropriating some and purchasing all the rest from others who obtained it without otherwise violating the Lockean proviso. If the proviso excludes someone's appropriating all the drinkable water in the world, it also excludes his purchasing it all. (More weakly, and messily, it may exclude his charging certain prices for some of his supply.) This proviso (almost?) never will come into effect; the more someone acquires of a scarce substance which others want, the higher the price of the rest will go, and the more difficult it will become for him to acquire it all. But still, we can imagine, at least, that something like this occurs: someone makes simultaneous secret bids to the separate owners of a substance, each of whom sells assuming he can easily purchase more from the other owners; or some natural catastrophe destroys all of the supply of something except that in one person's possession. The total supply could not be permissibly appropriated by one person at the beginning. His later acquisition of it all does not show that the original appropriation violated the proviso (even by a reverse argument similar to the one above that tried to zip back from Z to A). Rather, it is the combination of the original appropriation *plus* all the later transfers and actions that violates the Lockean proviso.

Each owner's title to his holding includes the historical shadow of the Lockean proviso on appropriation. This excludes his transferring it into an agglomeration that does violate the Lockean proviso and excludes his using it in a way, in coordination with others or independently of them, so as to violate the proviso by making the situation of others worse than their baseline situation. Once it is known that someone's ownership runs afoul of the Lockean proviso, there are stringent limits on what he may do with (what it is difficult any longer unreservedly to call) "his

---

[1]For example, Rashdall's case of someone who comes upon the only water in the desert several miles ahead of others who also will come to it and appropriates it all. Hastings Rashdall, "The Philosophical Theory of Property," in *Property, its Duties and Rights* (London: MacMillan, 1915).

We should note Ayn Rand's theory of property rights ("Man's Rights" in *The Virtue of Selfishness* (New York: New American Library, 1964), p. 94), wherein these follow from the right to life, since people need physical things to live. But a right to life is not a right to whatever one needs to live; other people may have rights over these other things (see Chapter 3 of this book). At most, a right to life would be a right to have or strive for whatever one needs to live, provided that having it does not violate anyone else's rights. With regard to material things, the question is whether having it does violate any right of others. (Would appropriation of all unowned things do so? Would appropriating the water hole in Rashdall's example?) Since special considerations (such as the Lockean proviso) may enter with regard to material property, one *first* needs a theory of property rights before one can apply any supposed right to life (as amended above). Therefore the right to life cannot provide the foundation for a theory of property rights.

property." Thus a person may not appropriate the only water hole in a desert and charge what he will. Nor may he charge what he will if he possesses one, and unfortunately it happens that all the water holes in the desert dry up, except for his. This unfortunate circumstance, admittedly no fault of his, brings into operation the Lockean proviso and limits his property rights.[m] Similarly, an owner's property right in the only island in an area does not allow him to order a castaway from a shipwreck off his island as a trespasser, for this would violate the Lockean proviso.

Notice that the theory does not say that owners do have these rights, but that the rights are overridden to avoid some catastrophe. (Overridden rights do not disappear; they leave a trace of a sort absent in the cases under discussion.) There is no such external (and *ad hoc?*) overriding. Considerations internal to the theory of property itself, to its theory of acquisition and appropriation, provide the means for handling such cases. The results, however, may be coextensive with some condition about catastrophe, since the baseline for comparison is so low as compared to the productiveness of a society with private appropriation that the question of the Lockean proviso being violated arises only in the case of catastrophe (or a desert-island situation).

The fact that someone owns the total supply of something necessary for others to stay alive does *not* entail that his (or anyone's) appropriation of anything left some people (immediately or later) in a situation worse than the baseline one. A medical researcher who synthesizes a new substance that effectively treats a certain disease and who refuses to sell except on his terms does not worsen the situation of others by depriving them of whatever he has appropriated. The others easily can possess the same materials he appropriated; the researcher's appropriation or purchase of chemicals didn't make those chemicals scarce in a way so as to violate the Lockean proviso. Nor would someone else's purchasing the total supply of the synthesized substance from the medical researcher. The fact that the medical researcher uses easily available chemicals to synthesize the drug no more violates the Lockean proviso than does the fact that the only surgeon able to perform a particular operation eats easily obtainable food in order to stay alive and to have the energy to work. This shows that the Lockean proviso is not an "end-state principle"; it focuses on a particular way that appropriative actions affect others, and not on the structure of the situation that results.

Intermediate between someone who takes all of the public supply and someone who makes the total supply out of easily obtainable substances is someone who appropriates the total supply of something in a way that does not deprive the others of it. For example, someone finds a new substance in an out-of-the-way

---

[m]The situation would be different if his water hole didn't dry up, due to special precautions he took to prevent this. Compare our discussion of the case in the text with Hayek, *The Constitution of Liberty*, p. 136; and also with Ronald Hamowy, "Hayek's Concept of Freedom; A Critique," *New Individualist Review*, April 1961, pp. 28–31.

place. He discovers that it effectively treats a certain disease and appropriates the total supply. He does not worsen the situation of others; if he did not stumble upon the substance no one else would have, and the others would remain without it. However, as time passes, the likelihood increases that others would have come across the substance; upon this fact might be based a limit to his property right in the substance so that others are not below their baseline position; for example, its bequest might be limited. The theme of someone worsening another's situation by depriving him of something he otherwise would possess may also illuminate the example of patents. An inventor's patent does not deprive others of an object which would not exist if not for the inventor. Yet patents would have this effect on others who independently invent the object. Therefore, these independent inventors, upon whom the burden of proving independent discovery may rest, should not be excluded from utilizing their own invention as they wish (including selling it to others). Furthermore, a known inventor drastically lessens the chances of actual independent invention. For persons who know of an invention usually will not try to reinvent it, and the notion of independent discovery here would be murky at best. Yet we may assume that in the absence of the original invention, sometime later someone else would have come up with it. This suggests placing a time limit on patents, as a rough rule of thumb to approximate how long it would have taken, in the absence of knowledge of the invention, for independent discovery.

I believe that the free operation of a market system will not actually run afoul of the Lockean proviso. (Recall that crucial to our story in Part I of how a protective agency becomes dominant and a *de facto* monopoly is the fact that it wields force in situations of conflict, and is not merely in competition, with other agencies. A similar tale cannot be told about other businesses.) If this is correct, the proviso will not play a very important role in the activities of protective agencies and will not provide a significant opportunity for future state action. Indeed, were it not for the effects of previous *illegitimate* state action, people would not think the possibility of the proviso's being violated as of more interest than any other logical possibility. (Here I make an empirical historical claim; as does someone who disagrees with this.) This completes our indication of the complication in the entitlement theory introduced by the Lockean proviso.

CHAPTER 19

Philosophical Dialogue on Justice: Allan Bloom on Traditional Political Philosophy

The previously described condition of mid-twentieth-century American philosophy before Rawls (and Nozick) actually mostly applies to philosophy as practiced in academic departments of *philosophy* of many major American universities. In the *political science* department of the University of Chicago in the 1950s, however, German émigré Leo Strauss almost single-handedly kept the classical tradition of philosophical discourse on economic justice and other ethical and political questions alive. In Strauss' view, the most needful task of the day is to read . . . and reread . . . and read again the great texts.

Leo Strauss' passion inspired a whole generation of students, many of whom have gone on to important scholarly careers of their own. But far and away the best known "Straussian" is Allan Bloom, whose name so surprisingly burst onto the best-seller list in 1987 with *The Closing of the American Mind.* Previously best known as a classical scholar—perhaps the best contemporary translator of Plato and Rousseau—Bloom managed to phrase his blistering attack on contemporary American academia, including analytical philosophy, in a manner that effectively moved many beyond the ivy walls.

A foretaste of Bloom's approach appeared in an article he wrote in the mid-1970s on Rawls' *A Theory of Justice.* It is difficult to think of a more fitting

conclusion to a book of "classic" readings intended to put the fundamental questions of economic justice in perspective than Bloom's concluding remarks on
Rawls:

> The greatest weakness of a *Theory of Justice* is not to be found in the principles
> it proposes, nor in the kind of society it envisages, nor in the political tendencies
> it encourages, but in the lack of education it reveals. Rawls's "original position"
> is based on a misunderstanding of the "state of nature," teachings of Hobbes,
> Locke, and Rousseau. His "Kantian interpretation" is based on a misunder-
> standing of Kant's moral teaching. His "Aristotelian principle" is based on
> a misunderstanding of Aristotle's teaching about happiness. . . . An authentic
> understanding of these thinkers would have given him an awareness of the
> problems he faced and of the nature of philosophic greatness. We are in no
> position to push ahead with new solutions of problems; for as this book demon-
> strates, we have forgotten what the problems are.
>
> The most essential of our freedoms . . . consists in the consciousness of the
> fundamental alternatives. The preservation of that consciousness is as impor-
> tant as any new scheme for society. The alternatives are contained in the
> writings of the greatest men in the philosophic tradition. This is not to assert
> that the last word has been said, but that any serious new word must be based
> on a profound confrontation with the old ones. . . . Rawls is the product of a
> school which thinks that it invented philosophy.[1]

[1]Allan Bloom, "Justice: John Rawls and the Tradition of Political Philosophy," *American Political
Science Review*, Vol. 6, No. 2 (June 1975), p. 662.

Justice: John Rawls and the Tradition of Political Philosophy"

Allan Bloom

THE PROMISE AND THE PROBLEM

John Rawls's A *Theory of Justice* has attracted more attention in the Anglo-Saxon world than any work of its kind in a generation. Its vogue results from two facts: It is the most ambitious political project undertaken by a member of the school currently dominant in academic philosophy; and it offers not only a defense of, but also a new foundation for, a radical egalitarian interpretation of liberal democracy. In method and substance it fits the tastes of the times. Professor Rawls believes that he can provide persuasive principles of justice that possess the simplicity and force of older contract teachings, that satisfy utilitarianism's concern for the greatest number without neglecting the individual, that contain all the moral nobility of Kant's principles, that will result in a richness of life akin to that proposed by Aristotle, and that can accomplish all this without falling into the quagmires of traditional philosophy. This is a big book, not only in the number of its pages, but in the magnitude of its claims, and it deserves to be measured by standards of a severity commensurate with its proportions.

Liberal democracy is in need of a defense or a rebirth if it is to survive. The practical challenges to it over the last forty years have been extreme, while the thought that underlies it has become incredible to most men living in liberal democracies. Historicism, cultural relativism, and the fact-value distinction have eroded the bases of conviction that this regime is good or just, that reason can support its claims to our allegiance. Hardly anyone would be willing to defend as truth the natural right teachings of the founders of liberal democracy or of their philosophic masters, as many, for example, defend Marx. The state of nature and the natural rights deriving from it have taken their place beside the divine right of kings in the graveyard of history. They are understood to be myths or ideologies of ruling classes. One need only recall the vitality of the thought of liberal democracy's great opponents, Marx and Nietzsche, and reflect on the absence of comparable proponents to recognize the magnitude of the crisis. A renewal in the light of these challenges, theoretical and practical, is clearly of the first importance.

But, disappointingly, A *Theory of Justice* does not even manifest an awareness of this need, let alone respond to it. In spite of its radical egalitarianism, it is not

Allan Bloom, *"Justice: John Rawls and the Tradition of Political Philosophy,"* American Political Science Review, *Vol. 6, No. 2 (June 1975), pp. 648–662.*

a radical book. Its horizon does not seem to extend to the abysses which we have experienced in our own lifetimes; the horrors of Hitler and Stalin do not present a special or new problem for Rawls. Rather, his book is a correction of utilitarianism; his consciousness is American, or at most, Anglo-Saxon. The problems he addresses are those of civil liberties in nations that are already free and of the distribution of wealth in those that are already prosperous. The discussion is redolent of that hope and expectation for the future of democracy that characterized the late nineteenth and early twentieth centuries, forgetful of the harsh deeds that preceded it and made it possible, without anticipation of the barbarism that was to succeed it.

Just as the political concern which appears to motivate Rawls is narrow and thin, so is his view of the theoretical problems facing anyone who wishes to accomplish what he proposes to accomplish. Simply, historicism, whether that of Marx or that of Nietzsche and the existentialists, has made it questionable whether an undertaking such as Rawls's is possible at all; yet he does not address himself to these thinkers. He takes it for granted that they are wrong, that they must pass before his tribunal, not he before theirs. Marx is not treated, and Nietzsche is quickly dispatched, improbably, as a teleologist. I am aware that it is not Rawls's intention to write a history of political philosophy, and it is not incumbent on him to present a critique of Marx and Nietzsche. But the issues raised by Marx and Nietzsche must be dealt with if Rawls is to be persuasive at all. If liberal democracy is just a stage on the way to another kind of society, then Rawls is merely an ephemeral ideologist. And if rational determination of values is in the decisive sense impossible, then Rawls is only a deluded myth maker. He supposes that his method makes a detour around these roadblocks, that there is no need to discuss nature and history. Throughout this book one wonders about the status of Rawls's teaching. Is it meant to be a permanent statement about the nature of political things, or just a collection of opinions that he finds satisfying and hopes will be satisfying to others? One finds no reflection on how Rawls is able to break out of the bonds of the historical or cultural determinism he appears to accept, and no reflection on how philosophy is possible within such limits or what it means to be a philosopher. Is he a seeker after the truth, or only the spokesman for a certain historical consciousness?

What Rawls explicitly undertakes to do is to provide principles for our pre-existing moral sense, to elaborate the implications of our intuitions or convictions, to tell us what we mean when we speak of justice, to find a basis of agreement among our contemporaries. He believes that there is a *via media* between subjectivity pure and simple and telling us what the world is really like. But, again, the question always present is whether that moral sense is anything other than a mere preference, one conditioned by our time and place. Rawls takes it for granted that we are all egalitarians. Aristocratic teachings are inadmissible, but it is not clear whether this is because they are based on an untrue understanding or because we do not like them any longer. Conversely, it is unclear whether our egalitarianism is a result of the revelation of the fact of men's equality or whether it is just what we happen to like today.

Rawls thinks that his procedure is Socratic. Socrates, however, did not begin from sentiments or intuitions but from opinions; all opinions are understood by Socrates to be inadequate perceptions of being; the examination of opinions proves them to be self-contradictory and points toward a noncontradictory view which is adequate to being and can be called knowledge. If opinion cannot be converted into knowledge, then the rational examination of opinions about justice, let alone of senses about justice, is of no avail in establishing principles according to which we should live. It is even questionable whether such examination is of any use at all. Rawls begins with our moral sense, develops the principles which accord with it, and then sees whether we are satisfied with the results; the principles depend on our moral sense and that moral sense on the principles. We are not forced to leave our conventional lives nor compelled, by the very power of being, to move toward a true and natural life. We start from what we are now and end there, since there is nothing beyond us. At best Rawls will help us to be more consistent, if that is an advantage. The distinctions between opinion and knowledge, and between appearance and reality, which made philosophy possible and needful, disappear. Rawls speaks to an audience of the persuaded, excluding not only those who have different sentiments but those who cannot be satisfied by sentiment alone.

Thus, those who turn to Rawls hoping to find a reasoned statement of the superiority of liberal democracy to the other possibilities or a defense of the rationalist tradition of political philosophy will not find what they are looking for. They will find reassurance that their sentiments are sufficient, that they need not enter the disputes of the philosophers; they will be made to feel at home rather than made to long for distant worlds; they will be nudged in the direction of more reform and tolerance in accordance with the prevailing tendency of our regime; and they will be given a platform that would appeal to the typical liberal in Anglo-Saxon countries: democracy plus the welfare state—leaving open whether capitalism or socialism is the most efficient economic form (so that one need not be a cold warrior); maximum individual freedom combined with community (just what is wanted by the New Left); defenses of civil disobedience and conscientious objection (the civil rights and anti-war movements find their satisfaction under Rawls's tent); and even a codicil that liberty may be abrogated in those places where the economic conditions do not permit of liberal democracy (thus saving the Third World nations from being called unjust). This correspondence, unique in the history of political philosophy, between what is wanted by many for current political practice and the conclusions of abstract, rigorous political philosophy would be most remarkable if one did not suspect that Rawls began from what is wanted here and now and then looked for the principles that would rationalize it.

JUSTICE AND THE ORIGINAL POSITION

A theory of justice must show what a decent regime is and what duties citizens owe to it. Rawls's problem is the classic one: what kind of a civil society would a reasonable man choose to live in and why should he obey its commands when they go against his grain? Rawls assumes that there is a form of civil society that can reconcile public and private interest and hence that a true political philosophy is possible. He argues that the principle of utilitarianism—the greatest good of the greatest number—is the one generally accepted today and that it does not suffice. Out of the many possible criticisms of that principle he selects the one that it does not satisfy the demands of the few, in particular of the economically disadvantaged few. He accepts the utilitarian position that each individual's view of his good *is* his good and that it is the business of society to attempt to satisfy the individual to the extent the fulfillment of his wishes does not do harm to others and not to propose or impose a view of the good on the individual or to have a collective end. The objection to utilitarianism is that it does not insure consideration of each individual and that, in spite of its individualist basis, the disadvantaged are sacrificed on the altar of the collective. Rawls proposes a contract according to which every man gives his adherence to civil society only on condition that he be guaranteed certain minima which one might call rights. Such a contract serves to set the goals and limits of civil society, to prescribe duties to rulers and to motivate the citizens' adherence as well as to define their legitimate claims.

Although Rawls goes back in time to seek a model for his theory of justice, he brings a fresh set of concerns to the contract doctrine. It must somehow be transformed to accommodate sensibilities that have emerged historically out of utilitarianism and popular dissatisfaction with it. Men must have equal rights not only to "life, liberty and the pursuit of happiness," but to the achievement of happiness. Inequalities, whether they stem from birth, fortune or nature, should be offensive to us. Thus to the familiar principle of liberal democracy that each person is to have an equal right to the most extensive basic liberty compatible with a similar liberty for others, Rawls adds a second principle that all goods are to be equally distributed or, if unequally distributed, this unequal distribution must be agreed to be to the advantage of all as measured by the desires of the least advantaged member of society. Rawls seeks a new morality which will constrain the advantaged to admit that the possession or use of their advantages depends upon the permission of an egalitarian society, one which will persuade the disadvantaged that whatever inequalities exist are to their advantage. Rawls's innovation is to incorporate the maxims of contemporary social welfare into the fundamental principles of political justice. Not only must material goods be provided to each citizen, but also an equal sense of his own worth, recognized by others; for, after all, man does not live on bread alone.

The disadvantaged, or, to say what Rawls really means, the poor, must be listened to, not condescended to or told how they should live; and the attention paid them must be grounded on the most fundamental right which precedes institutions and in accordance with which institutions are formed. A man does not, as Plato said, have a right to what he can use well; or, as Locke said, to that with which he has mixed his labor; or even, as Marx said, to what he needs; he has a right to what he thinks he needs in order to fulfill his "life plan," whatever it may be. With respect to ends, government for Rawls must *laisser faire*; with respect to the means to the ends, it must *beaucoup faire*.

Once Rawls has determined what is wanted, he seeks for a way of deriving or demonstrating his two principles of justice that will be persuasive and that will exclude conflicting principles. A contract made by all the future members of the new society to abide by these principles would fill the bill. But why would superior men agree to a contract that requires them to make sacrifices for the benefit of the disadvantaged? A common ground of advantage, more fundamental than any particular advantage, must be found in order to gain unanimous consent. This need for a common ground is the source of the elaborate construction of "the original position" which is *the* feature of this exceptionally complex book.

Every understanding of man must have some vision of the fundamental situation, free from the accidents and trivia which distract us from the one thing most needful, a situation in which a man can discern what really counts and on the basis of which serious men guide their lives. The Best Regime of Plato and Aristotle, the City of God of Augustine and the State of Nature of Hobbes, Locke, and Rousseau come immediately to mind as powerful alternatives according to which we are asked to take our bearings. Now comes Rawls's "original position" which, if we are willing to assume it, will compel us to accept his two principles of justice and his version of society.

The "original position" amounts to something like this: Ask a man, any man, what kind of a society he would like to live in, assuming that he wants to live in a society. He would describe one that fulfilled his idea of the good, one that would make him happy. But he knows that other men have different ideas of the good that conflict with his, so that it is unlikely that his idea will prevail; and even if it were to do so, those other men would be deprived of their happiness. If he were to imagine that he did not know what view of happiness, what "life-plan," he were going to have, but did know that he would have a "life plan," what kind of a society would he choose? In this case he would be choosing under what Rawls calls "the veil of ignorance." Since there are many possible "life-plans," none belongs to man as such; therefore, it is not unreasonable to assume that men in the original position do not know their goal but know only that they must have one. The different final goods cannot be reconciled, and it is undesirable that they be so. Inevitably, according to Rawls, a man in this situation would choose a liberal society, for at least he would be permitted to pursue his goal, if it did not do harm to others, whereas he would otherwise risk losing his happiness altogether. Better a little than nothing—so cautious calculation would seem to indicate. This provides a ground for agreement among men who are similarly situated. They would accept Rawls's first principle of justice.

Further, although this man does not know the good, the final end, he knows that there are certain things that will contribute to the fulfillment of his life-plan, no matter what its content. These things one can call primary goods, good because they serve whatever good is final. They are things like rights, liberties, birth, talent, position, wealth, a sense of one's own worth. Our typical man would want to have as much of these primary goods as possible. Some are natural and others are effects of social arrangements; but possessing them depends on chance. He would want a society which encourages the use of what nature gives and assures that he gets the most of what society can give. But, if the veil of ignorance descends again, he would opt for equality, since, given the fact of the relative scarcity of primary goods, he would be likely to have less rather than more of an unequal distribution. The natural primary goods he would choose to use and develop only insofar as they contribute to the happiness of all and they are harnessed by the institutions to that end. The social primary goods, like wealth, he would allow to be unequally distributed only to the extent that the least advantaged member of society, which he might be, would gain from that unequal distribution and could hope to improve his own situation thereby.

In this condition of ignorance, calculating men will agree to Rawls's second principle. A contract is made for mutual advantage on a basis of equality. This contract sets down the rules of the game; justice in a man is abiding by his agreements, keeping his word. Justice is fairness in the sense that it is only fair to abide by the results of a game the rules of which are seen to be reasonable and just, even though one might have wished for another result and would like to alter the rules for one's personal advantage. Rawls's recipe contains equal measures of selfish calculation in the original position and public spiritedness—in the form of fair play—after real social life has begun. A man cannot be expected to join a group in which his happiness is not promoted equally with that of others. A society which gives him that equality of treatment deserves his adherence. Once men are aware of the original position they will abandon their overreaching: they will recognize that there are no legitimate claims to special privilege and will be dissuaded from using the power deriving from any unequal possession of primary goods to command such privileges.

The "original position" is an imaginary foundation which Rawls wishes to insert beneath the real edifice of liberal society in order to justify that society. It is invented rather than discovered, and one may well doubt whether it is substantial enough to support such a structure.

THE "ORIGINAL POSITION" VS. THE STATE OF NATURE

In order to see the difficulties inherent in the "original position," it must be compared to the "state of nature" in the contract teachings of Hobbes, Locke, and Rousseau, for Rawls intends his invention to play the same role in his presentation of justice as did the state of nature in theirs. And the change of name is indicative of the decisive difference in substance. Rawls banishes nature from human and political things. The state of nature was the result of a comprehensive reflection about the way all things really are. Hobbes, Locke, and Rousseau could not be content with a figment of the imagination as the basis for moral judgments. Nature is *the* permanent standard; what the good man and the good society are, depend on human nature. The state of nature is the result of a specific under-standing of nature founded on a criticism and a rejection of an older understand-ing of nature and its moral and political consequences. The state of nature theorists, therefore, agreed with Plato and Aristotle that the decisive issue is na-ture; they disagreed about what is natural. Metaphysics cannot be avoided. If there is to be political philosophy, they believed, man must have a nature and it must be knowable. Rawls does not wish to enter into such disputes, the validity of which has once and for all been refuted by his school. And his political goals are furthered by the imperatives of his method, for he does not wish to accept the iron limits set by nature on the possibilities of transforming the human condition. Although he sometimes rests an argument on what he calls human nature, his thought is directed not only at overcoming those injustices which are against nature but at overcoming nature itself. He wants the advantages of the state of nature teaching without its (to him) unpleasant theoretical and practical consequences.

The state of nature presented a picture of man as he really is, divested of convention, accident and illusion, a picture grounded on and consistent with the new science of nature. Man, according to the real contract theorists, is a being whose primary natural concern is to preserve himself, who enters into the contract of society because his life is threatened and he fears losing it. That fear is not an abstraction, a hypothesis, an imagination, but an experience, a powerful passion which accompanies men throughout their lives. This passion is sufficient to pro-vide a selfish reason, a reason that men can be counted on having, for adherence to a civil society which is dedicated to preserving them. The conflict between particular interest and public good disappears. The reason why this passion is not ordinarily effective enough to guarantee lawful behavior is that men in civil socie-ties which protect them forget how essential that protection is. They get notions of self-sufficiency; they pursue glory; they break the law for their pleasures. And, above all, their religions persuade them that there are things more important than life or that there is another life, thus calming the fear of losing this one and encouraging disobedience to civil authority. The state of nature is intended to reveal the nullity or secondary character of these other passions and these hopes of avoiding the essential and permanent vulnerability of man. Death is the natural sanction for breaking the contract, and the state of nature shows both that this is so and that the goods which might conflict with desire for life are insubstantial. The positive law is merely derivative from this sanction and gets its force from nature. The state of nature demonstrates that the positive goals of men which vary are not to be taken seriously in comparison with the negative fact on which all sensible men must agree, that death is terrible and must be avoided. They join civil society for protection from one another, and government's sole purpose is the establishment and maintenance of peace. This origin and end of civil society is common to the contract theories of Hobbes, Locke, and Rousseau in spite of their differences. And whether they believed the state of nature ever existed or not, it was meant to describe the reality underlying civil society. Man's unsocial nature and the selfish character of the passion that motivates men's adherence to civil society limit the possible and legitimate functions of that society.

Now, Rawls's "original position" fails to achieve what the state of nature teaching achieved. Apart from the fact that there is nothing in the original position that corresponds to any man's real experience, the fear of death disappears as the motive for joining civil society and accepting its rules. Rawls is very vague about the reasons for joining civil society and, because he does not want to commit himself to any view of man's nature, it cannot be determined whether the attachment to society—attachment in the sense of obeying its laws—is really so important for a man in fulfilling himself. With the disappearance of the fear of death as the primary motive, the sanction for breaking the contract also disappears. In civil society contracts are protected by the positive law and the punishment it can inflict. Prior to civil society, there must be a natural punishment or none at all. A man whose desires or view of happiness urge him to break a contract that has no sanctions, no authority, would be foolish not to do so. After all, life is not a game. He exists naturally, while civil society is merely conventional. Either there is some essential harmony between private and public good or there is none. If there is none, on what basis can one arbitrate between the two? Rawls does not provide a basis for the reconciliation or anything more than a sermonizing argument for the nobility of sacrifice to the public good.

What Rawls gives us in the place of fear is fairness. But that is merely the invention of a principle to supply a missing link. Why should fairness have primacy over the desire for self-fulfillment? Once we leave the "original position" and the "veil of ignorance" drops, the motive for compliance falls away with it. When we leave the state of nature, the passions found there remain with us and provide powerful reminders of that earlier state and our reasons for preferring the civil one. But the "original position" is a bloodless abstraction which gives us no such permanent motive. Fairness is a reasonable choice of enlightened self-interest only in the "original position." Fairness as something more, as choiceworthy for its own sake, cannot be derived from the "original position." It is a tattered fragment of an earlier tradition which argued that man is naturally political and that the practice of justice will make a man happy. The state of nature begins from the natural isolation of man and teaches that society and its justice are good only as means to an end. The natural sociality of man is inconsistent with individualism or anything like the freedom of choice among ends which Rawls wishes to preserve, or the notion that man's relation to society is in any way contractual. It requires a rigorous subordination of particularity to the community and all the harder virtues of self-restraint about which Rawls never speaks. He is an individualist, but he does not wish to accept the harsh practical and theoretical consequences of that individualism. In order to pose the issue clearly he would have to confront the opposing views of human nature underlying the contract teaching and the one that asserts that man is by nature a political animal. Fairness simply does not cohere with his shrewd, calculating individual in the "original position."

Rawls's egalitarianism is similarly without foundation, for he does not want to accept the low common denominator of the true state of nature theory. He wants an equality which extends beyond mere life to all the things social men care about. All men, no matter what their qualities of mind or body, no matter what their virtues or their contributions, must have a legitimate claim to all goods natural and social, and society's *primary* concern must be to honor that claim. He must therefore abstract from all the evident inequalities in men's gifts and achievements, but he can find no firmer ground for this abstraction than that it is what he wants, that it is required for his "original position" to work. But it is a long way from the rights of nature to the rights of the original position. The latter rights are hardly likely to inspire awe in anyone who believes himself to be superior. The contract theorists consciously lowered man's sights and his view of himself in order to make equality plausible and found a common interest. It is not in a situation of neutral "reflective equilibrium" that man chooses civil society, but in the grip of powerful natural passions which control and direct his reason and reduce him, willy-nilly, to the level of all other men. Rawls does not want to follow these theories in this respect, although he wants to have all the advantages he sees in their teachings. The state of nature teachings are connected with a denial of the nobility of man and thereby of the nobility, if not the utility, of morality, and their authors were aware of this. Rawls does not wish to stoop low enough to benefit from their solidity, but what he adopts from them prevents him from soaring to the moral heights to which he aspires.

As opposed to the contract theorists who taught that the strongest thing in man is his desire to avoid death and who took their bearings by that negative pole, Rawls insists on the positive goal of happiness. The contract theorists took the tack they did because they denied that there was a highest good and hence that there could be knowledge of happiness; there are only apparent goods, and what happiness is shifts with desire. Men have always disagreed about the good, indeed, this has been a source of their quarrels, particularly in matters of religion. The contract theorists tried to show that this factual disagreement reflects a theoretical impossibility of agreement. Out of this bleak situation which seems to make political philosophy impossible, they drew their hope. If the importance of all particular visions of the good can be depreciated, while all men can agree on the bad and their inclinations support its avoidance, then solid foundations can be achieved. But it has to be emphasized that a precondition of this result is the diminishing of men's attachment to their vision of happiness in favor of mere life and the pursuit of the means of maintaining life. Rawls, while joining the modern natural right thinkers in abandoning the attempt to establish a single, objective standard of the good valid for all men, and in admitting a countless variety of equally worthy and potentially conflicting life plans or visions of happiness, still contends, as did the premodern natural right thinkers, that the goal of society is to promote happiness. Thus he is unable to found consensus on knowledge of the good, as did the ancients, or on agreement about the bad, as did the moderns. He is able to tell us only that society cannot exist without a consensus, but he does not give any motive for abiding by that consensus to the man who is willing to risk the breakdown of actual society in order to achieve his ideal society—which is what any man who loves the good must do. Only the "veil of ignorance" in the "original position" makes consensus possible; but once the scales fall from a man's eyes, he may very well find that his life plan does not accord with liberal democracy. Rawls asks that only those life plans that can co-exist be accepted, but he is not sufficiently aware of how far this demand goes and how many life plans must be rejected on this ground—and all for the sake of a peace the value of which is improved.